How the RiverCats Won

Lessons on Relationships and Competition

Kyle Wagner

Contents

Preface

What makes you qualified to write this book?

What a fabulous question. It's a question that I struggle with as I sit down to write a book. I have two degrees. A B.S in Business from Wake Forest University and a degree in Mathematics from Penn State University. I do, however, have 19 years of teaching experience in public education. I currently teach at Red Land High School in Lewisberry, PA. I have coached baseball from tee-ballers up to professionals. More importantly, I read, observe and reflect.

I wasn't always a reader. It took a very special relationship to change that. My grandfather, Harold Wagner, was important to me. I noticed as he aged, he tended to remember less and less about "today." But, his memory of when he was a younger man was strong. I started to read anything about baseball from his era to have meaningful conversations. I read about Lou Gehrig. I read about Germany Schaefer (if you're a baseball fan you need to read about this man). I read about Hank Greenberg and Joe McCarthy and Casey Stengel and Ernie Lombardi. I read about Van Lingle Mungo because Pap used to tell stories about these people. I wanted to make the most of my time with Pap while he was still alive. I became a voracious reader of baseball books. Pap died Sept. 2015. I stopped reading baseball books. They became too painful. I started reading other books.

We live in an age where information comes at us like a water hose. If you're willing and you're observant there's a chance you might pick up a thing or two. This book is an account of a travel baseball team I coached called the GoWags RiverCats. The events unfolded in real time in our daily lives. As I look back and think about our time together, my hope is that the events I share might be able to shed some perspective on all of our lives.

I do not claim to be an expert on any of this. I do claim to be curious enough to consider these possibilities and courageous enough to share them with the population at large. Hopefully, there is something to be gained by writing *How The RiverCats Won*.

What Can I Expect to Find in This Book?

For five years of my life, I coached a travel baseball team. For all intents and purposes, we were simply a team that consisted of some young boys, their families and me as their Head Coach. Yet, the GoWags RiverCats were our lives. I'd like to tell their story. I'd also like to paint a broader picture that everyone could learn from.

The book is broken up into nine chapters (I called them innings) and a tenth chapter called "The Clubhouse." In each chapter, I'll communicate a message that I believe is important to developing great relationships and a message for "winning." The message is shared from the Ninth Inning to The Clubhouse. As I sat down to write the book, I kept thinking "begin with the end in mind." So, that's what I did. I started with the end. I think it flows better that way.

You'll see highlights as you read. These are my mental timeouts. I've told my students those highlights are the book's cheat code. If you wanted to read the book in fast forward, I suppose you could read the highlights. I know that more and more people want to get on with their lives and sitting down and reading an entire book is tough. I also know that today's world has so many mediums in which a message can be shared. I'm honored that you've chosen a book as your medium. There are more than 280 characters (I love Twitter) so I hope you have the energy to pace yourself as you read through the book.

The book format is a special format in that you can't respond in real time. Once upon a time, the book was a sacred source of information. The information in a book had to be vetted thoroughly and only the best pieces of information made it through the filtering process. Our world doesn't work that way anymore. Today, you can get almost anything to print and into the public forum. Whereas, the burden used to be on supply of information, now the burden has fallen on demand. Supply is ubiquitous. Demand is the new key to communicating information.

Everyone seems to be distracted. We're over stimulated, over motivated, over complicated. This book is yet one more information laced opportunity that I'm asking you to consider. This is my first "real book"[1] and I'm aware that in todays over exposed culture, that's a risk. It's a risk that I'm willing to take. One of the quotes I've come to share with my students is "Don't share your art, unless you're willing to defend your art." The things we share with the public will be criticized. It's inevitable. There are too many eyes and too many opinions to think you can share your work without others attacking your work. I'm ready to share my art!

In 2011, when I became the RiverCats coach, I believed I was a good coach. I had my ideas and I believed I knew how to create winners between the lines. Winning baseball games was validating. Every win and every championship confirmed in my

---

[1] I wrote a book called Green Light Hitting for the very focused baseball development fan.

mind that I was in fact on the right path. Years later, I still believe I was on the right path. But I was on the right path for different reasons. With the benefit of hindsight, I now realize the true victories and the championships that were won are the relationships that the 'Cats still have to this day. Coaching the GoWags RiverCats didn't pay well (actually it paid me $0). Coaching the GoWags RiverCats was often challenging and stressful. I often asked myself "Is it worth it to care so much?" You're damn right it was worth it!

Life is a cycle of love and growth (The Ninth Inning). Life will present opportunities that will be motivating in the beginning and get so darn hard in the middle (The Eighth Inning). Life will scream hold onto the status quo while everyone around you demands change (The Seventh Inning). Life will tempt you to chase the confident road while it quietly beckons you to see the competent road (The Sixth Inning). Life will ask you to subjugate your personal goals in favor of team goals (The Fifth Inning). Life will challenge your why by making the what so pleasurable (The Fourth Inning). Life will provide opportunities to learn and it will demand that you separate what is valuable with what is not (The Third Inning). Life will create incredible pain and joy on the inside and detachment and curiosity from the outside (The Second Inning). Life will reveal, over time, the only difference with right and wrong is time and perspective (The First Inning). In the end, there will be only love.

"Hey Kyle. What did you just say?"

Theoretically, my opinion should mean nothing. I'm hoping you might disagree. The words beyond this point are meaningful through two lenses. The micro lens is a story about a team and the lives they lived. The macro lens paints a broader message that's applicable for all.

The Ninth Inning
The Love Growth Cycle

"When people say to me how do you get through life each day, it's the same thing. To me, there are three things we all should do every day. We should do this every day of our lives. Number one is laugh. You should laugh every day. Number two is think. You should spend some time in thought. Number three is, you should have your emotions moved to tears, could be happiness or joy. But think about it. If you laugh, you think, and you cry, that's a full day. That's a heck of a day. You do that seven days a week, you're going to have something special." - Jim Valvano

The excerpt above came from a famous speech. It's known as the ESPY speech by Jim Valvano. He was honored with a lifetime achievement award called the Arthur Ashe award. According to story, Valvano's attendance that night was dubious. He was riddled with cancer throughout his body. Somehow, he managed to attend and what you see written above is a portion of his legendary speech. His message was simple. Life is precious. To get the most out of life you should laugh, think and cry every day.

Jim Valvano was stricken with terminal cancer when he uttered these words. He lived his life passionately and when time had become limited his focus narrowed to what was important. Valvano realized, as everyone eventually does, when life itself is at risk, all that really matters is love. The theme is repeated over and over throughout all of time. When someone is confronted with the reality that the end is near or even if it has arrived, they shrink their circle and they focus on what really matters: love.

"If we learn nothing else from this tragedy, we learn that life is short
and there is no time for hate."
—Sandy Dahl, wife of Flight 93 pilot Jason Dahl, in Shanksville, Pennsylvania, in 2002

Valvano wasn't always sick. Valvano was a self-admitted passionate Italian that was motivated to be the best. Valvano lived his life wanting to win. He didn't sit on the sidelines laughing, thinking and crying. Valvano had too much to achieve to spend the day embracing only those in his closest circle. He had mountains to climb and championships to conquer.

"My job. My goal, what I want to do each year, is to win a national championship. I want to cut the nets down...Each year, season ends, doesn't matter what I did last year, we won a conference championship last year, doesn't matter. Starts over again.... I think everybody has to have a personal philosophy of how you live your life. Here's mine. Very simply put, you, plus motivation, equals success. I have that only thing in my locker room, nothing else in my locker room but that sign. You, plus motivation, equals success. I have it on cards, bookmarks. I have it on everything. It drives me. It's a passion." -Jim Valvano

The excerpt from the above speech was given in 1987. By that time, Valvano was a circuit speaker. He had won the 1983 National Championship. The speech was presented at the Million Dollar Round Table Meeting in Chicago, IL. In attendance were other motivated professionals hoping to find value in a message from a well-respected basketball coach. His message was simple. To achieve success, you must be motivated.

Have you ever heard anyone say, "With the detriment of hindsight?" I'm guessing no. What I have heard is, "With the benefit of hindsight" Hindsight, apparently, is infallible. Hindsight is the rearview mirror that allows for clarity. It takes all the jagged edges out of our poor decisions. It smooths them over so the answers that eluded us in the moment are crystallized as we look in the past. Unfortunately, most of us only use hindsight selfishly. We only look in our rearview mirror. For the lucky ones we use it to cement our current beliefs. For the unlucky ones we use it to live in regret and fear. What if we could use someone else's rearview mirror? What if we could learn from those that have preceded us in life? What could we learn from them? I think they'd say....

Life isn't about love. Life isn't about growth. Life is a constant cycle between the two. Growth without love would be unsustainable. To achieve with no one to share your glory with is hollow. Love without growth would be stagnant. Men aren't born simply to bask in each other's existence. We're meant to improve the world around us. This cycle permeates everything we do. Yet, it feels like many of us are driven to the extremes by the emotion of the day. Both emotions must be in our lives. Both emotions create balance in a chaotic world. Both emotions must be embraced. But, in the end, there is only love.

In the End
Carter Christopher

The travel baseball family has developed a unique view of the weekend. This perception changes imperceptibly over time. Prior to travel baseball, the weekend is often perceived as a time for leisure. The activities vary on the season but by in large the time is yours to do with as you please. Everyone looks forward to the weekend because they reclaim time as their own. That's a very powerful incentive.

But then you make a commitment to play travel baseball. The weekend becomes competitive. There are targets to hit and progress to be made. Leisure as we once knew it only becomes leisure if the game was won and "the son" performed appropriately. Furthermore, the weekend has multiple games. That seems attractive until you realize it means more emotions. What used to be one win to enjoy and one loss to dissect now gets multiplied. The weekend becomes a roller coaster of emotions.

Travel baseball relationships on the weekend aren't always by choice, but rather by convenience. Over time, these convenient relationships become friendly but competitive travel teams require selection over a very broad area. Having intimate friends to associate with is a luxury very few are provided. By the time the RiverCats were 14 years old, most of them had been playing baseball together for 4 years. The families enjoyed their time together. Convenience evolved into choice. In many respects, the weekend post game activities trumped the game activities. The games were stressful as the parents watched with a very critical eye. If expectations weren't met, at least there were understanding friends to commiserate with after the game.

By chance we played the New Cumberland All-Stars in 9U Tournament in Wormleysburg. Our team blew through everyone except New Cumberland. For the first time in a long time, Carter was not the best player on the field. Your team had 6-7 kids as good as Carter or better. I knew you and what you and your brother had accomplished as players from growing up in the area. GoWags was in its early stages and the RiverCats were just forming. -Judson Christopher, RiverCats Dad

As the RiverCats players shared their game experiences with each other, the RiverCats parents began to share their children's dreams with each other. Parents opened up and invited each other into their lives and their homes. Experiencing the weekend became much more than rooting for doubles and wins. Parents knew that there was a level of play that was expected if these dreams were to be achieved. Success was shared by many. Losses hurt for more than just individual families. The RiverCats parents grew into their own extended family. As often happens with families, the closer you become, the more pain you sometimes invite into your lives. On one particular weekend, the pain felt by someone in the RiverCats family was palpable.

By in large, these weekends are very predictable. On Saturday, you're given a schedule of two games. When the games are over you wait for your seeding. Evening plans can be made based upon the conclusion of the last game. Most teams prefer games to end around 3 PM so the evenings are free. If your team is the host team you can generally schedule your game times appropriately. The RiverCats never hosted events so we were always at the mercy of the tournament host.

Sunday, on the other hand, is designed around the winner. Losers are eliminated and go home. Ostensibly, this is punishment for not playing well. However, by the time your son is 14, going home early has some benefits. You get home at a decent hour. You can sit down and have a dinner with your family. You can mow the grass. You can take advantage of things that you used to take for granted prior to travel baseball.

The RiverCats generally played very late into the day on Sunday. The weekend commitment engulfed every bit of the 48 hours it seemed. But, the time away from home had become a very enjoyable experience for most every family. The boys were improving at a rate that brought college attention and the Perfect Game rankings. In other words, 14u baseball was giving many of the boys an opportunity to stand out on an individual basis. Prior to 14, the attention that baseball players received socially was an Instagram photo holding a trophy.

There is another difference between Saturday and Sunday for the travel baseball family. Saturday is when coaches grant opportunities much more freely. The consequences aren't as dire. Coaches know that playing time on Sunday, if they want to keep playing, often gets dispensed on a meritocracy. The best players play more. Saturday is more of a democracy. Granted, your seeding might be affected if you don't win by a large enough margin, but you'd have to be an awfully calloused coach to not recognize the obvious difference Saturday and Sunday make regarding playing time.

The summer of 2014 was a big summer for the RiverCats. They were rising freshman and the boys felt an urgency about their performance. High School baseball was a mere winter away and colleges were recruiting baseball players as young as their freshman year. The summer circuit would set the stage for much bigger and brighter things. On this July weekend as I recall, the RiverCats were playing in Vineland, NJ in a Perfect Game event. I'm not sure why I remember this but there was some national exposure to be gained. Perfect Game was taking individual mug shots of some of the players for their web site and subsequent featured articles.

On the surface, coaching the game of baseball is a fairly straight forward proposition. Two teams enter their respective dugouts. The coach writes a lineup. The game is played. The umpire officiates the game. The team that scores more runs is declared the winner. Both teams shake hands. The game is concluded.

Here's how it plays out. Teams arrive. They judge each other from how they play catch to how they run. They size up their chances of success based upon the looks test and previous track records. They wait impatiently to see who is pitching. "Does he throw hard?" Once that matter is settled the players form their plan of attack. The coaches and the umpires meet at home plate to address "the ground rules." The meeting is designed as a formal discussion of the playing field and conditions. What it actually serves is a chance for the umpires to assert their initial authority and for the coaches to demonstrate whether they are willing to comply with the umpires on all thing's baseball: from out and safe calls to how to run onto the field to appropriate and inappropriate coaching advice. The parents anxiously await who takes the field. There is always an uneasy feeling at the beginning of every game. The coach has made a decision as to who are the "insiders" and who are the "outsiders." Every person on the team has a role but some roles are more important than others. When the game begins, the umpire often demonstrates his incompetence to both teams. This is usually just confirmation bias though. The umpires are generally very good. The parent's judge bad umpiring as calls that go against their team. As the game plays out full of emotions at every turn, parents often form their own plan of attack for after the game. What should I say to my son? What should I say to the coach? Will my son be happy? Will my son be angry? Psychologists would have a field day in the heads of baseball parents.

There are a lot of perspectives when viewing a baseball game from the sidelines. Watching a game through the lens of a parent/former successful player (The Second Inning) can be one of the most challenging. The RiverCats' parents were very competitive people. But very few carried Judson Christopher's perspective. Judson Christopher played college baseball at Elizabethtown College in Elizabethtown, PA. They had plaques of him in the hallways.[2] In other words, he knew what excellence looked like.

In Vineland, NJ on this particular Sunday in July, Judson Christopher didn't see excellence. I know it scared him. His son Carter was a catcher on the RiverCats. Carter had been on the RiverCats since our first practice, since our first game. Carter Christopher, in all reality, might have been the face of the RiverCats. Following a Sunday game, Judson Christopher summoned up enough courage to have a conversation with Kyle Wagner, the Head Coach of the RiverCats. It wasn't a comfortable conversation.

Some of the most contentious conversations involve coach and parent. Whatever the particulars of the discussion, the parent generally represents the athlete's selfish motives. I don't mean to imply selfish as wrong. I mean to imply selfish as looking out for number 1. If the family doesn't look out for the athlete, who will? These ambitions represent his dreams and his goals. The parent is

---

[2] I coached at Elizabethtown College for 2 years.

the advocate for opportunity. When it comes to chasing dreams and goals, selfish is to be celebrated.

The coach, on the other hand, takes a less emotional position. His position usually is the position of distributive justice. Whereas the parent is keenly aware of an athlete's dreams, the coach recognizes that chasing these dreams doesn't happen in isolation. Providing opportunities for your son at the expense of another player isn't always the appropriate course of action. At some point in the conversation, whether it's said or unsaid, the coach must convey a message of "your son isn't good enough."

Kyle Wagner and Judson Christopher had this conversation. Kyle Wagner played the role of Head Coach. Judson Christopher played the role of Dad. Tears were shed and hugs were shared. It wasn't the official end of a relationship, yet. But the premise was easy to interpret. Carter Christopher was no longer a RiverCat.

In the world of travel baseball this isn't a big deal. There are more than enough teams to provide opportunities to anyone that wants one. Carter was a catcher. This would mean that there was DEFINITELY a team that would want his services. Catchers are a commodity. Gaining a catcher that played for the RiverCats would be an easy sell if Carter wanted another team. But, being a RiverCat for the last 4 years removed this option. Carter was a RiverCat or he was nothing at all.

It's easy to understand why the Christopher's were so committed to the RiverCats. The team was more than a team. The Christopher's were a part of a family. But the Christopher's had two older daughter's that navigated the rough and choppy waters of travel competition. They knew that life didn't always deal a fair hand when it came to opportunities. There had to be more than just a family feel. There had to be more at play to be a part of this team. There was.

A Professional Must Become an Amateur Again
A Beginner's Mindset

"The End" is relative. Every ending is a new beginning. I think it's safe to say that every coach, new or old, is a former player. There may be exceptions to that rule but by in large it's true. Before handing out information and being "in charge" you must have received the information and been "under one's influence." This isn't true just in sports, it's true in just about everything. The student and the teacher cycle of information.

The Head Coach of the RiverCats was a former professional baseball player. That sentence elicits different responses for different people. For the novice baseball person and novice family that sentence is called CREDIBILITY. If I played professional baseball, then I must be qualified to teach the game of baseball. Unfortunately, although this perspective isn't entirely wrong it's also not entirely accurate. For the seasoned baseball person that sentence is called UNCLEAR. People in the game of baseball know that being a professional implies a myriad of possibilities. A former professional baseball player could have had a long-storied career or a professional could have played one season and been unceremoniously dismissed. For Kyle Wagner, being a former professional baseball player meant that I was good enough to get drafted, but I was never really good enough to be considered a prospect.

Eventually, professional baseball players that aren't prospects must come to terms with their "end." Hanging up the spikes (baseball's vernacular for retirement) isn't always a press conference and a formal good-bye to one's endearing fans. Most times, it's a handshake followed by a "thank you and good luck." That's pretty much how I remember my farewell to the game but since it's my personal story the details are emotional. Here's the end in a nutshell for Kyle Wagner.

Following a game in some remote location in the short season Northwest League, the Boise Hawks manager pulled me aside to have a conversation. Tom Kotchman was and still is widely respected in baseball circles. My brief experience with Kotch solidified his reputation. Kotch was honest, passionate and extremely competent. He oozed professionalism and demanded respect. The respect that he demanded stemmed from a lifetime worth of conversations similar to the one he had with me.

Kotch: "Wags, we don't think you're ever going to hit enough to be a Big League, front-line catcher. We love the way you think, catch and throw. Thankfully, you play a position that doesn't require a ton of offense. I'm telling you this early in your career so you can decide if investing in bus rides and a backup role is worth your time. If you're patient enough, someday maybe you could be a back-up catcher in the Big Leagues and maybe even a coach in our organization."

I retired the following spring after one valiant attempt at trying to resurrect a floundering hitting career. I don't remember retiring as difficult. The act of walking into Ken Forsch's office was merely a formality. Retirement was the culmination of repeated failures in the batter's box coupled with high expectations that I wasn't equipped to handle.

That was it. The dreams that Kyle Wagner, the player, had dreamed for as long as he could remember were gone. There would be no Major League debut. There would be no microphone in my locker asking me how I felt being a Major Leaguer. There would be no call home telling Mom and Dad "I made it." There would be no article in the Harrisburg Patriot News exclaiming "Local Star rises to the Big Leagues." Not only did I have to come to grips that my dream was over, I had to come to grips that in many aspects, some people might be disappointed in me.

That experience was unique to me. It didn't make me the man I am, but it certainly helped to craft some very strong perceptions of the game of baseball. Perhaps, the one value, belief, opinion that it cemented for me was…*The game of baseball isn't owned by anyone and the game of baseball doesn't owe anyone.*

Maybe this value, belief, opinion is something that I formed because of the failure I had? Maybe if I never experienced this failure I would have never come to this conclusion? Maybe if every opportunity to play the game of baseball resulted in success I would have come to a different conclusion. Quite possibly, the conclusion might have been...*The way I'm conducting myself is THE RIGHT WAY.* I mean, if it ain't broke why fix it? I suppose that's the danger of success. Success is very affirming indeed. But, for a former player entering a new arena called coaching, success as a player just might be very dangerous.

Of course, what I'm about to suggest might be pure speculation. But, it's certainly fun to develop hypotheses and then test your hypotheses empirically. Maybe, success in the game promotes THIS value, belief, opinion…

The game of baseball is to be played a certain way. I'm entrusted to show my players the way.

In my opinion, this is a very dangerous mindset to take. It isn't dangerous in the sense that it's entirely wrong. There are absolutely nuances to the game of baseball that need to be shared and communicated to a younger, less experienced crowd. There are incredible opportunities to be passed along through modeling proper behavior, techniques and protocol. The game's tendencies are passed down from coach to player and this rite of passage should never be dismissed. What I'm suggesting is this very small insidious notion that the coach controls the message.

"Hey Kyle. What did you just say?"

Success and failure both teach. Failure teaches us to find another way. Success teaches us that our way is THE WAY. As players become coaches, THE WAY is a dangerous mindset to endorse.

Let's consider what a "game of baseball" looks like. I'll offer up 3 different "games of baseball."

Game 1 (The Backyard): A game of baseball in the backyard is a skeleton of what it could be. A pitcher's rubber is more than likely a rubbed-out dirt area. Home plate, more than likely, is a worn-out glove. If you're lucky you've got tattered and torn drop down bases. If you're unlucky you've got more worn out dirt spots in the grass. Teams were selected by offending the last person picked. Umpiring is more a mutual understanding than firm commitment. Do-overs are often used to settle a disagreement that can't be resolved. The time of the game is a function of the constraints placed on you by your Mom. In other words, whenever you must be home. THIS IS A BASEBALL GAME. This game is rooted in *imagination.*

Game 2 (The Schoolyard): A game of baseball played in the confines of a school has more structure. Uniforms are worn and teams are a privilege and honor not to be taken lightly. The stakes of winning and losing are much higher. The coaches receive money for providing this structure to the team. The players are required to sacrifice for the betterment of the team. Individual agendas are taught to be secondary to the primary objective of the team. There is an accepted level of play. Those that don't meet this level aren't to wear the uniform. They're to be cut. THIS IS A BASEBALL GAME. This game is somewhere in between *imagination* and *precision.*

Game 3 (The Professional Game): The game is played with an expectation of being the best. Before the competition takes place on the field, scouting your opponent is expected. Meetings take place highlighting the strengths and weaknesses of your opponent. Strategy is designed around winning the game and the player's role is crafted towards that end. Development is usually catered to "early work." If a player wants to improve or to work out any kinks he must do so on his time. Team time is generally set by the organization. THIS IS A BASEBALL GAME. This game is rooted in *precision.*

For anyone that has experienced "The Professional Game," precision is a mindset that is essential for survival. The competition is so fierce and so talented that advantages are gained only through an optimization approach. Combing the finer details with respect to scouting involves embracing the new age of analytics. The latest trends are adopted, and coaching is crafted with those trends in mind. From a player's perspective, constant growth is required. Threats to one's job are everywhere. The global game demands that anyone with a dream of playing in or staying in the Big Leagues continues to adjust his craft to the requirements of "today's game." The player is at the mercy of "today's game."

The Head Coach of the RiverCats was a former professional baseball player. I played The Precision Game. I dedicated my craft to constant improvement. I acquiesced to those in positions of authority that asked me to change my technique to their technique. It was required of me. But I also knew that emotionally it broke me. It wasn't my coach's fault. It wasn't professional baseball's fault. I broke because I wasn't built on a foundation of love. I was built on a foundation of success. As the Head Coach of the RiverCats, it was my duty for the next generation of baseball players to be built on a foundation of love. That's what I set out to do. To do that, I needed to know that the professional game demands precision. But I also needed to know that this was not the game these boys were playing. The game these boys were playing demanded imagination and love. Placing a Precision Game ahead of an Imagination Game is dangerous territory to tread. My experience taught me it's not IF it will blow up, but rather WHEN it will blow up.

Before a game can be played on the field, it must be played in your mind.

Great players have great imaginations. This is true for anything. Before you can be it, you need to see it!

I believe the biggest mistake that the professional coach makes is they overvalue information and they undervalue motivation. My experience taught me if I was going to make a mistake as a coach, I was going to err on having too much fun rather than too little fun. I wanted my players to want to play for me. I wanted my players to run from the house to the car to the field. I wanted my players to see their time as a RiverCat as the highlight of their day. Yes, I was going to teach them baseball. Yes, I was going to give them everything I knew so they could play quality baseball on the field. But, more importantly, I wasn't going to be the coach that made them stop loving the game. I owed it to their future coaches. In the end, I owed them love.

The game of baseball isn't owned by anyone and the game of baseball doesn't owe anyone.

Baseball coaches are servants to the game. We're tasked with passing the game from generation to generation. When we lose sight of this fact one of two things generally happens.

The first danger that a player encounters could be a GROWTH ONLY coach. This coach is motivated to be the best! This is a good thing. But he's motivated to be the best on his time frame. This is a bad thing. This coach believes that his time with a player is more important than it actually is. This mindset comes from a position of power. In this sense, he owns the game. He might pretend that it's his team and his agenda and his time, but this control is an illusion. A player's attendance doesn't always imply consent. In other words, just because a player submits himself to a coach's message, doesn't always mean he's bought into the message. The best a coach can offer is an environment to learn. He cannot control if something is learned.

The second danger a player encounters is a LOVE ONLY coach. This coach doesn't develop or grow a player. This mindset comes from a position of love but unfortunately a position of entitlement. The game of baseball is an extremely competitive game. If your intentions aren't to improve a player's skill set or give the player more skills to use, you're eventually setting him up for failure. The coach that doesn't grow a player is overvaluing the present and not recognizing the dangers of tomorrow. Players need challenged and they need to know that today's best might not be good enough for tomorrow.

The LOVE GROWTH CYCLE COACH (BALANCED APPROACH) recognizes the standard to which the game must be played but he also recognizes that the player dictates the pace and control of the message.

"Hey Kyle. What did you just say?"

The game of baseball means different things for different people. I also said that there are different types of coaches. Some coaches are more loving and care less about winning. Others care more about winning and are less forgiving. I believe all things being equal, the best coach is the one that finds balance between love and winning.

We Talkin' Practice
The Task, The Organism, The Environment

Coaches are chameleons. They adapt to the environment in which they work. The gameday environment isn't always the best place to evaluate a coach. There are so many variables that can affect a coach and his best laid plans. The best place to evaluate a coach is in a practice setting. Here's how I envision each coach and how he functions under a practice setting.

BEGINNING AND ENDING TIMES: The LOVE ONLY coach just enjoys practice time. When we start and when we finish is secondary to the team merely being together. The GROWTH ONLY coach has every second mapped out. Being late is tantamount to treason. If an error is made it's made in over extending practice time. There is information that must be taught. Running late is a byproduct of hard work sometimes. The BALANCED coach demands players arrive on time. He knows that being late is disrespectful to those that value their time. This is true for coach and player. The BALANCED coach also knows that practices should end on time. If being late to begin practice is an offense to the players and coaches, being late to end practice should also be an offense; to someone.

DELEGATION OF AUTHORITY: THE LOVE ONLY coach isn't obsessed with what is said. He only cares that it's well received. He's obsessed with maintaining a positive environment. The GROWTH ONLY coach is obsessed with perfection. He demands his assistant coaches have a consistent message to his. Any error in the message causes confusion for the player. This is simply unacceptable. The BALANCED coach understands the target and works tirelessly to hit the target. But he recognizes that human beings assist him. In that regard they get tired and they are sometimes distracted and exhausted. Compassion trumps perfection in the short term. But perfection isn't a bad goal to shoot for in the long term.

THE PLAN: The LOVE ONLY coach often has no plan. They will do whatever it is they feel like doing. The GROWTH ONLY coach is married to the plan. The plan is sacred. It must be followed at all costs. Abandoning the plan is an admission of weakness. The plan is where success lives. Sub optimal is a sign of imperfection. The BALANCED COACH writes a plan but adapts to the needs of his athletes. He believes that optimal is important but optimal is framed through a player's lens rather than a coach's lens. He knows intent precedes content. 100% commitment to half an executed plan is better than 50% commitment to an entire plan.

PRAISE / "WRONG SPOTTING" RATIO: The LOVE ONLY coach praises more than he "wrong spots." In fact, "wrong spotting" seldom occurs. The GROWTH ONLY coach "wrong spots" as it is critical to address less than optimal. As The Imagination Game becomes The Precision Game, identifying errors is critical for survival. Furthermore, complimenting someone for meeting an acceptable level of performance seems excessive. Everyone has a job to do. The GROWTH only coach often sees praise as "kumbaya" for the group. The BALANCED coach knows that although "wrong spotting" is essential for growth, it will eventually fall on deaf ears if performance is never seen as acceptable. The BALANCED coach is well aware that there is an optimal level of performance and although doing what is expected should not always merit praise, everyone enjoys a compliment. Recognizing performance creates influence over the "long game." The BALANCED coach also knows that not every "transgression" needs recognized. Allowing mistakes to exist without mentioning it, can often lead to a better opportunity later.

LANGUAGE: The LOVE ONLY coach never offends. His word is sacred, and his message never changes. There is no room for anything other than authentic messages. Sarcasm is to be avoided. The GROWTH ONLY coach works towards the goal. He has no time for sensitive players. Time is of the essence and he can't worry about bruising egos to get the message across. Sarcasm adds value in that sarcasm is merely another tool in the communication tool belt. The BALANCED coach is sensitive to the player. His language is crafted to the time sensitive nature of the sport and the environment in which the message is sent. Threatening environments are no place for sarcasm. Safe environments are more accommodating to sarcasm. The BALANCED coach respects his position enough to place demands on the athlete, yet he respects the athlete enough to never send ambivalent messages when direct is required.

PACE: The LOVE ONLY coach walks. His pace isn't too fast. This communicates that time isn't of the essence. Again, if we're together everything is fine. The GROWTH ONLY coach is constantly sprinting. He's hyper sensitive to his packed schedule. He's as obsessed with missing something as he is with covering something. The BALANCED coach has a good pace to his practice. There are times that he sprints. There are times that he laughs. There are times that he huddles the guys up. The BALANCED coach uses a constant variety of pacing to impart his message.

TECHNIQUE: The LOVE ONLY coach doesn't structure technique too much. Imposing a certain type of technique on someone might be considered oppressive. The LOVE ONLY coach has no preference on style. To each his own. The GROWTH ONLY coach has studied technique. He knows the optimal style. It's essential that this method be taught. Incorporating best practices is an essential ingredient to good teaching. The BALANCED coach has studied technique. He has a preference on style too. He's just sensitive to the fact that he's asking another human being to try this preference. In order to influence someone to try a new technique, he must build trust. Trust takes time to build. The BALANCED coach plants seeds until the player is willing to ask a question. Once the question is asked, he'll embrace the opportunity to affect change.

IT'S *JUST* BASEBALL
IT'S JUST *BASEBALL*

Being labeled a baseball coach seems to be such a superficial assignment outside of baseball. If influencing people is a high priority, teaching baseball players how to swing a bat and throw a ball hardly seems like a noble cause. The BALANCED coach understands that baseball is just a game. The BALANCED coach knows that not everyone shares this passion and in reality, it's a mere game. The BALANCED coach sees a different ending than a LOVE coach or a GROWTH coach. When the players move beyond their playing careers, there is always life yet to experience. The BALANCED coach embraces this and understands that equipping his players with skills for life is more important than the skills between the lines. Baseball's shelf life is transient. Life, on the other hand, has limitless possibilities.

But the BALANCED coach knows that life is meant to be experienced. Today is meant to be pursued passionately. Discounting the game of baseball as superficial is discounting the meaning of a baseball player's life. Everyone has a passion. Discounting the game of baseball as a mere game often means discounting the lives of thousands and thousands of players over the years. So, if they're declaring winners and losers, we'll play to win. Baseball, for many, is an avenue to express one's art. It occupies the baseball player's mind on most waking moments. It's important. In that regard, the coach that equips the player with skills to achieve his loftiest of goals is someone to be cherished, loved.

In the End
Carter Christopher

Eventually, every RiverCat met the fate of Carter Christopher; they left the RiverCats. The RiverCats no longer play baseball. Many of the 'Cats moved on to other national level travel baseball teams. Many of the 'Cats have signed and or committed to prominent programs throughout the country. As these players don a collegiate or professional uniform their RiverCats experience will hopefully continue to resonate. And that's the way it must be in baseball. The BALANCED coach must coach his players knowing that the ultimate success a player experiences will often occur outside his scope. He must develop his players with a standard in mind that will never be achieved. He must love his players with that standard in mind knowing falling short of that goal will always lead to disappointment. He must develop his players with a patience that understands success always falls on their terms. He must love his players enough to know that some other coach will more than likely enjoy the fruits of his labor.

The game of baseball isn't owned by anyone and the game of baseball doesn't owe anyone.

The game of baseball in 2019 is almost unrecognizable to the game I grew up playing. The pitchers throw much faster. Their development has been augmented by analytic driven coaches and ruthless specialization. The hitters are more precise. They're developing in an age that not only requires them to hit elite pitching but also defeat advanced scouting. The actual on field product might not even be the hardest adjustment of all. That honor goes to the social pressure they feel to be great. Is an extra base hit even an extra base hit if a Perfect Game rep doesn't tweet about it? Is a home run a home run if it wasn't seen on Instagram? The perception to be great is real. Perception can open doors in a social media world.

But, thankfully, the true aspect of the game hasn't changed. My hope for the RiverCats is they've been enriched in this aspect of baseball. The game at its core is an imagination game. Deep down beneath the layers of Perfect Game write ups and StatCast exit velocities is a love for the game. Deep down beneath the ubiquitous, inflated expectations is a love for the game. Deep down, buried under the professional scouts and agent's obsession with analytics and metrics is a love for the game. When the RiverCats eventually hang up their own spikes, the struggle they endured and the growth they experienced may not amount to more than some memories worth reliving. But, their love of the game will remain. Their love of the game will eventually drive them back into the coaching profession. The cycle will repeat itself. In the end, there is only love.

Carter Christopher was and always will be one of my favorite players I've ever coached. When you talked to him, he would look at you differently. Most athletes return your coaching with a gaze that says "I hear you. I'm listening to what you're saying. When the next opportunity presents itself, I'll try it." Carter was different. Carter's gaze was more like "I'm sorry I let you down. I want to get this right for both of us. You're important to me and I'll give it my best effort next time." There were many times when I was coaching Carter, I felt like stopping and just giving him a hug and saying "You know you're not going to be a baseball player, right? But I've never coached someone that was so damn focused on being so good. I'm honored that you allow me to push you."

Hugs would have to wait so long as Carter was willing to grow. Some of my fondest memories of Carter revolve around our Tuesday 3:30 lessons. Judson and Carter would often be the first to arrive at the facility. I'd hustle over after school to find them together in a cage prepping for our lesson. My thoughts usually centered along, "I hope they are getting along." The Christopher family dynamic at GoWags was unique to them but it was also a microcosm of every father and son relationship we had in our building. Father knew the danger around the corner. Sons knew how fun the game was in the present. Balancing the need to grow and the love of the game was my job as instructor. I needed Carter to believe in himself today, but I needed him to know it wasn't good enough for tomorrow. Dads appreciate that message. It usually takes a very mature son to do the same.

When it comes to the swing, I break it down into five phases. Those five phases are Anticipation, Initial Impulse, Acceleration,

Error Correction, and Deceleration. In more basic terminology, you have to be ready, be quick, be fast, adjust, and finish. Carter and I spent most of our days working on his "be quick" phase. Carter had power, but I knew it was artificial power. As the velocity improves in The Precision Game, a player's swing must become quick. Any extra movements eventually get exposed by elite pitching. This, in my opinion, was undeniable. We had to improve if Carter was to keep progressing in the game he loved.

But I was always balancing this mindset with a "is it healthy for me to keep pushing Carter if he wasn't capable of implementing the change?" What if the best use of our time was to fill Carter with adjustment skills to navigate the present, knowing that the future might never materialize? Happiness comes in many forms. The GROWTH coach knows it's found through achievement. The LOVE coach knows it's found by accepting who we are without the burden of achievement. The BALANCED coach knows they are both right. I would often tell Carter and all of my lessons, "I can make you feel good anytime I want. I am challenging you. It is uncomfortable. That is where we get better."

Only Carter can say if he looks back on his time as a RiverCat as a happy time. I certainly challenged him. There were many times he left the cage frustrated. There were equally as many times he left the cage ecstatic. We competed together.

"Simply stated, I wanted Carter to play with the best players and be coached by the best coaches in the area. At that time, Carter wanted to be a college baseball player, I wanted to give him every chance to be the best player he could be and that was playing for the RiverCats." -Judson Christopher, RiverCats Dad

---

Carter Christopher never played organized, competitive baseball after leaving the RiverCats. Instead, he dedicated himself to football. The cerebral catcher became a run stopping defensive lineman. Carter was recently named to the prestigious Big 33 football game held in Hershey, PA. Every Super Bowl ever played as had a former Big 33 football player in it. Carter Christopher will represent himself, his family and most assuredly his RiverCats family when he takes the field in Hershey, PA. I see ya workin' Carter.

Carter Christopher currently stands at 6'2" 290 lbs. He'll be attending Princeton University in the fall of 2019. Carter was recruited to play defensive tackle for the Ivy League school.

The Eighth Inning

Goals Change; Discipline Persists

Why are we so attracted to greatness? What is it about witnessing the best on this planet achieve great things that makes us honor them? We're spellbound by their abilities. They make the difficult look easy. They give us a vision into what the human spirit or in some cases "not so human" spirit could look like. We imagine the possibilities when it comes to those that are great. They inspire hope and promise. Imagine what they can do next. They connect to our soul because they're the best of us. Our people, our country, our team produced that.

Three souls that I admire in this very way are John Wooden, Robin Williams and Secretariat. I can't help but admire them and think about what they did with their time on this planet. Maybe it's because Wooden made me think. Maybe it's because Williams made me laugh. Maybe it's because Secretariat made me cry. In a very simple sense, it could be just that. But, on a visceral level, I love them because they inspired others around them.

John Wooden was a humble man. But, John Wooden competed. John Wooden was by all accounts an incredible husband, father, teacher and humanitarian. He was and still is the model for all coaches to shoot for. He was a man that won a lot of basketball games. But he was a man that was revered by his players long after the games ended. John Wooden built his teams and the people he influenced on his principle of the Pyramid of Success. Wooden cared enough about greatness that he developed a model for others to use. If you've never explored Wooden's model do yourself a favor and check it out. John Wooden inspired others around him to be great because he challenged them. He didn't challenge them by asking them to work hard. Working hard was to be a given. Why do anything at all if you're not going to give your best? Wooden challenged them to see a better future for themselves by instilling the greatest gifts our world has to offer; the gifts that propel the human character forward. John Wooden was a teacher of principles that was so respected that others were attracted to his mere presence. Wooden was great.

Robin Williams was hilarious. Robin Williams gave anyone that saw him one of life's greatest gifts. He gave us laughter. He could disarm a room full of tension with his arrival. Williams knew that eventually the only thing that matters is love. All the tasks that are so important today, are probably just a task for today. The agendas that drive our urgency? It's not really that urgent. Robin Williams was great because Robin Williams seemed to understand that at our core, we want to love people. Love can be expressed in so many ways, but you can't hide authentic laughter. I'm not talking about I'm amused with your thought laughter. I'm talking about that's so damn funny I might pee my pants laughter. You don't forget those moments. Williams lived to make those moments. Put a bunch of people in a room together. The room could be full of dignitaries, authorities, statesman, and yet Robin Williams would get them to laugh. Williams never seemed impressed with titles and labels. If you had a pulse, Williams assumed laughter would help you enjoy the day. So, Robin Williams gave you a gift. He always made people around him laugh. Williams was great.

Secretariat was a fast horse. Racing seems to be one of life's easiest forms of competition. Who is faster? Let's race. The anticipation of the gun going off and the suspense at the finish line. It's simple and yet it's profound. The world of horse racing lumps three races into a collection of races they refer to as the Triple Crown: The Kentucky Derby, The Preakness and The Belmont Stakes. The races are all different lengths. They recognize The Triple Crown as a very prestigious accomplishment because great racers, humans or horses, aren't supposed to be great at varying lengths. Long distance runners aren't built for sprints and vice versa. Winning the Triple Crown says, "I can do it all." Secretariat did it all by captivating a nation along the way. Maybe it was Secretariat's owner Penny Chenery that assisted the cause. Chenery played the role of attractive female owner that had enough bravado to compete in a man's world. Maybe Secretariat had an adoring fan base well before the 1973 Kentucky Derby ever was run. To me, I can't help but adore Secretariat because of the '73 Belmont Stakes. The Disney movie *Secretariat* embellishes the final stretch. I love the final stretch with the music and the drama. I cry every time. Secretariat was great.

I find myself asking probing questions all the time. When I think about greatness, I ask myself...

1) Would they have been great if life dealt them a different beginning?

2) Would they have been great if the people in their lives would have been different?

3) Would they have been great if they were born in a different time?

When I ask these questions, I appreciate them even more. Yes, they were amazing, and their exploits are now a part of our collective memories. But, thinking about a world without Wooden's teams, without William's antics, without Secretariat's speed makes me grateful they existed at all.

Here are some interesting notes about each of their lives that makes me stop and think "What if they had chosen a different path?" What if their lives had gone in a different direction?

John Wooden would have been the coach at The University of Minnesota if not for a major snowstorm. Wooden wanted to stay and coach in the Midwest where he grew up. As he waited for a Golden Gopher coaching offer, the UCLA Bruins offered him the same position out on the West Coast. Not hearing from Minnesota due to the weather, he assumed they weren't interested, and he accepted the position in California. The "Wizard of Minneapolis?"[3]

Robin Williams was voted by his high school graduating class as "Most Likely to Not Succeed." I should also add that he was voted "Funniest". Knowing what I know now, "funniest" often implies "smartest." High School students interpreted his "funny" as "inappropriate." That's awfully unfortunate but completely understandable. There are tasks to be accomplished in school, life. Only the most aware realize the idea is more important than the task. Thankfully, Robin Williams didn't allow others to promote the task over the idea.

Horses call their dads sires and their moms dams. Secretariat's sire was Bold Ruler and his dam was Somethingroyal. As documented in the movie, Penny Chenery's ownership of the legendary racehorse was due to a coin flip. In theory, this makes the circumstances to Secretariat's training a 50/50 proposition. The movie leads us to believe that Chenery would have wound up with Secretariat regardless of the outcome of the coin. Nonetheless, it's crazy to imagine how Secretariat might have turned out with different ownership and a different trainer.

Moving forward in life requires goals that attract us. They are these nebulous events in the future that excite us, inspire us. They are the reasons we wake up. They are the reasons we challenge ourselves. They are the promise of a better future.

But the path that leads to that goal isn't always fun. The path that leads to that goal is riddled with pain, adversity, uncertainty, doubt, and fear. At any moment along the way, the emotion of the path can sabotage the future goal. If the pain is too great, just quit.

---

[3]John Wooden's nickname was "The Wizard of Westwood." Westwood, CA is a suburb of Los Angeles, CA.

It's gone just like that. If the adversity is unbearable, just quit. It's gone just like that. And that's the way goals and discipline interact. Once you set a goal, you invite in all the pain that prevents you from achieving that goal. The only way to find the prize at the end is to embrace the uncomfortable. The pain isn't a result of doing something wrong. The pain is a result of doing something right; chasing the goal.

Dream Chasin'
Nick Embleton

Nick pitched. He was the pitcher that every team knew existed in the other dugout and hoped wasn't slated to pitch against you. Nick was a hard throwing young athlete and Nick was a competitor. One of my first memories of Nick was watching him throw a baseball with a radar gun behind him. He was firing balls as young kids do simply trying to make the number go higher and higher. At the time, I happened to know that the highest velocity I had seen from a 9-yr. old was 64 mph. I told Nick this. Nick was throwing 60-61. The next pitch was 64 mph.

Nick joined the RiverCats as an 11-yr. old. He was immediately our staff ace. Being a staff "ace" for an 11-yr. old travel team simply meant he threw late on the weekends. If you could hold your ace until the championship that was preferred. Sometimes, the semi-final would foil your plans and you'd have to use your ace to get to the championship. One memory of Nick Embleton occurred in this very fashion. The RiverCats would need Nick in a semi-final game in Cooperstown, NY.

Cooperstown, of course, is home to baseball's Hall of Fame. It's a bucket list event if you're a sports fan. The town wreaks of nostalgia. The quaint little town is also home to one of travel baseball's major events. Cooperstown, NY hosts week long tournaments all summer at their prestigious Dreams Park. Weekly, over 100 teams flock to Cooperstown to indulge in the festivities that only a baseball mecca can provide. For most teams, attending Dreams Park is the culmination of years of fundraising and often a youth travel team's last event together before tackling "the big field." For the RiverCats, Dreams Park felt like a business trip. Yes, we had procured the necessary pins to trade. Yes, we had our banner we'd walk with as we paraded around campus. But, for the players and coaches, leaving Cooperstown without the championship would very much feel like a disappointment.

At the prestigious tournament, Thursday is the championship day. Thursday is survive and move on day. To make it to the championship as one of the last two teams requires deep pitching and as always, a little bit of luck. The RiverCats reached the semi-final round with our two best pitchers remaining. We thought we had a chance at this thing. As Head Coach, I decided to hold Nick for the championship. The Louisiana Padres, our semi-final opponent, would get Adam Maring instead. Adam Maring was, for all intents and purposes, our most productive pitcher all year long. I was conceding nothing. Adam would be just fine. By the 2nd inning we were down 6-0.

I love emotion in a baseball game. I think baseball would be well served to adopt more emotion. Baseball's stodgy old traditions of throwing at batters when they celebrate home runs seems like an entitled little brat when you think about it. When a guy celebrates because he bettered you, how about "get better?" Of course, there are grandiose forms of celebration that can't be tolerated. But, often, a team's ego gets bruised and they use an outdated mode of retaliation to get even. During this semi-final game, I was trying to decide if the Padres celebration was inappropriate or if I was that stodgy old man. As I was debating the authenticity of their celebration, I decided it was time for Nick to pitch.

We started to chip away at their lead. Nick started to set them down. A six-run deficit became a four-run deficit. By the 5th inning, we brought the tying run to the plate. By the 6th inning, we had the lead. Nick gave them nothing. In a game witnessed by what felt like the entire Dreams Park community, Nick proved to everyone there he was in fact our "ace." I'm sure there are a lot of reasons that that game sticks in my memory. A Pennsylvania team beat a very talented Louisiana team. Jimmy Losh homering to put us ahead. The Padres coach celebrating in a slightly over zealous manner. But, make no mistake, without Nick Embleton those memories aren't nearly as sweet.

The Embleton family had every right to dream big following Nick's 12u campaign. Nick was proving time and time again he was a "dude." I mean, if Nick couldn't dream about his future on the mound, few could. If 12-yr. old Nick never openly talked about playing baseball in the SEC or the ACC, it's only because Nick wasn't always the most outspoken kid. But rest assured, Nick was thinking about it. Nick Embleton deserved all the attention he received. He was the best pitcher on the best 12u travel team Pennsylvania could muster. Then, Nick got hurt.

If you polled most youth baseball coaches, they might collectively agree that 13u baseball is the hardest time to be a player and a coach. It's almost not even worth it. The field is gigantic compared to what the boys were playing on as 12-yr. olds. The pitchers' arms aren't strong enough to consistently throw strikes. The pitchers' egos aren't mature enough to embrace batted ball contact. The position players make much longer throws than they're accustomed to. Outfielders can't cover enough ground and more balls fall. It's generally a recipe for injury. This was Nick Embleton's fall following his magical 12U season.

For the first time, Nick Embleton was forced to wrestle with thoughts of doubt. The tamest of those doubts centered around, "What if I'm not ready to pitch by the spring?" The most severe became "What if I'm never the same again?" This is where all decisions eventually stem from. A thought sprouts up in one's conscious. The more you feed it, the more it starts to become you.

The brave, the committed, the disciplined refuse to succumb to those thoughts. They realize the thoughts might not be wrong. But they also realize there is still a goal worth pursuing.

If you want to know how much value something has in your life, take it away. Only when something is gone do we value what it means to us. Nick eventually regained his health. Baseball was no longer a guarantee. The time on the mound wasn't to be taken for granted. Success would be appreciated.

Routine
The Good, The Bad, The Ugly

Routines are driven by rewards. Nothing is more rewarding for a pitcher than a healthy arm. Nick Embleton knew that a healthy arm was the key to his long-term success and regaining the form that made him so effective. Chasing that healthy arm isn't quite as easy as simply resting the arm. Arm health and pitch velocity have been packaged together in an attractive option for many aspiring pitchers. If you want a healthy arm, you might as well throw harder in the process. The reward of health and velocity create an opportunity to engage in a habit loop. Whether you become aware of the routine, determines if it is dangerous.

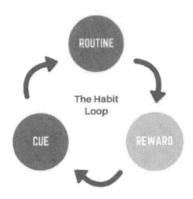

Charles Duhigg created this visual called *The Habit Loop* in the book *The Power of Habit*. Special attention must be paid to the reward as it will determine the routine.

Duhigg succinctly states the danger of the habit loop when he writes, *"When a habit emerges, the brain stops fully participating in decision making."* If the brain isn't going to help with decision making, it sure better know if it's on the right track. This routine that becomes our de facto decision making isn't always beneficial.

The Good:
Routines are the backbone of good habits. Not everything in life is fun and exciting. To create an opportunity for beneficial life choices, we often need to build life habits that choose for us. Without these routines, we're left with an infinite amount of daily choices and invariably we'll succumb to the wrong choice. Peer pressure, temptation, and the gratification of now can overwhelm productive. Routines provide the necessary structure to eliminate the noise of distraction. Routines provide the necessary structure to prevent avoidable exhaustion. Routines must exist if progress is to be made. As Jocko Willink, author of the book by the same name likes to say, *Discipline Equals Freedom*.

Routine is useful if the journey is safe. Routine can be harmful if the journey is threatening.

The Bad:
Routines are not only the backbone of good habits, but routines are the backbone of bad habits. Routines provide the ability to move faster. As we transfer from awareness of the world around us to auto-pilot we take for granted the dangers that are lurking. I like to refer to this as running scripts. Running scripts are the GPS mindset of our modern-day world. We plug in the destination and without enjoying the journey we arrive. Did you notice the lake on your left? No, I was just running the script. Did you notice the ambulance approaching behind you? No, I was just running the script. Despite our need to create predictable, the world is not

predictable. Running scripts instead of reacting to the world is a dangerous proposition. At best, you'll miss opportunities to better your life. At worst, you'll miss threats that can damage your life.

Routine is useful if the journey is safe. Routine can be harmful if the journey is threatening.

The Ugly:
People interact with other people. If the Golden Rule is, treat others the way you would like to be treated, routine can compromise the Golden Rule. This happens when people are running their scripts of life. Is it important to do your job? Absolutely. A job well done is satisfying. Is it important to do your job if doing your job hurts someone else? Maybe. Sometimes people get hurt. A utopia has yet to be created. Is it important to do your job if doing your job hurts someone else **AND THERE IS AN ALTERNATIVE SOLUTION?** The jobs, tasks, goals that we're asked to do can be very rewarding. The incentives that we receive monetarily and the rewards that we receive socially become self-fulfilling. We repeat these things craving more and more. The status quo becomes accepted because the status quo is addictive and powerful. Why would I consider an alternative if this solution is successful? That's what Charles Duhigg would call a *Habit Loop* in his book *The Power of Habit*. Often, by no fault of our own, people in positions of authority are trained to run dangerous habit loops. They're not necessarily dangerous for those running the scripts, but rather dangerous for those around them. As we run the scripts of our life, we often develop unintentional blindness to the needs of those around us.

Routine is useful if the journey is safe. Routine can be harmful if the journey is threatening.

"Hey Kyle. What did you just say?"

Close attention must be paid to whether our actions are by choice or out of habit. The rewards that enter our life are addictive. Chasing these rewards becomes the script we tend to engage in. Awareness that rewards create unintended consequences is the first step in reclaiming discipline to meet your long-term goals.

Pitching Lessons
From Imagination to Precision (The Hard Middle)

Most of my lessons at GoWags were hitting lessons. Every now and again, when Bret[4] was too busy or when one of my families wanted a change of pace, they'd ask me to give them a pitching lesson. "Hey, you know pitching too, right?" I'd reply "Well, I've been catching them my whole life so I think I can add some value." Here's the thing about catchers. We don't know what it feels like, but we sure know what it looks like.

Here's how my pitching lessons would usually go. They'd get loose with some form of warmup and then I'd squat behind a plate and catch their stuff. I wanted to make sure I knew what I was dealing with. After catching their pitches, I'd walk up and tell them what I believe made up a pitcher and I'd follow it up with a question.

I'd say "Pitchers demonstrate four qualities with every pitch they make. 1) Velocity. Every pitch leaves the pitcher's hand with a certain amount of speed. 2) Location. Every pitch has a final destination that determines its accuracy. 3) Movement. Every pitch moves a certain degree on its way to home plate. 4)

---

[4] Bret Wagner is my twin brother and best friend. Reducing him to a footnote as an introduction hardly seems appropriate. Yet…

Competitive grit. Every pitch is thrown under the pressure and context of a game." After sharing these pieces of information with the pitcher, I'd ask "Which one are you best at and which one do you need more work at?" Many times, the young pitcher would recruit the dad for help. The dads whom I respected would look back at the son and say, "He didn't ask me, he asked you." Eventually, a reply would come either from the dad or the son. Most of my pitchers happened to be good strike throwers that wanted to throw harder.

That's the "hard middle" in a nutshell for pitchers. They've survived the beginning of the Imagination Game and they know the need for more velocity is real to survive The Precision Game that lies ahead. The hunt for more velocity takes center stage in the lives of all pitchers. What's also very real in the hunt for more velocity is it can never happen in a lesson format. There's absolutely zero chance I can make quantifiable gains in a 30-minute lesson if in fact you truly believe that velocity is what you need to improve upon. Here's a story that I've told my lessons from time to time to explain the importance of velocity.

Bret and I were outsiders on the Wake Forest baseball team. Not because we weren't welcomed by our teammates and our coaches but because we were from Pennsylvania. At the time, Bret and I were the sole Keystoners on the team. Apparently, we had an accent. As is always the case, a fish "out of water" implies a fish is at home in the water. Bret and I had never been told we had an accent because Bret and I had never ventured out of state for any extended time. As we were having a catch one day[5] and I made the comment "Was there controversy, Bret?" The boys from Carolina hooted and hollered about that question. Apparently, when you're from New Cumberland, PA the inflection of your voice rises at the

---

[5] Growing up in Pennsylvania, we called this "passing." We were trained to call it "have a catch" by our North Carolinians.

end. I can still hear Chris Smith, a Wake Forest teammate, laughing at me today. Each of us use the English language to communicate with each other. The subtle dialects that we use are unique to us and define us. Velocity is like an outsider's dialect. Throwing at an acceptable speed allows you to fit in easier. Throwing at a substandard speed doesn't necessarily exclude you, but you need to be aware of your limitations and find a way to work around them.

The quest for velocity has become a huge market to exploit. Everyone knows it's in high demand and with demand comes opportunity. The challenge for the pitcher is who to trust and what's at risk. There are better people than me to speak about how to develop velocity. These are the people with an INSIDE VIEW (The Second Inning) of velocity training. I have an OUTSIDE VIEW and that's what I'd like to discuss.

The OUTSIDE VIEW of velocity training recognizes that everything has a cost. Time spent developing one thing is time lost developing another. I believe there is a holistic way to improve your velocity and I believe there is a fractured isolated way to improve your velocity. The fractured isolated way looks at velocity through an independent lens. This suggests that 86 is better than 85. That's easy. Higher is better than lower. Separate lenses can get people in trouble. It was that same separate lens that never considered that people from New Cumberland, PA talk different than folks from the Carolinas.

I realize that some kids don't have the luxury of taking a holistic view to velocity training. If velocity doesn't allow you a chance to play, it might require a separate lens to focus on. I get that. But it doesn't mean it won't have consequences in the long run. Bowing down at the altar of more and more velocity can make for a tough existence when it comes time to play The Precision Game.

Pitching in The Precision Game requires sequencing of pitches and it requires this sequencing to occur in the face of great adversity.

Taking an isolated, fractured approach to velocity improvement can lead a pitcher into a bad habit loop. Here's how the bad habit loop occurs.

A pitcher is lured into believing that improved velocity improves your ability to pitch. This very well might be true. But equally it might not be true. It's certainly not a fact that increased velocity makes you a better pitcher. Increased velocity only means you have sharpened one of your tools in your pitching tool belt. Potentially, this can be used to your advantage. The best measure to a pitcher's effectiveness is best quoted by Randy Sullivan of the Florida Baseball Ranch. *"Did the dude with the bat in his hand go back to the dugout?"*

Before I go any further, I need to make this comment. If I had a choice between throwing 85 or 86, I'd choose 86. Throwing harder is better than throwing softer, **all things being equal.** But all things aren't always equal. A pitcher's effectiveness comes down to his velocity, his command, his movement and his competitive grit. If you're pitching at LakePoint, Georgia with a giant radar gun at your back and every pitch you throw you check the radar gun, I have to question if you're competitively focused.[6] If your goal when taking the mound is to "post a number" I have to question how much value, you actually place on the process of pitching.

---

[6] I recently saw a video of Trevor Bauer checking the scoreboard while pitching. Once you are competing at the highest of levels, your competitive grit has already been established.

Numbers
Let's Sort Them

I'm not naive. I realize that college coaches require a certain number on the scoreboard in order to offer you money. The cost of attending college is so high it's gotten to the point that many can't justify the expense. A scholarship to defray that expense can be a huge break in the life a student athlete. It is indeed a reward.

Afterthoughts	Can't Miss Dudes
Fred Flintstone **81 mph**	Barney Rubble **93 mph**
George Jetson **77 mph**	Astro The Dog **92 mph**
Laverne **75 mph**	Shirley **92 mph**

We live up to the labels we're given.

If I see myself as a kind person, punching someone in the face won't sit well with me. If I see myself as a smart person, failing a Biology test won't sit well with me. If I see myself as a fast person, losing a race to half the track team won't sit well with me.

The hard middle is still the middle. You haven't arrived anywhere yet. You're not pitching in the Big Leagues. You're not on a 40-man roster. You're not about to sign your first pro contract. Those folks have survived the middle. They're playing The Precision Game that the end requires. The people languishing in the middle still have miles to go. The last thing they need is a label to distract them from their true purpose.

The **Afterthoughts** are often led to believe they're not pitchers. They might not be. But, quite possibly they're late bloomers with a passion to pitch. Maybe they're 5'4" 135 lbs. and can command 3 pitches for strikes. Maybe, once they grow their velocity becomes another tool in the tool belt and they become a **Can't Miss Dude.**

The Can't Miss Dudes are often led to believe that they're a finished product. They're courted by colleges and advisors and they believe they're on the cusp of the Hall of Fame. It's just a matter of time before Cooperstown is calling. How could I not be? Uhhhh…maybe because you're just a big fish in a small pond. The **Can't Miss Dudes** that overvalue the velocity will pay a huge price when they realize the guys that hit baseballs in the Big Leagues prefer the better fastball. It's the command and movement they despise. Hello **Afterthought.**

And, that's the reason that external motivation makes the hard middle very hard. When pitchers get labeled as **Afterthoughts,** they must fight the temptation to think the game doesn't have a future for them. If you kill their dream, you kill the game for them. When pitchers get labeled as **Can't Miss Dudes,** they must fight the temptation to think they've already arrived. If you kill their drive and determination to chase the actual goal, you've also killed the game for them, the "long game."

The hard middle is a wilderness of danger. The goal hasn't yet come into view and the beginning's motivation was forgotten a while ago. Surrounding us in the wilderness are adults helping us navigate this dangerous and threatening world. In an idealistic world, these adults only have our best interests at heart. They tell us what we need to hear and when we need to hear it. The truth is, these adults are motivated by things. These adults are afraid of things too. These incentives and fears can often manifest in advice and critiques that become distractions to our true end game.

What's the solution? Ignore all advice and bury your head in the sand when it comes to radar guns? Absolutely no. The adults in your life are there to help you. You need as many advocates for your cause as you can find. Alienating another human being because he's simply doing his job isn't a recipe for success. The radar guns aren't going away. Sports are becoming micro managed by technology. More and more the athletes that play the game are merely a number on some critics' computer screen. The solution isn't a solution at all. It's more like a concession. The concession is 1) recognize you're in the hard middle and 2) don't ever allow one man's opinion to define you. Coaches provide information to assist you. Coaches do not provide judgment to define you. Radar guns provide information to assist you. Radar guns do not provide judgment that defines you.

Nothing stays the same. The minute you dive into the pool of competition, every day is more challenging than the previous one. The competition improves. The coaches become more demanding. The critics become more judgmental. Mom and Dad often become more protective. Some people continue to strive towards that goal. That's commendable and it's what defines grit and perseverance. Some quit and that's perfectly ok too. Survival Systems[7] can't be enjoyed by everyone. But those that quit better never quit on the discipline that is required to chase whatever that next goal becomes. Life without goals seems worthless. But those same goals that you set and those same goals that move you and motivate you won't always be achieved. Others may even claim those goals and laugh at you when you don't achieve them. Set a new goal anyway. Chase it with the same determination and conviction of your old goals. The goals give life meaning not because we achieve them, but because we set them. The discipline

---

[7] I call any competition a survival system. If the pool of competition narrows as you play it, it is a survival system. Survival systems cause people to be on "high alert." Dangerous!

required to pursue them becomes the sustaining virtue that is a skill for life.

Not everyone is meant to be John Wooden, Robin Williams and Secretariat. Not everyone is meant to be a champion. Not everyone is meant to be celebrated and called great. The world honors those "champions" with applause and fame. But everyone is meant to demonstrate discipline. Everyone is required to find value in their life and pursue the goals that give meaning to it. Maybe the reason we celebrate greatness is the human spirit found motivation to start, the discipline to get through the hard middle, and had enough courage to finish and capture the prize at the end. Maybe, subconsciously, we know that's no easy task for anyone.

"Hey Kyle. What did you just say?"

Whenever you attach something to an object, the attachment takes on more significance than it should. Often the price of an object becomes more important than its value. This is what happens when athletes fall victim to caring more about how hard they throw than learning to pitch.

The Hard Middle of Survival Systems
When Other People Make Us Reach for Rewards

"Justice is not only about the right way to distribute things. It is also about the right way to value things." — Michael J. Sandel, *Justice: What's the Right Thing to Do?*

When people *do* things, other people *judge* things. It's the nature of the artist and the critic. The artist creates. His imagination is free to concoct whatever comes to mind. The critic determines if that art falls within the bounds of social norms. If that critic is tasked with ranking the art, often the task becomes more about pleasing the critic than making great art. In survival systems, the critic often provides most of the stress and subsequent pleasure that distracts from the goal. In survival systems, the critic is often valued more than the artist.

A critic believes his job is to dole out distributive justice. The art that is created must be evaluated. The critic believes it is his duty, based upon his experience, to rate the artist's work upon the standard to which he thinks art should exist. The critic's perception of the world is "art centered" but the feedback provided is seldom "artist centered." The artist believes his job is to create great art. He understands that creating great art tends to elicit the critic. He believes the critic doles out procedural justice. The artist doesn't interpret the feedback as a rating against the standard. The artist interprets the feedback as an indictment on his work. Both the artist and the critic see the rating or critique as "art centered." The difference exists in the interpretation. The artist is always "artist centered" while the critic is "art centered." The distributive justice, procedural justice perspective is where all the tension lives.[8]

Seeing the role of justice through Charles Duhigg's habit loop model reveals the reality of the Bad Habit Loop and the Ugly Habit Loop when it comes to the artist and the critic. The artist falls prey to a bad habit loop the minute he recognizes the reward he's chasing (velocity) was an external motivator that doesn't necessarily mean he'll become a better pitcher. The critic falls prey to an Ugly Habit Loop when the job he's performing takes precedence over the artist he's serving. The habit loops we engage in affect more of life moments than we realize.

---

[8] Teachers grade tests through a critic lens. Students perceive tests through the artist lens.

Every school year that I can remember we have an inspirational speaker come and talk to the teachers in attendance. I love the idea. I hate the timing. If you want to have the greatest impact on the lives of students, the motivational speaker needs to come in the middle of the year when routines are at their peak. In August or September, teachers know the grind lies ahead. They're essentially playing The Imagination Game. They know what challenges they'll surely face, and they've had three months to prepare. In February, they're stuck in the routine of lesson planning, grading and discipline. The mission (idea) often gets lost under a stack of "to do" lists. The best time to bring on a motivational speaker is when the motivation to start has worn off and the goal of finishing feels too distant to dream about.

Most people enter a survival system exactly how teachers start a school year, on high alert. They know it will be tough. They anticipate the struggle and they're prepared to meet it. They may overestimate their skill level, but they know the competition isn't going to lay down and concede the prize. The beginnings of survival systems are generally met with an expectation of struggle, challenge and competition. When it arrives, we're generally not caught off guard. We knew it would be tough. Here it is. The perception of the system matches the reality of the system. No psychological warfare needed. In the immortal words of Dennis Green[9]…*" They are who we thought they were."*

Getting to the middle of the survival system has an implication that can't go unnoticed. We survived the beginning. People that find themselves in the middle of a survival system have gained experiences that form their new perception. They've been successful. Success breeds success. Unfortunately, the success that was won isn't the ultimate goal. That lies further down the road. The middle gets hard because often the competitor mistakes

---

[9] An NFL football coach who offered up that quote in a post-game rant.

45

the rewards received along the way as accomplishment. The more rewards we collect the more we're affirmed that our path is the right path. This feeds the brain's dopamine circuit. The hard middle gets very hard because the ever-threatening survival system takes on an element of safety. What I've done to this point has proven successful. So long as I stay the course, the future is bright. But these rewards are often fool's gold tricking the competitor to leave his guard down only to be surprised when danger is found lurking around the next corner. The habit loop becomes real.

The danger eventually manifests itself and causes pain. The pain could be in a loss. The pain could be in losing a starting position. The pain could be a bad grade on a test. The pain could be being cut from a team. But the pain we experience in the middle is essential to get to the end. Without the pain, we'll never truly understand the discipline required to achieve as the survival system narrows.

The end of the survival system is for the very select few. These people survived the hard middle as they recognized that the discipline required to keep chasing their goal is in fact fun. Discipline isn't fun as in instant gratification scratch my back fun. Discipline becomes fun as in my hard work has earned me the right to see my big dreams come into view fun. The prize is within reach. I've sacrificed the allure of now for the promise of tomorrow. As tomorrow emerges from a cloud of uncertainty, only the disciplined can enjoy the satisfaction of knowing that their hard work was in fact worth the effort.

"Hey Kyle. What did you just say?"

Discipline is hardest when we forget the reason for starting and can't see the light at the end of the tunnel. The people in our lives often contribute to this as they influence us in so many ways; many of which aren't good.

Navigating the Middle
Nick Embleton

Nick Embleton was and is a very good pitcher. The folks that have entered Nick's life as he's progressed towards his goal have made the middle very difficult for Nick. It's not their fault they have made it difficult. The middle is hard for everyone. They're doing their job. They, in this case, are the people that value radar guns. They are the college coaches that hold the dreams of many aspiring athletes in their hands. They are the college coaches that decide who is worthy of receiving an athletic scholarship to play Division 1 college baseball.

Today's game is different than the game I played growing up. I saw my future self on This Week in Baseball every weekend. That was the goal that motivated me. Today's players have their dreams scrolled across their face more frequently. Today's players can check out their dreams every nanosecond on Instagram if they choose. Today's players are confronted with a much more realistic dream than playing in the Big Leagues. They are confronted with playing Division 1 college baseball. There are decisions in our life that are important. Who you marry is a very big decision? The companion you choose to interact with on a daily basis is life's biggest decision. If that is true, choosing where you spend your time between the ages of 18 and 22 probably factors in as much, if not more, than who you marry. You can't marry the right person if you can't meet the right person. College is where many people find their eventual spouse. It's a big decision.

The undeniable reality is many athletes choose where they go to college based upon where they can play their sport in college. The college coach holds more power in their hands then they realize. An offer to play baseball at a school could be extrapolated to mean an offer to start a new life. I love college baseball. Many young athletes love college baseball. The invitation to a beautiful, appealing life flashes across our eyes as often as you can refresh your Instagram feed. And, now that ESPN has their app anyone can watch college baseball much more frequently. College baseball has become a marketable commodity. The young people that play the game are identifying more and more with towns like Baton Rouge, Nashville, Corvallis, and Chapel Hill. The college game is a passionate game. The college game is romantic. The college game is innocent. But the college game has an underbelly that most don't see. The college game is pure on the outside but often rancid on the inside.

The college coaches I know are great people. They're giving. They're committed. They're compassionate. But they're handicapped. They're handicapped by a number. 11.7. That's a number that only an aspiring baseball player's family can appreciate. Three tenths short of an even dozen. It's just a number. But it determines the fate of athletes all over the country. It sets the rules by which baseball players play. It creates urgency. It pits good people against other good people. It promotes unethical behavior. It facilitates decisions that run counter to good logic and rational thought. The number sets the tone for our lives. The number creates an ugly habit loop that often has unintended consequences for the aspiring baseball player. The number is the amount of scholarships a Division 1 baseball coach has available to hand out to prospective student athletes. 11.7 scholarships to create a roster of 35. That'll certainly make the middle hard for those accepting and those offering the scholarships.

I've known Nick since he was that little 9-yr. old firing rockets into a net. Nick hasn't won every goal he's ever set. They're called losses, setbacks and failures. They're inevitable. What isn't inevitable and what separates the disciplined from the undisciplined is how you respond. The beginning and the ending are easier than the middle. Nick's in the middle. If his behavior is true of his motivation, Nick's finding a way to move towards his goals. He shows up on time. He does the work required of him. He doesn't seek artificial attention and fake rewards. He's got his head down and it appears he realizes the true target is still miles away. I see ya' workin' Nick.

Nick Embleton will be attending St. Joseph's University (Philadelphia PA) in the fall of 2019. Nick Embleton developed an insurance policy as he pursued his dream of being a division 1 pitcher. Nick had enough discipline to know that the goal is worth chasing but the discipline to plan for a new goal might prove important. Nick is an outfielder / pitcher.

The Seventh Inning

People Seek Stability; Teams Seek Change

> *"If you want to go fast, go alone. If you want to go far, go together." – African proverb*

Here's a question worth pondering. When do people choose pain and misery over happiness? It's so common, in fact, that it makes you question the basic sanity of those that do it. Here's how it plays out. The work week ends, and these insane people devote countless hours of their weekend to making themselves miserable. I would argue the misery could be so powerful that it might even take until the following Thursday until the wound is entirely healed. Sports fans have to be insane when it comes right down to it. What compels an entire fan base to pay money and devote time to what many would consider inevitable pain?

Cleveland Browns fans are the extreme of this insanity, but every fan base goes through it from time to time. Why do we choose to root for teams that inflict pain and misery every year? In reality, the fans could switch allegiances as often as they switch their wardrobe or dinner plans. There's no contract that commits a fan to his team. There's no national oppressor forcing one's obligation to a team. It's so rational to switch teams that young children are forced to adopt the irrational behavior the older they grow.

In 1979, there were pictures of me sporting the Pittsburgh Steelers gold and black. It must have been a Christmas present that six-year-old Kyle and Bret Wagner asked for. The Steelers were Super Bowl Champions in 1979. Later, there was evidence of Bret Wagner sporting 49'ers gold and maroon. Kyle chose the Bengals. My choice wouldn't pay the same dividends that Bret's would. Still, other memories involve the Baltimore Colts, the beloved team of the Wagner men before Kyle and Bret. But they moved away from Baltimore in 1983 leaving a void that was to be filled by some other team. Today, Bret and Kyle Wagner pull for the Philadelphia Eagles. 2018 Super Bowl Champions baby.

Of course, the fickle nature of young fans speaks more to their inexperience than anything else. As we age and gain experience in the ways of competition, we cement our fandom so securely that even winless seasons can't deter fans from their team. Emotion always finds a way to win the battle with the rational brain. What anchors someone so strongly to a team that they're willing to endure countless hours of misery over a very rational choice of switching teams?

February 22nd, 1980. Anything? How about Miracle on Ice? The date doesn't evoke the same memories as the name synonymous with arguably the greatest sporting event in the 20th century. I was six years old at the time. I had never watched a hockey game in my life. It wasn't a sport that Gary Wagner had introduced to his twin sons. On February 22nd, 1980 we would sit down to watch our first hockey game.

At the time, Gary Wagner probably said something like "Boys, sit down and watch this game. You'll thank me later." I'm sure Bret and Kyle resisted a little. Sitting down and watching a sport that didn't interest us hardly seems like it would hold our attention. Yet, it did. I remember looking at an emotional man and thinking "This looks important. I better pay attention." Years later, I am thankful that I have that memory with my Dad. I remember nothing about the specifics of the game. The only game highlights I recall are from watching replays and YouTube videos. I do remember my Dad telling us very roughly that "The United States isn't supposed to win. We're a bunch of college guys. The Soviets are professionals. This is more than a hockey game."

Teams aren't formed to pick strawberries. Teams are formed to achieve. That's what makes teams special. They are to be a collection of people with a common goal. The goal not only unites the players, it also galvanizes those that identify with the team. A team becomes a symbol of hope and a symbol that binds generations. Declaring allegiance for a team isn't an act of preference. Declaring allegiance for a team is an act of commitment. It's a bond that becomes unbreakable over time. It's a lesson that can only be learned with experience. When you're young, rational logic chooses success over failure. As you age and start to identify with a team, the emotion of a team anchors people into positions of loyalty. The reality is, experience teaches us that becoming a part of something bigger than us exceeds the transient joy of winning one game on the weekend.

In 1980, the emotion of US vs. THEM was never more powerful. The United States, as a nation, was lacking confidence and our sense of self-worth was tenuous. Our "losses" were mounting. We needed a "win" desperately. In living rooms all over the country I can only imagine fathers, like Gary Wagner, took an opportunity to teach their children what being a part of a team meant. This is who we are! This is what we believe in! This is what we're willing to fight for at any expense!

This passion that some teams evoke demonstrates a common theme often seen in great teams. Teams that anchor themselves to our soul have a central idea that permeates through the players, the coaches and the fan base. The idea becomes the central theme as the players act out the drama on the playing surface. In 1980, the idea that governed everything from what type of offense will we run to who played on what shift to who made the team to where will we practice was **TO ACHIEVE INCREDIBLE THINGS, YOU MUST DREAM SELFISHLY BUT PARTICIPATE UNSELFISHLY!**

This idea often goes undiscovered through many people's lifetimes. Without an opportunity to play on a team, an unselfish team, many never come to realize that a team consists of parts that sacrifice to a greater good. This idea is so uncommon that it usually takes an extreme person of influence to convince a group it is a value worth committing to. The default mode for most every human being is to take what is rightfully theirs. When someone butts in line in front of me, most every human being feels wronged, as a default setting. How dare you violate the unwritten rule of waiting your turn? Don't you realize that we're all here waiting for an opportunity? It often takes an extreme person of influence to say, "That might be so, but on this team, there will be times when one person will be told to butt in line and when they do, it is your responsibility as a teammate to accept that." That simple act of recognizing on a team, everyone has a role but not everyone's role is equal, often becomes the greatest obstacle for someone leading the team.

On the 1980 United States Hockey team that Herculean task fell to head coach Herb Brooks. On the outside, it's easy to believe Brooks' goal was to compete and medal in the Olympic Games. On the inside, there was a much more important goal that preceded that obvious goal. On the inside, Brooks' goal was to turn a bunch of selfish college kids into unselfish teammates. How do you make ambitious, goal oriented, testosterone filled, competitive young men willingly commit to a cause that requires sacrifice over immediate pleasure? Herb Brooks' greatest challenge wasn't Boris Mikalhov or Vladislav Tretiak. It was finding a way to convince college men that their college team and their college success was actually a superficial attachment compared to the honor and glory that representing the United States of America would be. If Herb Brooks could somehow get these kids to dream selfishly about winning a gold medal but commit acts of unselfishness in achieving it, the who they played would be insignificant.

Herb Brooks was a master motivator and a keenly observant man. Following a tie with Norway leading up to the Olympic Games, Brooks decided this would be an appropriate moment to bond the selfish dreaming with the unselfish participating. He would make them skate to exhaustion all the while reciting the team for whom each player played. Following each sprint, Brooks would ask a player to repeat his name followed by who he played for. It went something like this, "Mike Ramsey, University of Minnesota." It continued for a very long time. In all reality, it was probably physical abuse. In 1980, it was still seen as appropriate for a coach to use it as motivation to bond a team. Finally, after each player's will was taken to the brink of quitting, one player stood up and gave Brooks what he wanted. "Mike Eruzione, United States of America." And there it was. One moment in time where a player crossed over. Brooks never even asked Eruzione to be the one to offer his information. Eruzione volunteered his information. I can only imagine what compelled Eruzione to chant "The United States of America" as his team while others were responding with their college team. My belief is Eruzione, who was the captain of the team, knew that a jersey worn is only an external sign of commitment. True commitment comes from within. True commitment doesn't need a jersey to signal US vs THEM. True commitment starts in one's soul, travels to one's heart and eventually manifests in one's words. Mike Eruzione's declaration for the United States of America was confirmation to Herb Brooks that he finally had a team that was willing to sacrifice for the greater good. They were giving themselves a chance.

All Progress Comes from Change...
Anthony Volpe

The idea that the RiverCats were formed under was unusual. It wasn't an ordinary 10u travel baseball idea. The RiverCats mission (idea) was masked under the fun of our practice environment and the success of our weekend events. To an outsider, the idea probably looked like most travel baseball teams. It could have been...

1. To develop baseball players.
2. To provide a great environment for baseball players to grow in.

3. To enjoy the game of baseball while developing young
    baseball players.

Those were great ideas, but they weren't for the RiverCats. The
RiverCats main idea was built under a premise on playing the
"long game." The RiverCats began as a 10u baseball team but the
RiverCats main idea couldn't be seen from an outsider. They
didn't have the proper lens through which to evaluate the
RiverCats. The RiverCats were built with the end in mind. The
main idea for the GoWags RiverCats was

Practice and Play with Good Players as Often as Possible.

Some teams are formed for six months. This was true of the
United States hockey team. They had to improve, and they had to
improve quickly. The RiverCats were 10-yr. old little boys. They
had so much of their future ahead of them. The reality was this
team was a cute team that eventually would fade away as high
school engulfed the boys time. With the understanding that the
RiverCats were never designed to exist past a certain point, the
idea for the RiverCats was to *identify* with as many good players as
possible. This was the essential point for player development.
Great players eventually become great because they see
themselves as baseball players. If baseball is just a fun game to
play, when the fun disappears it's then a former fun game to play
and a current game to quit. The easiest way to create a baseball
player for the "long game" is to give him teammates that also see
themselves as playing the "long game." In this sense, the game of
baseball is experienced holistically. Players begin to identify with
their success and their failure. The same players watch their
teammates succeed and fail and learn appropriate ways of handling
that success and failure. Practicing and playing with good players
creates an ecosystem that allows for success in the moment, but it
promotes a mindset that sustains itself for the "long game."

This idea of practicing and playing with good players as often as possible is an easy message to swallow so long as you're one of those players. That's incredible validation. Yes, I'm good. Yes, I like practicing and playing with other good players. But there is a very dark unspoken message that lies underneath it all. If you're not "good" there might not be a place for you.

Truth be told, I wasn't actively looking for other "good" players in 2011. The RiverCats were very talented and we loved our squad. The weekends were a great event full of camaraderie with boys and parents alike. We didn't win all the games we played but we won more than enough to know we were one of the best 10u teams around. It was a lot of fun. When we didn't win, we'd chalk up the game to a learning experience and figure out how to improve with our next game or our next practice. There were some teams out there with some very talented players but no one that made me wish I had a chance to coach that boy instead of my beloved RiverCats. Then, we played Anthony Volpe.

Anthony Volpe was the best player the RiverCats had played to date. The strange thing about Anthony was he wasn't a pitcher. He was a slick fielding shortstop. At the 11u level, it's usually the pitcher that gets people to stop and take notice. The strong arm that overpowers young hitters is so enticing that it's what catches most people's attention. Anthony not only didn't pitch; he wasn't physically intimidating either. Anthony's presence was a matter of his athleticism and fluidity in which he played the game.

Imagine going to a music concert for 5th and 6th graders. You sit down to watch the event expecting novice musicians to play their instrument. Collectively, the sounds of the individual instruments combine to create the sounds of the concert. Noticing any individual instrument would only occur as your eyes scan the orchestra. With Anthony, it was an orchestra with this one musician demanding attention by the brilliance of his play. It was undeniable. His actions attracted you. Once you witnessed the ease at which he played the game, it was hard to divert your eyes. Anthony Volpe was different than anyone I had seen to date.

I think recruiting youth athletes to play for one travel team over another travel team is generally bad for youth baseball. The game is predicated on friendships just as much as development and opportunity. Anthony Volpe would be the first challenge that Kyle Wagner would face in maintaining the RiverCats idea. If the RiverCats were founded on the idea that practicing and playing with good players was a tenet to our existence, I'd need to consider coaching Anthony. I had no idea if Anthony wanted to play for us.

"So even though I really wanted him to play with you I had to ask him first, and I wasn't sure what he was gonna say, but when I asked him, he immediately said yes. He said those guys are awesome! It really was like a family and you guys all welcomed us and made us feel a part of something right from the beginning. It was so much different than anything else.... Anthony wanted to play with good players, and I guess he liked winning. I think being around boys who were really good motivated him to get better."
- Mike Volpe, RiverCats Dad

Discussing Anthony Volpe, the 11-yr. old RiverCat, is impossible without also discussing Jimmy Losh. Anthony was an incredible shortstop. Jimmy was an incredible shortstop. Both were premier players at the positions they played. Practice and play with good players is an easy pill to swallow. Practice and play with good players when they take your position is a different pill altogether.

It's one thing to tell hockey players they should sacrifice for a goal so noble and incredible that it's self-evident. It's yet another thing to tell a 11-yr. old that you're adding a player to the team from a different state and it's in your best interest. As a matter of fact, it wasn't in Jimmy Losh's best interest to accept Anthony at face value. Anthony's acceptance to the team was an easy one. He made us better the minute he put the uniform on. But, Anthony's acceptance as Jimmy Losh's teammate would take some time. People and athletes specifically aren't equipped to handle change.

...But Not All Change is Progress
Jimmy Losh

I love how athletes assess each other the first time they make eye contact. Every competitor does the eyeball test. Ostensibly, they're deciding in a split second "Can I take him?" I'm not exactly sure what it is they're looking for, but you know danger when you see danger.

When I first saw Jimmy Losh as an 8-yr. old playing in the New Cumberland Pony League, I saw danger. Of course, in a sports setting danger only means loss but loss is painful, so danger. I was a 30 something man so the loss I sensed wasn't for myself but rather for the team I coached. Jimmy Losh was a special baseball player the minute you laid eyes on him.

Jimmy wasn't a big kid. Jimmy was the stereotypical red-haired fire ball that could beat you on will alone. Coaching a team of 7 and 8-yr. old's is more about intent than anything else. If you have a team full of kids that care more about winning than eating hot dogs, you're probably going to do all right. No one cared more than Jimmy Losh.

Like all talented young baseball players, Jimmy pitched. Throwing balls over the 17" wide pentagon is a skill set that not too many young players possess. Jimmy could do this, and he could do it very well. There were harder throwers in the league, but Jimmy's intimidation had more to do with his determination than his velocity.

In the game I recall, Jimmy took the mound first as his Tigers were the home team. The Yankees and the Tigers were evenly matched. Truthfully, I think the Yankees probably had better players than the Tigers, but the Tigers did have Jimmy. It would certainly be a challenge for the Yankees in this pre-season scrimmage.

Jimmy faced Luke (my son) with nobody on base and 2 outs. He struck out the first two batters of the inning. As I recall, Luke "ran into one." In baseball jargon, that means he hit the ball very well. I believe the official scorer would have called it a home run, but it very well could have been a single and a 3-base error. Official scorers at the Pony level aren't exactly meticulous in their judgment. Obviously, when your 7-yr. old has success against a kid of Jimmy's level there's a sense of pride. I probably said "I see ya' workin' Luke" as that phrase has become one of my calling cards for achievement. But, as hard as it is to remember what I said exactly to my son, it's much easier to remember the reaction of Jimmy.

For any competitive adult male, if I could conjure up visions of Rocky Balboa against Clubber Lang in Rocky III that would be just about right. "He ain't gettin' killed, he's getting mad." And that's how it was with Jimmy. My blink test was right. Jimmy was dangerous because he was as determined a Pony baseball player that I had ever seen. He had just given up a home run and the visceral instinct for this 8-yr. old was retribution. Jimmy's intensity was often misdiagnosed as bad body language. This is another disconnect between The Imagination Game and The Precision Game. Most baseball coaches realize that composure is needed when you play a team sport like baseball. Huge emotional displays are a no, no. When a teammate makes an error, you can't show him up. When you strike out, you can't throw a temper tantrum. When you give up a home run, you can't react with anger. Teaching baseball players how to harness their competitive grit is essential for The Precision Game. But given the choice between a talented 8-yr. old that competed like crazy and one that didn't, I'd take the competitor always and forever. If a dog will bite, he'll bite as a pup. It is much easier to teach restraint than aggression. Jimmy would get his retribution.

In the bottom half of the inning, Jimmy hit a home run off of Luke. The pitch was about shoulder high and he tomahawked it over an outfielder's head. Jimmy set a New Cumberland Pony League record for his time around the bases. I think the record still stands today.[10]

The rest of the game is forgettable. I have no idea who won or how the rest of the game played out. But, on that particular night in New Cumberland, Jimmy Losh's intensity would be indelibly etched in my head. I had no doubt that Jimmy would be competing in this sport for a very long time. As they say, Jimmy had "it." Anthony would test Jimmy's "it." Jimmy would be forced to demonstrate some restraint.

Understanding Basic "Team" Chemistry
Why? How? Who? What?

I'd imagine the first "teams" were designed to win wars. In a threatening world, winning had a much more significant prize than championships. I'd imagine that armies were the first teams built to achieve a very ambitious goal. As the size of the army grew, creating proper dynamics between the men in the army would be paramount for success. How do we communicate the grand idea to each and every man on the front lines? How do we make sure they have the latest up to date information to act appropriately? How

---

[10] I'm joking.

do we ensure that the leaders of the armies understand the basic motivation needed to fight daily battles?

In the book *The Utility of Force,* British General Rupert Smith highlights the manner-in-which armies achieve this success. The same lessons that he purports can be applied to the teams designed to win championships. Smith acknowledges that "teams" consist of 4 levels of decision making. When these 4 levels work in harmony, teams function correctly. When these 4 levels have communication breakdown, teams function incorrectly. Smith calls these 4 levels in descending hierarchy...

1. **Political...**This is the top of a food chain in a hierarchy. These are the people, the person, tasked with creating a broad mission for why the team exists. The political nature of every team doesn't have to be noble in any way. By suggesting the top of the food chain is political, it's recognizing that all teams exist under a basic notion that there should be a common purpose for them being together. Reminder: teams aren't formed to pick strawberries. Teams are formed to achieve something. Smith calls this level of decision making political. Emotionally, it's the WHY of every team.

    1980 United States Hockey Team's **WHY**: To medal in the 1980 Olympic Games and renew the American spirit.

2. **Strategic**...Smith calls the next level strategic. This is the level of the team designed with organizing the people into clusters. These clusters are to accomplish the broad goals designed by the political level of the team. The clusters of people won't always have direct contact with other clusters. Getting these clusters, the most up to date information would become a primary challenge to the political agenda. Emotionally, this stage of the team is the HOW.

1980 United States Hockey Team's **HOW:** Hire a driven, ambitious coach that can mold boys into men and foster a spirit of unity.

3. **Theatrical...**Smith refers to the third level of team as theatrical. This is the WHO of the political agenda. In sporting parlance one of my favorite quotes is "It's not the X's and O's, it's the Jimmy's and Joe's." This is the theatrical level of team. Finding the right people to execute a broad mission becomes a critical stage of teamwork.

1980 United States Hockey Teams **WHO:** The 20 players who will best complement each other, not necessarily the 20 best players.

4. **Tactical...**The last level of a great team is the tactical level. This level is the WHAT of successful team implementation. You could have the best idea, the best plan and the best people to run the plan but if the men aren't motivated to move or are too sick to fight, you've got a disaster on your hands.

1980 United States Hockey Team's **WHAT:** Brooks would motivate them tactically by becoming the villain in their eyes. Their collective animosity for him was reason to achieve. Later, he'd marshal this collective energy into the vision of defeating the Soviets.

Every team enters into these levels whether they know it or not. It's the undercurrent of every team. Travel baseball teams shouldn't have the same difficulty in achieving harmony as a national army or a national hockey team. However, these same challenges definitely exist. With respect to Anthony and Jimmy it would be essential to make sure there was a link from the political to the tactical, from the why to the what.

The GoWags RiverCats **WHY**: Practice and play with good players as often as possible.

The GoWags RiverCats **HOW**: Create an environment that good players want to be in. Make practices fun while teaching them new skills. Give them a chance to win every game they compete in.

The GoWags RiverCats **WHO**: A collection of players, parents, coaches that can learn from each other and can offer something to be learned.

The GoWags RiverCats **WHAT**: Motivate them in the present by convincing them they are good baseball players. Motivate them for the future by convincing them that they're not good enough, yet.

The hardest connection to make is from the **WHAT** to the **WHY**. I believe this is ultimately why most teams fail. The easiest and most convenient way to achieve tactical motivation often undermines the broad goal of teamwork, the **WHY**. Unfortunately, coaches that don't occasionally retreat and use the broad lens of perspective, will live in the very narrow **WHAT** and **WHO**.

In order for the RiverCats to be the team that both Anthony and Jimmy wanted to play for, it would require a very broad perspective and a "long game" approach. This isn't always easy for young athletes and quite frankly for ambitious parents. Taking a back seat to another person in the quest for greatness is hardly motivating. The teams' greatest threat often simply becomes can a leader keep his players motivated to chase personal goals while sacrificing to chase team goals.

"Hey Kyle. What did you just say?"

Teams are more than meets the eye. Teams have a structure that must always be considered. At the top of the team model is the WHY. At the bottom is the WHAT. Integrating the two, requires recognizing the WHO and the HOW. Many teams never understand this relationship. They lose sight of the WHY trying to execute the WHAT.

Servant Leadership
No Task is Too Great, No Task is Too Small

Hierarchies make it very difficult to ignore labels. Generals are superior to privates. It's the foundation of hierarchy. People's experience provides them certain rights that others haven't yet earned. Hierarchies exist to protect the collective group and to achieve a dangerous goal. But hierarchies are meant to only exist in threatening environments. When environments are safe, we don't need authority to demand us to act in a certain way. Safe environments allow for free will.

Most people fail to make a difference in the lives of other people because they're too busy doing their job mistaking a safe environment for a threatening environment. A job goes by many different names. It is often called a task, an objective, a goal. The focus is all the same. There is something to get done. It's my responsibility to do it. That's a commendable mission. Everyone should take pride in a job well done. But, doing one's job at the expense of a greater idea (**THE WHY**) is where most teams break down. The focus on achieving one's goal creates a blind spot in that person's mind. Without proper perspective, the goal becomes all there is, and relationships become strained. This happens to all of us in our daily routine. We set out on a course to do our grocery shopping. The task is to bring home food for the family. Tasked with the job of securing food, we often feel rushed and neglect the other people in the grocery store. If your job is to get the groceries and you ignore an acquaintance, that's probably a transgression worth forgetting. If your job is to coach a baseball team and you ignore the basic needs of the players you're coaching, that's a tragedy. A tragedy is an overstatement. But, it's definitely gut wrenching.

Consider a team consisting of 12 players and 4 coaches. That's 16 people. 16 people acting together on a team have the potential to create 120 unique relationships. Each relationship has the opportunity to add value to that person's life. When one person's job takes center stage over 120 different opportunities that better be one very important job.

Labels create entitlement. My name is Kyle Wagner. Some people call me "Coach Wags." Some people call me "Mr. Wagner." Some call me "Uncle Kyle." Many, even call me "Bret." Regardless of what they call me I'm the exact same person. The titles and the labels merely reflect the nature of the association. Far too many people with a job to do lose sight of the big picture or the **WHY** because they become enamored with their titles.

There's a scene from one of my favorite movies *A Few Good Men*. It involves Jack Nicholson playing the role of Colonel Nathan R. Jessep. In this scene he and the judge throw around their titles that they've earned as justification for how they're permitted to act. Certainly, I don't mean to pretend that these two don't deserve respect, but it highlights how attached we become to the labels we're given.

Col. Jessep: I'd appreciate it if he would address me as "Colonel" or "Sir"... I believe I've earned it.

Judge Randolph: Counsel will refer to the witness as "Colonel" or "Sir."

Col. Jessep: I don't know what the hell kind of unit you're running here.

Judge Randolph: And you will refer to this court as "Your Honor" or "Judge"... and I'm quite certain I've earned it. Take your seat, Colonel.

The labels we're given create pride in what we do. Pride is fulfilling. People must have a sense of pride for what they do. But the labels often create hubris-bad pride. Pride in doing a job well affirms people from the inside out. This is where competence lives. Knowing you don't need validation from others is liberating. But, identifying with the labels that others give us is dangerous territory when you interact with other human beings. The pride of being seen as something more than "your best self" is very difficult to live up to.

President of Pixar Animation and author of *Creativity, Inc.,* Ed Catmull explains the health of his organization like this. "*...we never wanted to foster a culture in which some workers were viewed as first-class, and others as second-class, where some employees were held to a higher standard and others were effectively relegated to the B-team.*" In order to play the "long game" with Anthony and Jimmy the title of "shortstop" would need to become just a place between 3rd base and 2nd base. Young baseball players fall in love with the label of a position. This attachment to a position creates hubris that ultimately will fracture a team. Only one player can play shortstop. But 9 players can play the game of baseball. If players attach themselves to a position, it limits the opportunity for a coach to implement **THE WHO.** The RiverCats were at our best when Anthony and Jimmy were both on the field. Finding a way to marry **THE WHAT** to **THE WHY** started with making sure Anthony and Jimmy both knew the right question to ask.

I'd Rather Have the Wrong Answer to the Right Question Than the Right Answer to the Wrong Question

Anthony Volpe and Jimmy Losh

Young people don't want to be told "Here's what you have to do to be great tomorrow." That's for older people to think about. Young people want to be told "Here's how you can be great today." As we gain more experience, we develop a future thinking lens. Jimmy and Anthony needed to know that they both were on a winner and they both were contributors to that winner.

Every athlete, at their core, wants to play for a winner and they want to contribute. The allure of winning is so powerful it needs no justification. Winning is preferable to losing. The other core motivator is more misunderstood. Athletes know that teammates sacrifice for each other, but they need to know that their sacrifice is appreciated. Sacrifice without appreciation quickly becomes punishment. Athletes need to know they're contributing to the winning. The ability to manage these two basic needs of both players would prove to be essential for the RiverCats evolution.

Practice and Play with Good Players as Often as Possible.

Jimmy was a regular at practice. This meant whatever information was passed on to the players, Jimmy had heard. Anthony, being out of state, couldn't always make every practice. This posed a problem one particular Ripken semi-final game. The 11U

RiverCats were playing the Chester County Bobcats.[11] As far as rivals go, this would be considered a rival. In the 6th inning of a 6-inning game, the Bobcats created a 1st (go ahead run) and 2nd, 0 out situation. For baseball people, that means the bunt was in order. I had to make a decision as to what I wanted to do. The easy decision would be to yell..." Get an out on a bunted ball." This means, if they execute the bunt, throw the ball to 1st base.

But I was greedy. I thought I could get more than just the out at 1b. Jimmy Losh was pitching, and Anthony was at SS. Could I teach them a bunt play in the time allowed for a mound visit? I believed I could. "Time" I yelled. By my calculations I had approximately 30 seconds to say
what needed to be said. The three primary targets for my instruction were Jimmy (the pitcher), Anthony (the shortstop) and Jared Payne (the 3B). I had to be succinct and I needed eye contact from those 3 specifically. Here's how I remember the conversation taking place in 30 seconds.

"Listen to me. We don't have much time. I want the out at 3b. Jared that requires you to stay home. Jimmy, since Jared is staying home, you're responsible for covering 3b after you pitch the ball. When you field it, you should have a play at 3b IF you and Anthony do your job together. Jimmy DO NOT pitch the ball until Anthony sneaks up behind the runner at 2nd and drives him back to the bag at 2nd base. Then and only then do you throw the ball home. If Anthony does his job, the runner will break back to 2nd with Anthony. Ok?"

I ran off the field thinking "What are the chances they do this right?" It often takes me weeks at the high school level to get them

---

[11] The RiverCats didn't have the market cornered on producing great baseball players. This small organization, also located in Pennsylvania, created many talented baseball players. In fact, Eric Grintz, Adam Grintz and Aaron Feld would all play for the RiverCats a time or two.

to execute this play correctly. Flawless!!!! Jimmy came set. He checked the runner at 2nd. Anthony broke on time. The runner broke back to the bag. Jimmy threw home on time. The ball was bunted at the 3B. Jimmy covered in the direction of 3B. He fielded the ball perfectly and turned and threw a strike to Jared. 1 out.

STILL, one of my favorite memories is when, against Grintz's team (Chester County Bobcats) in the last inning in the finals at Ripken, you called time and went out to the mound and taught the boys that bunt play, and they executed it to perfection. You never dumbed the game down to them. - Mike Volpe, RiverCats Dad

---

Most travel teams ask this question when deciding whether or not bringing a new player on is the right decision. *Can he help us win?* That's a good question but for the RiverCats it wasn't the right question. The right question was *Can we learn from him and will he learn from us?*
Central to being a RiverCat was the idea that our entire existence as a team was the end game. The end game for these boys was down the road wearing some other uniform. The RiverCats was just their youth travel team providing a venue to improve for some other opportunity that mattered entirely more than 11u baseball. I had no doubt that we could learn from Anthony. It appeared he was willing to learn from us.

What I most wanted Anthony to learn was his impact on a team goes far beyond the ground balls that he fielded. His impact went well beyond the home runs he would sometimes launch from the leadoff position. My hope for Anthony was he would come to appreciate the role that someone like him offered to the rest of the team. If your best players are willing to do whatever is asked of them, everything else falls in line. Coaches could spend months desperately trying to communicate the value of sacrifice and unselfish play. Yet, one unselfish act by the best player on the team immediately communicates that same message.

I'm not suggesting Anthony was the best player on the team. That's a label I wasn't willing to give Anthony and that's a label he wouldn't be willing to accept. But he was certainly one of the best. Anthony Volpe would sprint to 2b with the same energy and vigor as which he ran to shortstop. Anthony Volpe would relinquish an at bat to a teammate without batting an eye. Anthony Volpe would pitch if he was asked to. Actually, no he wouldn't. He would think he was letting his teammates down if he agreed to this. That's who Anthony was.

Jimmy Losh became the best center fielder on our team. Maybe if the RiverCats were younger it would have been a harder sell. At the 11u level, many hitters would challenge outfield fences. Jimmy understood his ability to cover ground in the outfield would go a long way in helping us win games and grow as a team. Jimmy would also play shortstop and 2nd base, but Jimmy took Anthony's emergence to add another tool to his tool belt.

In 2012, when the RiverCats took the field, Anthony or Jimmy would play shortstop. When the RiverCats took the field, both Anthony and Jimmy were on it. The simple fact that I could write Anthony Volpe and Jimmy Losh's name in the lineup at the same time might seem like an innocuous event. There are 9 spots in the order (travel baseball often affords a coach more than 9 lineup spots. This is something that makes our job much easier than traditional baseball coaches.) and Jimmy and Anthony only took up 2 of them. What's the big deal? Fair enough. But those lineups that coaches write can be extremely judgmental. The true success of the RiverCats existed when both Anthony and Jimmy looked at the lineup and didn't care if there was a "6" (the number that recognizes the position of shortstop) by their name.

Hope for the Best. Prepare for the Worst

Jimmy Losh and Anthony Volpe

Having Anthony Volpe as a member of the RiverCats was something that we all benefitted from. He learned from us and we learned from him. Once basic team chemistry gets settled, it's awfully comforting knowing you have someone of Anthony's skill set on your team. But comfort is a luxury that survival systems don't allow. Survival systems are always threatening. Most of the time, they are threatening because the team in the other dugout is trying to take what you want. Sometimes they are threatening because someone is trying to take your roster spot. The RiverCats would learn that sometimes survival systems are threatening because you are forced to compete shorthanded.

As we detailed in the Eighth Inning, Cooperstown, NY is home to Dreams Park and the venue for many travel baseball teams culminating event. The RiverCats had no such plans of disbanding but we did have plans of winning. Dreams Park would be a very big trophy for the collection. We would have to fight for that trophy without Anthony.

As will be discussed in the Fifth Inning, all baseball players have selfish goals that evolve with every team goal. One of Anthony's personal goals was playing for Team USA. It just so happened that Anthony made Team USA as a 12-yr. old. It just so happened that this opportunity of a lifetime would prevent Anthony from playing with the RiverCats in Cooperstown, NY. Jimmy would be our shortstop.

Baseball is a game to be played by the people on the field. The coach's responsibility is to provide the best opportunity for success. As will be detailed in the Third Inning, it's the coach's job to turn information into intelligence; practical intelligence that can be applied in the face of adversity. It is not the coach's job to become larger than the players playing the game. Coaches are servants to the players they coach. Coaches are competitive. Coaches are tasked with extracting the best out of their players. But coaches are not on the front lines of competition. The coach and his role stop at the theatrical level of team. When coaches make the game more about them, than about the people playing the game, I tend to get mildly irritated.

The coach of a team is authority. In survival systems, everyone needs to know who to look to when things start to unravel. Towards this end, coaches often insert themselves when justice is challenged (bad call from an umpire). Toward this end, coaches often insert themselves when team morale might be low. Sometimes, it is merely an ounce of inspiration that provides needed clarity when the fog of doubt sets in. As a baseball coach, I'm very sensitive to the nature of those inspiration laced speeches. Baseball is more execution than emotion. Getting "fired up" often leads to wrong outcomes. But, one speech I gave seemed appropriate in Cooperstown, NY. As authority, I needed to say my peace.

They think we're afraid of that guy. They think the RiverCats are like every other team they have faced getting to Cooperstown. They think when they bring that big dude back into the game, we shake and quiver in the batter's box knowing a strikeout is next. That is not who we are. That is not how you have been trained. The crowd you see on the hill is about to witness one of the greatest comebacks by one of the greatest teams to ever play in Cooperstown. Now, I cannot predict which one of you is going to be that guy. But rest assured one of you will be that guy. One of you will be in the batter's box with an opportunity of a lifetime. When that times comes, I expect you to compete fearlessly. I expect you to embrace the opportunity. The worst that can happen is you strikeout. Who cares? The best that could happen is you make a memory of a lifetime. I want to beat the big guy. One of you is going to be the hero today. Let's do this.

You see, the Louisiana Padres had a really good pitcher on their team. The Louisiana Padres were a very well coached team. Their coaches realized that they could save pitches by removing their best pitcher (a very big 12-yr. old) and relieving him with other arms during non-stressful situations. When the stress of the situation mounted, the big dude would march back in and squelch the fire. After witnessing this a couple of times, I began to feel disrespected. I was merely RiverCats' coach and although I wasn't on the front lines of the battle, I felt authority needed to interject his opinion.

If you want to know the truth, I think many RiverCats could have seized the opportunity. I think on this particular day, the memory that was about to unfold was unavoidable. I sensed the comeback would happen. Who was going to be that guy? Jimmy Losh would be that guy. Down 2, with 2 runners on, they brought the big dude back into the game. I honestly remember looking at the big guy coming in and looking at Jimmy on deck. Remember how I said I'd always choose the aggressive kid. Remember how I said, you can always teach restraint but it's much harder to teach aggression. It is moments like this, that confirm why. With the opportunity upon us, it was obvious for anyone watching the game and for anyone cheering for the team from Pennsylvania, Jimmy Losh had a chance to be the hero. Hero's do what is needed despite the quiet voice cautioning them to be careful. Jimmy Losh was always the aggressor. Jimmy Losh didn't know fear. Jimmy Losh got a very good fastball from a very good pitcher and hit a home run. Jimmy Losh became a hero for many on that day. Granted it was a 12-yr. old baseball game played by 12-yr. old boys, but competition teaches. On this particular Thursday, everyone who was watching learned that Jimmy Losh had the courage of a hero and the clarity of focus you only see in the best of competitors.

Jimmy Losh could have committed to a couple of Division 1 schools. He chose Division II power Millersville University instead. Jimmy, apparently, is still not into labels. I see ya workin' Jimmy.

Jimmy Losh

Anthony Volpe will be attending Vanderbilt University. Anthony will also have an opportunity to play professional baseball. He's still very fun to watch. Anthony sees himself as neither a shortstop nor a second baseman. He's simply a middle infielder. I see ya workin' Anthony.

Anthony Volpe

The Sixth Inning

The Courage of Competence

I believe it's dangerous to accept one man's opinion at face value. Conceding power to one person is a dangerous proposition. Sure, there will be times that one person loves what you're doing, but there will also be times that person doesn't think too highly of you. If that one man or one woman holds all the power, it can be discouraging and downright devastating to know they don't like what they see. But, it's also unrealistic to not recognize those "experts" in certain fields. The name "expert" is getting a bad rap in baseball circles since the analytic revolution has taken over. But, "experts" exist. Those are the people that Malcolm Gladwell in his book *Blink* refers to as thin slicers.

Gladwell coined the phrase thin slicer as someone that can look at a situation, event, pattern and quickly diagnose accurately what it is he's seeing. Whether it be art, music, acting or baseball, thin slicers don't need a huge amount of data to accurately determine what is and what isn't true. Becoming an expert thin slicer takes years of experience and years of critical thinking.

Is it possible to thin slice a coach? Are there "tells" or giveaways that could lead someone to know if a coach is an expert coach? Coaches aren't quite like players. Whereas a player performs on a stage, a coach is just the guide on the side. Could there possibly be a blink test to determine if a coach has the ability to be a great coach BEFORE his players play a game, a season?

As I mentioned in the Ninth Inning, the game of baseball evolves from an Imagination Game when you're young, to a Precision Game as you get older. By the time the game is played at major Division 1 college baseball, we're talking a Precision Game. Here's an example of how I see The Precision Game playing out for the act of bunting a ball down the third base line.

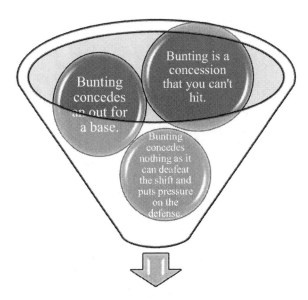

Imagination to Precision

Having precision coaching is essential to becoming an elite program. Finding the subtle nuances for ways to improve can be what separates teams. Moving from good to great to elite requires precision in every aspect of coaching. I happened to have a front row view of a coach that played The Precision Game better than his peers.

Mike Martin is the current wins leader in division 1 baseball. As of the start of the 2019 baseball season (his last) he has amassed 1,987 wins with a winning percentage of .736. My very personal stories give some insight into why Martin has achieved such incredible success.

In 1992, Florida State joined the Atlantic Coast Conference. I was a freshman at Wake Forest University. Florida State and Wake Forest would compete on the baseball field all four years while I was at Wake. Florida State was a perennial power. Wake Forest was very competitive against the Seminoles and even won a series in Tallahassee in 1993. But it was an observation that I made the first time I saw Coach Martin and an interaction that I had with him in 1994 that cemented his status in my mind.

Florida State's first series against Wake Forest took place in Winston-Salem, NC. The anticipation seemed awfully high. How would they play? How would they dress? How would they act? As the bus pulled up, we were curious to say the least. The team exited the bus, dropped their gear off along the first base dugout. Then, something strange happened. I had never seen it prior and have yet to see it since. Coach Mike Martin brought his entire team out to home plate with him. In his hand he had 3 baseballs. With the entire team fully attentive, he rolled the 3 baseballs down the third base line to see how the foul line would treat a bunted ball. He wanted to know EXACTLY the hand he had been dealt by playing at a new field. To me, at the time, this demonstrated a very weird method of coaching. In hindsight, Mike Martin was playing The Precision Game better than his peers.

The second interaction that demonstrated his exacting need for precision was one that affected me personally. Most people focus on themselves, their team. They identify with the players and create a level of expectation. When that level is met, they're happy. Yes, we won. When that level is not met, they're angry. We lost. Someone or something must be blamed. This is "wrong spotting" by its very nature. If we are to win next time, we must identify why we lost and make improvements. It's the nature of competition. Winning cures most of what ails you. It's extremely uncommon for a competitive person to take a big picture perspective and to look at things from a unique viewpoint. Mike Martin did just that following a weekend series my junior year in Winston-Salem. Following a Seminoles win against yours truly and Wake Forest, Mike Martin sought out a junior catcher that happened to play for a different team.

After every home game, college players have "field jobs" to assist in the daily clean up. My junior year, my field job consisted of sweeping the home dugout. That meant making sure the dugout was cleaned of sunflower seeds, making sure all drains were clear from debris, and general cleanup from any trash. As I was sweeping the home dugout, probably 15 minutes following the end of the game, I heard a voice from behind me say, "Wagner, come up here son." I turned around to see none other than Florida State's esteemed and veteran coach still wearing his mustard yellow uniform. Needless to say, I quickly put the broom down and hustled up the steps.

Memories fade over the years. I'd be doing the story an injustice if I tried to recall what Coach Martin said. Emotions don't fade. I remember exactly how Coach Martin made me feel. His message wasn't only inspirational in what he said but it was eventful and memorable because he simply chose to say it. Mike Martin could have gotten on the team bus following the last game in Winston-Salem. He could have chosen to dwell on the good that was the Florida State baseball team. He could have chosen to do what most every coach does, think about what his team did well and what his team didn't do well. Mike Martin chose to do something in addition to all of that. I'm sure Mike Martin didn't consider his act an uncommon act. Acting as a veteran coach with years of experience behind him, it probably was just the right thing to do. In the eyes of a 21-yr. old catcher, it was extraordinarily uncommon.

Here's how I remember the conversation 25 years later. "Kyle, I know you haven't received some of the same attention as your brother. (Bret was drafted later that year in the 1st round by the St. Louis Cardinals) but I need to let you know that you were a pain in our backside for the last two years. You are a game changer on defense, and we have to game plan around you whenever we play Wake Forest. Sometimes, offense gets all the glory. I just wanted to let you know that one coach in this conference thinks the world of you." Wow! One man's uncommon act changed the perspective of a defeated catcher in 20 seconds. Mike Martin chose to do what he thought was the right thing to do instead of getting on a bus and going home. No one would have thought less of him if he didn't act. In the span of 20 seconds, Mike Martin chose precision over acceptable and in turn he won himself a fan for life.

Playing The Precision Game means identifying an ideal level of "play." This is easy. There is an optimal standard to which we must aspire. Many coaches can identify optimal. Implementing The Precision Game is much harder. Implementing The Precision Game takes extraordinary competence and often, extraordinary courage. If you demonstrate the discipline to acquire good habits and subsequently the courage to act on those habits, sometimes you become the winningest coach in NCAA history; a model of competency.

Short Term Pessimism/ Long Term Optimism
Ryan Kutz

All of the successful athletes I have ever coached seemed to have a common belief that drove them. It seems obvious once you explore why it's essential for success. But, it's very uncommon. I think it's very uncommon because most athletes are afraid of admitting they're scared. Great athletes not only admit they're scared, they embrace it. Here's the mindset of every successful athlete that I've coached.

I'm not good enough today, but I'll be great tomorrow.

Successful athletes have an incredible amount of doubt. They're a worrying breed. Will I be good enough? Have I done enough? Is the time I'm putting in sufficient? Should I do more? They're admitting through their actions that danger is lurking around the corner. When it arrives, will I have given myself the best chance for success? At the most basic of levels, they're afraid.

But, ask them if they're going to be successful and they're unwavering in their answer. "Absolutely!" They're afraid they won't be good enough today but they're supremely confident they'll be great tomorrow. It's almost a paradox with their thought process until you dig deeper and see what's really at play.

Successful athletes that play The Precision Game demonstrate the courage to doubt themselves enough to get better. It can be very uncomfortable to be told "You're not good enough today." Yet, that's essentially what coaches do every single day in the life of an athlete. Coaches call this criticism feedback, but its criticism, nonetheless. If I walk up to a 16-yr. old and tell him the pimple on his face is unacceptable, that's callous and borderline abusive. Yet, if that same teenager dresses in a uniform and I tell him that his swing is unacceptable, that's feedback and expected behavior from a coach. Diving headfirst into the athletic realm and a survival system can be extremely threatening. Only the most courageous of those athletes are able to take feedback as important.

The reason they are able to handle the feedback is because they're able to play the "long game" in their head. If you're told you have a pimple on your face and you don't have the necessary tools to fix that pimple, tomorrow is going to be one frightening place. But, if you know that you can fix that pimple because you believe in your ability to overcome any challenge, that pimple is just a hurdle in a path full of hurdles. "Thank you for pointing that pimple out. I'm on it!" Feedback in the present is just feedback. The manner in which you paint your future world determines whether that feedback will be used to improve you or used to punish you.

Successful athletes paint a bright future for themselves by doubting their present is ever good enough but knowing their ability to jump hurdles will forever make them optimistic about whatever comes next.

I'm not good enough today, but I'll be great tomorrow.

"We realized early that there were a lot of good players around and if he wanted to get better, he needed to play with guys that were better or perceived better than he was in order to push him."
- Eric Kutz, RiverCats Dad

Ryan Kutz joined the RiverCats following our first two seasons. He wasn't an original RiverCat. He wanted to join the RiverCats after experiencing success with his previous travel team. Ryan had considerable success but, in his mind, he knew there was better. If better was to be had, he wanted in. Ryan would have to go through a very informal tryout process. The RiverCats didn't conduct tryouts in typical fashion. Typically, teams conduct tryouts in an industrial model. Run all the boys through all the necessary drills and evaluate as formally as possible. My mind is racing through numbers on the backs of jerseys and clipboards in evaluator's hands. Nothing says culture quite like numbers replacing names and clipboards instead of handshakes. The RiverCats consisted of a stable core group of boys and would on occasion evaluate additional players as needed. Ryan and his parents had asked for a tryout. I agreed to evaluate Ryan in the summer of 2012.

The manner in which I evaluate a player is probably a little different than most. Where many coaches value the PRESENT, I tend to value the FUTURE. Here's a great visual to demonstrate why I feel this way as first presented in Daniel Coyle's book *The Talent Code.*

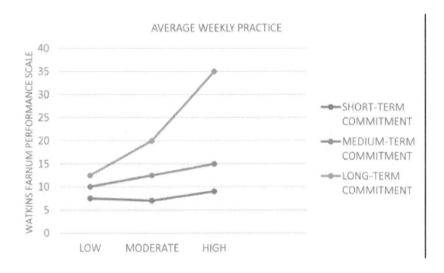

Coyle put into a picture what I had believed in my heart. By judging someone only on their present-day ability you fail to recognize what that person could become. As Ryan Kutz walked into GoWags, my first task was trying to decode what long term commitment Ryan had in the sport of baseball. Playing for me wasn't always easy. But, if Ryan had a long-term commitment, my coaching would be more than just insensitive feedback. It would become an opportunity to improve, an opportunity to play The Precision Game.

"Hey Kyle. What did you just say?"

Successful athletes are willing to be coached hard in the present day because they believe they have the discipline and courage to tackle anything that comes their way in the future. That belief stems from a long-term commitment they've made to themselves about who they are and what they want to achieve in life. Their baseball goals require precision.

What Malcolm Gladwell calls a "thin slicer" someone else might simply call prejudiced or biased. Essentially, that's all a thin slicer is doing. He's relying on years of experience and critical observation to judge one person based upon previous interactions. In a world like baseball, I've tried to rely less and less on what physical attributes I see and more and more on someone's willingness to improve. Of course, an athlete has to have the necessary skills to get in the door. I'm talking about the necessary motivation to keep working once he's inside the room. What I remember about that first tryout with Ryan wasn't the fastballs he threw or the balls he hit. What I remember is….

1. Ryan had a sister with Down syndrome.

2. Ryan had a firm handshake and looked me in the eyes.

3. Ryan's Mom Meg never once mentioned Ryan's previous accomplishments.

4. Ryan wore baseball pants, a belt and a jersey.

5. Ryan, as an 11-yr. old, did band work to warm up.

6. Ryan placed his glove in his bag after trying out.

7. Ryan thanked me for my time after working out.

Ryan would be a RiverCat.

The Achievement Trap
You're Never Going to Get There

I think every coach wants their athletes to be the most confident dude on the field but the most coachable guy in the classroom. This is easier said than done. Confidence says, "I'm the Man." Being coachable often implies "I have a lot to learn." Finding this balance between confidence and willingness to improve comes down to **NEVER OWN YOUR SUCCESS and ALWAYS OWN YOUR FAILURE!**

The minute you own something is the minute you can't afford to lose it. Ownership is a dangerous thing when it comes to growth. In fact, research has coined the phrase "loss aversion" to describe the dramatic effects of ownership. Owning a watch is simple. It sits in your dresser and it's yours. No one else wears your watch. Owning success is a much harder, abstract concept but it applies just the same.

A game is played. There is a winner and there is a loser. Among the winners are players that contributed to the win. Some contributed more than others. If your contribution is perceived as more than a part to a whole there is a very good chance that you're on your way to ownership. In other words, if you go 3-4 with 2 doubles and a walk off home run there is an extremely high probability that you might swallow that achievement whole. You might believe that your accomplishments won the game for your team. You're on the verge of owning your success. Danger!

The Game of Baseball: "Here, you can have this success as your own."

The Courage of the Athlete: "No. I don't want it. It's not mine to have."

Accepting success as your own tends to create false confidence. When success is framed because of what you did instead of what you contributed it can often lead to false confidence. Psychology has a name for this artificial superiority. It's called the Dunning - Kruger Effect. The graph below depicts the nature of the effect.

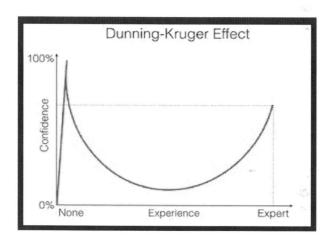

David Dunning and Justin Kruger may not have been baseball fans, but their work certainly lends itself to those of us that coach and play the game. Baseball is meant to be played with great emotion and great intensity. Trying to convince an athlete that he shouldn't own his double that he worked so hard for seems ridiculous. As a matter of fact, that guy on the mound throwing 96 mph with a nasty slider hasn't given up a hit in 15 consecutive innings. If I smoke a line drive off him, you can rest assured that I'm going to celebrate and own my success. Many baseball players do just this. Many baseball players can never handle the failure that comes following the success.

	Owning Your Success (Confident Player)	Renting Your Success (Competent Player)
Reaction to game winning double	Celebrate the success of MY DOUBLE.	Celebrate the success of a great at bat.
Attitude towards next at bat	"I'm the Man"	"Let's have another quality at bat"
Reaction to strike out	Assign blame for the strikeout because "I'm the Man"	Accept responsibility. Discover ways to learn from the strikeout.
Attitude towards next at bat	"I'm the Man"	"Let's have another quality at bat now that I've amended my approach."

The Achievement trap has become even greater now because of social media. What once was a celebration with teammates that ended after the game can now be saved forever. Instagram, Twitter, SnapChat have provided fertile breeding grounds for the confident player to sustain himself.[12] Not only can he relive his moment whenever he'd like, but he can swallow the success hook, line and sinker with every like and retweet. Confidence breeds on

---

[12] Social Media also promotes the other side of the "confident coin." The other side promotes the envious and anxious phenomenon. Social Media lives off of extremes. Only the loudest, most offensive, most absurd get our attention anymore. We're led to believe life is a series of dramatic spikes. When our spikes don't match their spikes, we live in a state of "we're not good enough."

applause from the crowd. Competence thanks the crowd and dismisses them just as quickly. Competence knows if he swallows the praise, he'll surely swallow the criticism.

Honestly, this is a very hard message for a coach to share with his players. It seems like "Old Man" speak. The guy that is a "has been" is telling the guys playing the game in the present moment to not enjoy the success that he's earned. Who is this guy to tell me that I'm not allowed to own my success when he wasn't the one to wake up at 5 AM and lift weights or do sprints? Surely, there is some other "Old Man" out there with a more appealing message. Surely, there is some other "Old Man" that will allow me to bask in my own success all the while helping the team become what it can be. That's the guy I want to play for. Yes, those guys exist. Yes, it's often very fun and rewarding playing for those guys. But those guys seldom walk across the field and congratulate a player on another team for being a great player. Those guys can't see the skills that are deeper than surface level. Those guys never experience the long-term success of instilling in players, of all teams, just what skills last a lifetime. Those guys aren't Mike Martin.

Handling success properly is only half the battle of a competent player. Truly, it's probably more like 25% of the battle. In a game of failure, the nature of handling failure is even more important.

Outcomes vs. Impact
Dealing with Failure

I was told one time by someone that I respect, "Dad, it's not that people are afraid to fail. They're afraid of being exposed." He was exactly right. Failure in privacy is entirely different than failure in front of the public eye. Having other's eyes observe your behavior can be very unnerving. It takes special effort to recognize that failure in the public arena is still just failure. It only has to feel like embarrassment if you concede more power to the viewing public than they deserve.

Let's step away from the game of baseball and all the emotion that comes with it. Let's talk about something less emotional like gossip.[13] You and some friends are sitting around having lunch. It's a relaxed carefree environment. You're sharing information. They're sharing information. Everyone is laughing. You decide to tell a story about a mutual friend. In your mind it's an innocent story with a hilarious plot twist. Your mutual friend, instead of drinking the water on the bathroom sink drinks the saline solution. Everyone has a laugh and the lunch ends with all of the traditional good-byes. Later that night, you get a text from the saline drinking mutual friend. She's beyond angry. You've got some explaining to do.

Confident people know she's overreacting. Competent people realize that a line may have been crossed. Confident people get angry at someone else for telling her about the story. Competent people realize that the emotion of the situation probably contributed to revealing more information than she would have been comfortable with. In short, confident people are certain that their position is right. Competent people allow for the uncertainty that always exists in relationships.

The same certainty, uncertainty dilemma occurs in the game of baseball. A pitcher doesn't get a call from an umpire. A confident pitcher demands justice. A competent pitcher allows for error and makes the next pitch despite the perceived injustice. A hitter misses a 2-0 fastball. The confident hitter comes back to the bench saying, "The pitcher is trash." A competent hitter realizes he just

---

[13] Again, I'm joking.

missed an opportunity. No one is to blame and certainly no one needs to be trashed.

The ability to handle failure is actually the ability to handle being vulnerable or as my son Luke said, "Being exposed." It simply comes down to the ability to handle fear of the unknown. Confident people need to know that the skills they have developed to this point will serve them well tomorrow. If the skills I have aren't helpful for tomorrow's world, what good will I be? Failure becomes a real sign that MY SKILLS MIGHT NOT BE GOOD ENOUGH. The confident player isn't sure what to make of this possibility. He needs to know that the tools that he has in his tool belt will work in tomorrow's world. The reaction of blame is simply fear. When a confident baseball player blames the umpire or calls the pitcher trash it's actually a desperate plea framed around fear. In my mind the conversation the confident player has with himself looks like this.

FAILURE OCCURS.

Confident player thought I gave it my best shot. I can't believe the result went against me. I'm not sure I can do that again.

FEAR SETS IN. THAT MAY HAVE BEEN MY ONE CHANCE.

Confident player demonstrates this fear in bad body language or in blaming someone else for his lost opportunity.

How does a competent player handle failure? The most important difference is the competent player doesn't need external validation to know he's good. Whereas a confident player relies on others to tell him that he's "The Man," a competent player simply knows that he's developed enough skills to be good enough in tomorrow's world. The competent player sees a single act of failure as just that. It's merely one moment in time that went against me.

Because this one moment in time doesn't define me or doesn't call into question my appropriate skill set, I can evaluate it for what it is. It's simply an opportunity to learn from.

Competent players see others not as a threat but rather an opportunity. They've worked so hard at their craft that they need others in the game to demonstrate the skills that they have. If it weren't for the others, how would I ever show the world all that I am. The fear of being exposed is actually replaced by the love of competing. It really is that simple.

I'm not good enough today, but I'll be great tomorrow.

The above quote embodies a LOVE of competing. It's conquered FEAR!! It's what every coach wants his players to demonstrate. Every coach wants his players to tackle every day with a thirst for wanting to get better coupled with a belief that they will. When this mindset consumes a player, he's no longer fearful of the outcomes of every little event that happens in the daily routine of life.

So, when your friend texts you that you crossed a line mentioning the fact that she drank saline solution your reaction as a competent person is simple. "Maybe I did cross that line." A competent person isn't a pushover. A competent person doesn't concede or waver on every serious issue. A competent person knows what issues are serious and what issues are superfluous. The reality is that she is in fact a friend. The reality is that she was the one being talked about and wasn't in attendance to hear what was being said. The reality is if someone was talking about me when I wasn't around, I'd probably be very sensitive to what was being said as well. A competent person has so many tools in his tool belt that he doesn't jump to conclusions using the only tool he has. Rather, a competent person hears his friend out allowing for the uncertainty of the situation. A competent person realizes that although his actions are perceived as threatening, it certainly wasn't the intent.

Yet, she's absolutely entitled to have that perception until I can mitigate the damage done. In my mind, the conversation the competent player has with himself goes like this.

FAILURE OCCURS.

Competent person thought I was just having some fun. It was an innocuous comment during a carefree moment. She's overreacting. But, seeing how as she wasn't there, she has no way of knowing this. I suppose I might react exactly like she did without all the information. I better fix this.

UNCERTAINTY ALLOWS FOR UNDERSTANDING AND A SUBSEQUENT APOLOGY.

Competent person apologizes providing context of the comment.

Athletes aren't always in uniform. Many times, athletes sit in classrooms. Many times, athletes drive cars. They go to movies. Athletes perform thousands of different roles besides playing the role of athlete. Demonstrating competence rather than confidence can be practiced in any of those roles. All it takes is a little imagination to see that complaining to an umpire that the call didn't go your way is very similar to complaining to the waiter that your service is unacceptably slow. It all might be very true, but it also might simply be your fear of being exposed.

"Hey Kyle. What did you just say?"

How an athlete reacts to an outcome determines his long-term success. When an athlete over values his contribution to a positive outcome, he's setting himself up for future despair. When an athlete doesn't allow for his contribution to a poor outcome, he can't grow from the incident.

Anchoring Quotient
Why Confidence is a Worthy Adversary

I grew up a Baltimore Orioles fan. In that regard, life hasn't been very kind. I did have the 1983 World Series to enjoy. Other than that, it was mostly enjoying Cal Ripken Jr. and his friends. Cal Ripken is known mostly as the guy that broke Lou Gehrig's consecutive game record. I remember exactly where I was the night, he broke the record (Boise, ID). It was a moment for the ages.

What many non-Oriole fans might not know about Cal Ripken is the number of times he changed his batting stance. It was so obvious that even young children like Bret and Kyle Wagner would notice from year to year. Imitating our favorite baseball players was a pastime in the backyard of the Wagner's growing up. You'd don the hard helmet of a certain team and you'd imitate their best player's stance. When you put the Oriole helmet on you either imitated Cal Ripken or Eddie Murray. Murray had the traditional low stance with the bat vertical. Murray was a switch hitter so you could alternate back and forth as well. But Ripken's stance changed with the wind. One year you'd lay it on your back. The next year you'd slightly cock it in the direction of the catcher back and forth. The next year you'd close your stance so pronounced that you'd struggle to see the pitcher. It was always something different. In fact, google Cal Ripken batting stance guy for some comic relief. Ripken wasn't anchored to any one stance. Ripken had the courage to try what was needed for that particular time.

I made up a quotient that helps me see why it is so difficult to change our viewpoint. In other words, why it is we get so anchored to our own opinion. There is absolutely zero scientific evidence that goes into this quotient. It's merely one man's opinion on why it is we are so hesitant to live in the fog of uncertainty.

$$\underline{\text{(Number of like-minded peers * Sunk costs/Monetary rewards *}}$$
$$\underline{\text{Social status)}}$$
(Exceptions to the Rule*Time Remaining)

Number of like-minded peers = Buddies that agree with you. Social Media has increased our number of "buddies."

Sunk costs = The amount of time and money you've dedicated to form your opinions.

Monetary rewards = Financial incentive to maintain this opinion.

Social status = How much of my perception is attached to this viewpoint?

Exceptions to the rule = Have I seen any evidence to the contrary? (Difficult to observe in a habit loop)

Time Remaining = Real or imagined urgency that is required for the opinion. Competition always creates urgency.

Imagine having 250 thousand Twitter followers that like your every post. Imagine having spent 300 thousand dollars and 8 years earning a degree. Imagine your reputation exists because of the opinions you hold. Imagine living your entire life in Shreveport, LA (I have never been to Shreveport. I'm sure it's a wonderful city). Imagine never visiting a foreign country. Imagine having deadlines that you must constantly meet. Consider what your perspective of the world would look like. I'm quite certain you'd have a very high Anchoring Quotient. In other words, there's no way I could change your mind. You'd be one confident person.

The danger of survival systems is it can breed a very high anchoring quotient. Surrounding yourself with like-minded people is essential for survival. You need people like you to protect you.

The longer you're in the system, the more time and money you devote to the system. The experiences you gain are awfully confirming. Less and less you see the black swans that exist. Before you know it, the coaches that exist at the end of survival systems are extremely anchored in their viewpoints. They must be in order to survive.

Maybe because Cal Ripken Sr. was a baseball lifer, it gave Cal Jr. the freedom to challenge convention. Maybe Ripken's courage to change was simply due to the fact that he knew baseball was a game to be played, not a skill to be perfected. So often in sports we demand our players play with confidence and wonder why it is they lack the creativity to compete. I believe competence promotes imagination as it removes the anchoring to ideas that confidence tends to promote. The courage of competence might simply be recognizing the fact that...

The game of baseball isn't owned by anyone and the game of baseball doesn't owe anyone.

The Mound Visit
Ryan Kutz

In major league baseball, typical protocol for visiting a pitcher on the mound is the pitching coach visits if information is to be communicated. These are the trips that don't involve a pitching change. If a change is to be made, that's handled by the manager. I'm not sure if it was always done this way but I'm sure it's evolved in this manner because competitors have a way of talking themselves back into a game. When a manager makes a decision in the safety of his dugout, he doesn't want the emotion of the mound visit to sway him. I think its great strategy for eliminating emotion.

Travel baseball teams aren't equipped to handle mound visits in the same manner. On most occasions, one guy takes the trip. On the RiverCats, that was usually me. On one particular occasion, the visit didn't go according to script.

Managing a pitcher's pitch count has become "the game within the game." Today's coaches must be cognizant of how many pitches a pitcher throws in one game, in one weekend, in one week, in one month. It's a juggling act that's critical for sustained health. Furthermore, when you have young and underdeveloped arms it takes on more significance. In the game of note, Ryan Kutz was a 13-year-old pitcher. His arm may not have been fully developed but his competitive spirit certainly was. That disconnect led to an interesting dynamic.

I, acting as Head Coach of the RiverCats, knew that Ryan was approaching the threshold for acceptable pitches. The tournament didn't have a specific number of pitches but as I recall I wanted to max Ryan out somewhere near 85. It was a semi-final game and our pitching wasn't especially deep. Getting to the championship game was important for everyone wearing baby blue but protecting Ryan's arm was more important for me. Before the start of the sixth inning I had a conversation with Ryan.

Coach Kyle: "Ryan, you've settled down, you look strong. Just know that you're approaching 70 pitches. I don't want you to go over 85. We have Luke ready to go so if you see me coming it's that time of the game. Ok? "

Ryan: "Yeah, that makes sense."

Coach Kyle: "They have 8,9 and 1 coming up so pound away at 'em and see if you can limit your pitches."

Ryan: "Gotcha."

Fist pound. Conversation over.

As we hit in the bottom half of the fifth, I started to have an inner dialogue with myself in the 3rd base box. I started to think about Ryan. Ryan struggled early in the game. I had considered taking him out in the 3rd inning but didn't. Mostly, I didn't take him out because I didn't have the pitching depth to be that liberal with the change. I left him in mostly because I didn't have any other options. But now that he survived up to the sixth, I did have more options. Luke hadn't pitched yet in the tournament and Nick Embleton was ready for the championship. I started thinking about the championship game and who was Nick's relief. Tyler Kehoe was capable of backing up Nick so I thought we would be fine in the championship. I started to regret the conversation with Ryan. I wanted Ryan to go out and start the sixth but if he got the 8 and 9 batters out, I was going to pull him before he had a chance to face the leadoff batter. Plus, it's always nice to be taken out on an up note instead of a down note. I made my mind up. I would tell Ryan as I ran into the dugout following the bottom half of the fifth inning.

The bottom of the fifth went a little longer than expected. We scored and they made a pitching change. In other words, I forgot to tell Ryan.

As Ryan was warming up for the sixth inning, I realized I had forgotten. I shrugged it off thinking, "Ryan's good. He'll understand." I would be proven wrong.

The first two batters were retired in order. Luke was sitting beside me in the dugout. I had told Luke when the leadoff batter comes up, you're going in. Luke was "hot" as they say in baseball lingo. As I looked at Luke and made my way out to the mound, I saw a look come over Ryan that was a little different than a normal Ryan Kutz expression. The look spoke volumes. "What are you doing? This isn't what we talked about. You lied to me." Of course, Ryan never said those words. He had too much respect to say that. But he didn't need to say it. His body language said it all.

Here's the thing about competent people. They compete like crazy. They're not any less competitive than a confident player. In the heat of the moment their reptilian brain acts exactly like the confident player. Ryan was angry with his coach. He had his heart set on finishing the inning and his coach took that away from him. Ryan was forced to go from 100 mph to 0 in the blink of an eye. Ryan would have to find a way to channel his emotions following this premature departure. Here's how I remember Ryan handling his emotions.

As Ryan walked off the mound, Luke received the ball. I gave Luke some basic obligatory instructions. I made my way back into the dugout knowing we had only 4 more outs to get before playing in the championship game. As I entered the dugout, I encountered a predictably angry Ryan Kutz who offered up an unpredictable outburst. For the first time since I had seen Ryan, he let his emotions get the best of him. That glove that he once treated with respect met a much different fate this time around. Ryan coupled the glove toss with a few choice words and needless to say we needed to have a conversation.

Coach Kyle: "You're allowed to be angry. But you're not allowed to act like that."

Ryan: "You said I could finish the inning if I got those first two batters out. I'm not at 85 yet."

Coach Kyle: "I changed my mind and I forgot to tell you. Sometimes, it's not about you. Luke needs some innings too. I just forgot. Now stop."

Ryan (teeth clenched): SILENCE

Ryan sat in silence the rest of the game. He wasn't a great teammate for those last 4 outs. I gave Ryan that time. I wish I had handled it differently. But, I didn't. It wasn't intentional. I got exactly what I wanted. Ryan had a solid, long outing and Luke got the last 4 outs. For all intents and purposes the outcome was exactly what I had wanted. The impact, however, was still up in the air. How would Ryan act once he created some distance between the game and his reaction?

20 minutes later leading up to the championship and with a hot dog or two in Ryan's belly we chatted.

Ryan: "Hey Coach. Sorry about the last game. I overreacted and it won't happen again."

Coach Kyle: "You don't know that. It very well might happen again. Emotion makes sane people crazy. You were just competing. I was just competing. The fact that you're apologizing speaks to your character. We're good."

Ryan: "Thanks Coach."

The courageous athletes are the athletes that know not every situation is exactly as it seems. As much as confidence feels so good it can deceive. The confident athlete has all the answers and can predict every future outcome. When those solutions and predictions fail, all he's left with are misery and blame. The competent athlete is built for the "long game." He's built for a tomorrow that is entirely unpredictable.
As The Imagination Game evolves into The Precision Game more and more it relies on the competent player. Adjustable and adaptable far exceeds optimal and efficient. The competent player can allow for the uncertainty of the situation to search for other, unexplored options. It isn't nearly as black and white as the confident player thinks. The competent player becomes much

more resistant to the dangers that are omnipresent in the baseball world.

Ryan Kutz has accepted a scholarship offer to attend Davidson College in Davidson, North Carolina. Ryan will pitch for the Wildcats. Since leaving the RiverCats, Ryan has competed for Lower Dauphin High School in Hummelstown, PA. In 2018, Ryan pitched in the state championship game for the 5A Falcons. Although they fell short of PIAA gold, Ryan lasted into the sixth inning. I see ya workin' Ryan.

The Fifth Inning
A Common Goal is Uncommon

Here's how I used to conduct my Green Light Hitting lessons. When the player would arrive, I would listen to the past week's events. I would ask probing questions listening to how each at bat transpired. I was actively listening. I was searching for a pattern, a sign of something that might indicate how I could help. I'd take my lesson into the cage and I'd assess their physical swing. Is it a swing error or is it a timing error? Sometimes, I'd find it quickly. If the naked eye failed to identify the error, I'd run for the camera. The "microscope" can usually find a problem.

Once the problem was identified using super slow motion, we'd often set out with a series of drills to work on a very specific swing flaw. The Green Light Hitting model was very easy to work with because it had markers that you'd look for. It was a progression of sorts. It worked for our guys and our instructors. Green Light Hitting was very popular with our GoWags teams and others in Central PA.

I've now been out of the baseball lesson business for two and a half years. I still teach the game of baseball, but I no longer take money for doing it. I still teach most aspects of Green Light Hitting but I no longer play the role of "expert fixer." Rather, I try and be "expert observer" and adjust accordingly. The difference between these two ideas is very important to reconcile. Billy White knew the danger before I knew the danger. Being removed from the lesson game has now allowed me to see the brilliance of Billy.

Billy White moved to Central Pennsylvania while I was the Head Coach of Red Land High School. When we opened GoWags it wasn't long until Billy was giving lessons in our facility. Billy played at the University of Kentucky and had a long professional career both as a player and as a coach. Billy had a lot of experience in the game of baseball. Any baseball facility would have been proud to call Billy an employee. Billy and I struggled to co-exist.

"First Do No Harm" is rule number one for doctors. When confronted with the noble endeavor of assisting another human being, the first order of business is don't make their life worse than when you found it. This seems self-evident but second and third order consequences complicate things a little. Prescribing medication for high blood pressure seems intuitive enough in the short term. Prescribing medication that creates a lifelong addiction and numbs the body's ability to experience life is never an intended consequence. Yet, it happens. It happens all too frequently.

Giving a lesson to a baseball player is very much like a doctor's visit. The baseball player is the patient and the instructor is the doctor. As is often the case, Mom and Dad don't schedule a visit unless they believe the patient has an ailment. The instructor serves as the baseball physician diagnosing whatever ailment he uncovers. The visit typically takes between 30 to 45 minutes and upon leaving, Mom, Dad and Son hope to have a plan that produces "baseball health". On any given night, the instructor performs this task multiple times (I think my daily record for lessons was 18). Instructors get tired.

Billy had a healthy amount of lessons while he worked at GoWags. He was busy. I was busy. Bret was busy. But, on occasion I noticed Billy didn't seem to diagnose an ailment. I'd question this internally. "Why isn't he giving Mom and Dad what they want?" They didn't bring their son here because he was healthy. They brought him here because they wanted a fix to whatever ailed him. I never told Billy this but, in some respects, I thought he was lazy. He wasn't lazy, he was smarter than all of us.

The lesson model is flawed because money changes hands. Instruction done right observes and corrects as appropriate. Instruction done with money attached observes and corrects as an obligation. That is a major design flaw in producing better baseball players. Looking at someone through a lens designed to see a problem will always find a problem. Whereas Kyle Wagner played the dutiful doctor, Billy White observed first and acted accordingly. Billy wasn't bound by the dollar.

Here's one specific example I remember. A college freshman came into GoWags for a lesson. I was one cage over and Billy was working with this Division 1 baseball player. The lesson was roughly 30 minutes long. Prior to the lesson, Billy talked with the Dad and Son and the reason for the visit was "There's just something off. We were hoping you could see what it might be." Billy said he'd do his best.

Billy started with some tee work and the athlete stayed in the middle of the cage. For baseball instructors this is a good thing. Often, when the tee work isn't hit precisely where it's intended to go there is in fact something worth addressing. On this night, everything looked fine. Billy proceeded to offer some front flips to see if he noticed something with his basic timing. Again, nothing too egregious. Billy commented it looked good. Billy then backed up and proceeded to throw classic Billy White batting practice for the next 10 minutes or so. The athlete, from what I could tell, seemed to be ripping pitch after pitch. Billy went from fastballs to breaking balls to an assortment of "unpredictable." Through it all, the athlete looked good. On occasion, he'd pop one up or rollover, but it was certainly a swing most everyone would be proud of. With 5 minutes to go, the Dad jumped in and said, "Well, do you see anything?" Billy's response makes me laugh just thinking about it now. At the time, I'm sure Dr. Wagner (The 2012 version of Kyle) wasn't amused but the 2019 version of Kyle Wagner thinks it's awesome. Billy said, "No."

Iatrogenesis is defined by Wikipedia as (from the Greek for "brought forth by the healer") refers to any effect on a person, resulting from any activity of one or more other persons acting as healthcare professionals or promoting products or services as beneficial to health, *which does not support a goal of the person affected.*

106

Doctors, teachers and instructors are servants. We are servants to the needs of our clients. We have an incredible responsibility. The first responsibility is to DO NO HARM. Unfortunately, sometimes we're too confident in our skills to realize that an attempt at "fixing" might in fact DO HARM. Baseball instructors have a huge responsibility to the dreams and goals of the athletes they serve. They must become competent and credible enough through the experiences they gain, but they must practice with humility and doubt that they might be wrong. Or, they might be tired.

I teach Probability and Statistics to high school students. One of the most misunderstood ideas that affects coaching is something that teenagers can understand rather quickly. The idea is *regression to the mean*. A regression to the mean in layman's terms simply suggests that scores go up and down. They are never constant. Let's use an example that demonstrates the simplicity of the idea and yet the enormity of the consequences. Let's say I'm a basketball player that has a scoring average of 10 pts. per game. My points scored might look like this over the course of a 20-game season.

14 8 3 20 11 15 9 7 11 5 1 10 12 15 6 7 3 20
8 15

Most coaches subscribe to a theory of "If it ain't broke, don't fix it." So, what that means is the coach would offer no coaching following the bolded games.

14 8 3 **20** **11** **15** 9 7 **11** 5 1 **10** **12** **15** 6 7 3 **20**
8 **15**

Notice what happens following the NO COACHING MODEL? Scores drop. Uh-oh! Time to fix the problem.

14 **8 3** 20 11 15 **9 7** 11 **5 1** 10 12 15 **6 7 3** 20
8 15

Here's what happens during the ACTIVE COACHING MODEL. Scores eventually go up after a coach intervenes. There you have it. My coaching helped the athlete. How could it not? When I offered up my advice, his scoring average improved.

"We are not made to view things as independent from each other. When viewing two events A and B, it is hard not to assume that A causes B, B causes A, or both cause each other. Our bias is immediately to establish a causal link."
Nassim Taleb, Fooled by Randomness

Coaches are human beings affected by the same biases that affect all of us. The regression to the mean is obvious. Coaches want to help when they perceive his substandard play as predictable. Coaches stay quiet when they perceive his play as above standard. When the player responds according to prediction, a habit loop is born. The reward was being proven right. The routine becomes do it again. You were fooled by randomness. You may have just participated in some iatrogenesis.

Iatrogenesis is the 3rd leading cause of death as reported by yourmedicaldetective.com. This book isn't designed to impugn doctors but rather to shed light on the fact that people in positions of power sometimes create unintended consequences. Athletes trust the coaches they work with. They don't expect us to be perfect. But they do expect us TO DO NO HARM. The best way to avoid harm is to be competent enough to act on what we believe is true yet vulnerable enough to realize two distinct reasons to pause. First, what we believe we know is probably less than we think. Second, and maybe most important, only the client gets to define success.

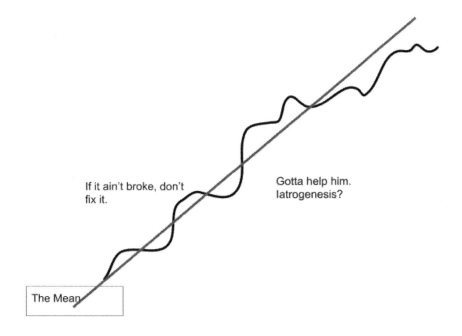

Saved by Inexperience
Justin Williams

When GoWags started training athletes we did private lessons and we did group training. Private lessons are essential for sharpening skills. Nothing can beat the one-on-one attention that a private lesson gives. But the group training also had a ton of value. Group training allowed the players to identify with others to see where they fit. Many times, the group settings were uncomfortable for people as they realized they were a little behind. Many times, the group settings were affirming, and they realized they were ahead. We sorted the athletes as broadly as possible, so each group had enough flexibility to see as many different faces as possible. Here's how we sorted the athletes.

Sampling Group: The Sampling Group was for our youngest athletes. We called them "Samplers" because we recognized that they might just be trying the sport out. They hadn't yet committed to the sport. Our primary purpose in the Sampling Group was to have as much fun as possible and to teach them the fun aspects of the game. As detailed in The Ninth Inning we were playing The Imagination Game with this group. Our primary goal with these young athletes was to get them excited about the game of baseball. If a mistake was to be made, we were going to err on too much fun.

Specialized Group: The Specialized Group was serious about baseball. They had chosen the sport. They wanted to improve in the sport. Yet, it wasn't their only sport. The focus of this group was to make sure we were teaching them something new every class period. Learning is fun and this group wanted to add more tools to their tool belt. Learning and having fun never go out of style. That was the focus of the Specialized Group. The primary difference between the two was we'd often trick the Samplers into learning while we often broke the Specialized Group down to make sure they knew why we were doing what we were doing.

Invested Group: The Invested Group were baseball players. This was their sport and they wanted to play this sport for as long as possible. These were often the older players, but we weren't opposed to allowing a Specialized player to jump up in groups. We didn't know it at the time but even then, we were following a model that would become the mission of the RiverCats.

Practice and Play with Good Players as Often as Possible.

Our focus with the Invested Group was to challenge them and find ways in which we could get them to fail in our group setting. For the Sampling Group and even the Specialized Group, failing may have been a sign to jump ship and pick something else. For the Invested Group, it was an invaluable resource for growth. Pain is the greatest teacher and our goal was to create some discomfort in a practice environment, so they had motivation to grow.

Justin Williams was a big kid. When he first came to GoWags he was a 9-yr. old in the fifth grade. Justin and his brother Josh could pound a baseball. They weren't naturals in the sport, but they were exactly the kind of kid that we loved at GoWags. The Williams boys had a very high ceiling and they had the motivation to challenge that ceiling.

When it came time to form the RiverCats we had a rough idea of who we wanted on our team based upon my previous coaching. In addition to coaching in the New Cumberland Pony League, I had been a coach on 9u Junior Colts team that had unearthed some serious talent as well. Furthermore, I had developed enough contacts to know who the better players in the area were. I had a hunch that finding a roster of 12 wouldn't be a considerable challenge. Justin Williams wasn't on my radar.

Experience is a double-edged sword. The more experiences you collect, the better you think you can predict. It's an essential tool for life. Yet, the more experiences you collect, the easier it is to be deceived by the "exception." Whereas a beginner isn't necessarily transfixed by the appearance of a black swan, the expert balks at it. Swans are supposed to be white. In the book *Rookie Smarts,* author Liz Wiseman calls the rookies the Hunter-Gatherers always on high alert scanning the horizon for danger. She calls the "experts" the Local Guide always advising on what it is we're supposed to be seeing. When it came to Justin Williams, I was observing him as a Local Guide. Thankfully, Teed Wertz was a Hunter-Gatherer.

Teed played for me at Red Land High School and was always a thinker when it came to the game of baseball. I hired him at GoWags because he was passionate, he was curious and most importantly he loved kids. As we were forming the RiverCats, Teed said to me "What about Justin Williams?" I replied, "Justin is too old to be a RiverCat." Teed looked at me with that Teed Wertz glare expressing both irreverence and surprise. "Kyle, Justin might look bigger than the RiverCats but he's RiverCat age."

Justin spent much of his time in the Specialized Group. In addition to baseball activities we'd do tests of speed and strength. It was a fun group challenging personal bests and competing with like-minded people. Justin always excelled. But I just assumed Justin wasn't age eligible to play for the RiverCats. His size betrayed his age. Teed, being Teed, struck up a conversation with Justin's dad, Mike. Low and behold, Justin was a grade older than most of the would be RiverCats, but he was in fact RiverCat age. Wow. Talk about almost missing a gold mine in your own backyard. Justin Williams was a Central PA kid and someone that would become a cornerstone of the RiverCats' success.

Daddy Ball
Mike Williams

Dads are getting an awful reputation in the world of sports. There's even a phrase called "Daddy Ball." It connotes a version of baseball that plays favorites and allows the entitled son an opportunity to experience certain things he hasn't earned. It has its merits. I've seen enough to know nepotism does in fact exist in the travel baseball world. But, if Justin Williams was a black swan when it came to playing the game of baseball, Mike Williams was a black swan when it came to coaching the game of baseball. Telling the Justin Williams story without telling the Mike Williams story wouldn't be fair to Justin.

Knowing what I know now, Mike's approach to coaching his son Justin might have been rooted in a deep appreciation for the game of baseball. Mike was and still is an avid baseball card collector. Ladies and gentlemen, that means Mike had a very broad perspective as to what this game actually was. Many dads fall in love with baseball mostly because they enjoy watching their son succeed in a sport that they love. In that regard, baseball has as much value as the legos on the floor. All dads enjoy watching their son find entertainment playing legos on the floor, but the game of baseball isn't meant to be appreciated like toys wrapped in a box. Baseball is nostalgic.

Mike saw the game of baseball through a very nostalgic lens. Mike appreciated Napolean Lajoie and Smokey Joe Wood. Mike could rattle off Cap Anson and George Wright just as easily as he could discuss Mike Trout or Mariano Rivera. I noticed very early that Mike could take a very broad approach with how Justin would be coached and trained. It was refreshing. It was actually something I aspired to be for my own son.

Mike wouldn't be a coach that first year with the RiverCats. I had my guys. Mike would be the fan on the side dutifully watching every pitch and competing from a distance. But Mike and I were getting to become more and more familiar with each other. I appreciated his perspective on things. I liked how he worked with Justin to become a better player and how he was honest with Justin when he wasn't at his best. But I always appreciated the love that he showed Justin by allowing Justin to be Justin Williams and not Mike Williams 2.0. As I was appreciating Mike's approach more and more, Mike was developing an appreciation for what the RiverCats were becoming. This appreciation was never more apparent than during one game at Cal Ripken's Aberdeen, MD complex.

The Ripken complex names their fields after Big League Stadiums past and present. This particular game took place at Citizens Bank Park. Luke Wagner was hitting, and Justin Williams was at third base, 70' away from scoring (The field dimensions allowed for 70' bases). With one out and Justin on third base, I gave my typical instructions that I have given since I've been called "Coach." Here's what I'm sure I said because it's literally scripted in my head. "Justin, contact read. If you're out by a lot get in a rundown. Work hard to get back with any lift." The contact read at third base on a line drive to an outfielder is a hard concept to teach young people. But we practiced it religiously. The RiverCats did this every practice. It was something Justin had done over and over again. On this occasion, Justin broke for home. The ball was caught. We didn't score the run.

I lost my mind. I'm not proud of my reaction now but the reptilian brain took over. The problem with coaching the boys like they're Big Leaguers (The Third Inning) is sometimes you have Big League expectations. This was one of those times. I immediately walked up behind Justin and I began a classic Kyle Wagner teaching moment. Did I embarrass Justin? Of course, I did. Was I more interested in the failed act of a contact read than the player I was coaching? Of course, I was. Were my actions influenced because my son was the player hitting? Of course, they were. Justin Williams had every right to be coached in that situation. Justin Williams had absolutely zero right to be embarrassed. I chose the latter option.

Mike Williams chose what I'd come to expect Mike Williams to choose. Mike walked up to the fence at Citizens Bank Park and he tersely said "Kyle, that's enough." Mike didn't make a scene like I had made. Thankfully, Mike had enough appreciation for my position has Head Coach to allow me to coach his son in the manner in which I chose. Thankfully, Mike knew enough to also know that being labeled Head Coach wasn't reason enough to embarrass his son. I remember turning and looking at Mike in a very heated state and chose to say nothing. Mike was right. I learned a lot on that day.

I learned that Dad is a label that carries with it a ton of emotion. I learned that although I might know more baseball than the rest of the dads cheering for the RiverCats, I wasn't necessarily the best Baseball Dad. I learned that Mike Williams, although he was for the RiverCats, would always be for Justin above anything else. I learned that high expectations are critical to becoming a great team but handling the disappointment when you fall short is critical to becoming a great human being.

Following that first year as a RiverCat, Mike Williams would serve as an Assistant Coach for me until Justin and he left to play for US Elite. Switching teams in the travel baseball world can be a sticky mess. Feelings get hurt and people play the victim card far too often. I actually believe it's very healthy to gain multiple perspectives and play for as many coaches as possible. Learning how to filter multiple messages is one of the baseball player's critical tools for long term growth. As was mentioned earlier, Justin was a grade older than most of the RiverCats. Mike and Justin believed that Justin needed exposure that the RiverCats weren't quite in a position to dole out. Justin and Mike opted for a different team as they started playing the 14U season. Essentially, they chose to play for one of our chief rivals. They were still following the mission of the RiverCats though.

Practice and Play with Good Players as Often as Possible.

"Hey Kyle. What did you just say?"
Coaches make mistakes too. Sometimes, it's appropriate for dad to correct them.

Hit or Error
I Thought We Were Keeping Score

The legend of Ty Cobb being disliked by his peers is a popular one. It might even be true. There appears to be an undeniable story of a batting average race that took place in 1910 between the aforementioned Cobb and the Cleveland Spider great Napolean Lajoie. Cobb and Lajoie competed in the Dead Ball Era. Before

Babe Ruth entered baseball's landscape, batting average was a much more glamorous award than home runs. The award was so popular that the Chalmers Automobile Company offered a new vehicle to the batting champion. The fact that Cobb and Chalmers both hailed from Detroit might have had something to do with the offer. From 1907 to 1915 Ty Cobb was crowned the batting champion. But, the 1910 race was the race that would prove both noteworthy and costly in the lives of many baseball men.

With two games to play in the season, Cobb led Lajoie .385 to .376. For all intents and purposes Cobb would be driving the new vehicle at season's end. Cobb, not wanting to risk playing the game and losing precious points (Refer to the Eighth Inning "rewards are dangerous because rewards detract from the true purpose") opted not to play. Lajoie's Spiders visited the St. Louis Browns in a season ending double header. The St. Louis Browns manager ordered the 3B to play absurdly deep. The bunt was all but a given hit for Lajoie. Lajoie recorded 6 bunt hits in the double header. Lajoie went 8 for 9 in the season's final two games. The only blemish on an otherwise perfect day was an error by the shortstop. Both the Spiders manager and the Browns manager, unconvinced that 8 hits were enough, tried to bribe the official scorer into ruling the error a hit. A 9 for 9 day would surely give Lajoie a better chance at the Chalmers automobile. The official scorer was unrelenting. 8 hits would have to stand for Lajoie. It wasn't enough. Cobb beat Lajoie .385069 to .384095. Or did he?[14]

Baseball coaches at all age levels deal with the athlete that asks, "Was that a hit or an error?" Baseball coaches have been trained to admonish such questions. The fact that you reached first base is all that matters. Be a team player and stop being so selfish. The

---

[14] Baseball Reference lists Lajoie as the batting champion in 1910. There still appears to be controversy.

audacity to ask such a question. The fact that coaches get angry and upset with this question speaks to the fact that baseball is a survival system game where the only thing that matters to a coach is hitting the target. Yet, outside the survival system mentality, there exists an athlete that's trying to achieve independent goals that are important to him. Would we begrudge a waitress that was angry because someone forgot to tip her? Would we begrudge a student for asking why a teacher marked a correct response incorrect?

Athletes enter a team sport like baseball with independent goals that are important to them. They adopt team goals that are important to the team. But athletes are allowed and expected to also have independent goals. Teams that recognize that these independent, often self-serving goals are every bit as important as the team goals create a much better chance of getting "buy-in" from their athletes.

Knowing that every athlete has their own goals unique to them isn't a difficult concept to accept. Allowing the athlete to chase their individual goals while in a uniform is a much harder concept to integrate. The "Was it a hit or an error?" question is a tangible question all coaches field from time to time. It's the athlete admitting in the form of a question. "I have a preference to how that was scored. It's important to me that it be ruled a hit because I care about my batting average." Having a high batting average is important. But, not nearly as important as playing time.

Nothing is more sacred than playing time. It's the great challenge for every coach. As a matter of fact, everything hinges on it. The parents that are your "friends" are your "friends" because you play their son. The after-game walk to the car is affected by playing time. The conversation at the concession stand is affected by playing time. The hotel room lobby chat is affected by playing time. The elevator ride is affected by playing time. The best of intentions, the noblest of causes, the "long game" mission will fall flat on its face if playing time isn't awarded justly. Coaches that don't recognize the importance of this very individual goal will never achieve the greatest of team outcomes.

"Hey Kyle. What did you just say?"

Being on a team doesn't eliminate the individuals on that team from having individual goals. We all have individual goals and they're important to us. The only way true progress can be made is to recognize these goals instead of labeling them "selfish" under a team umbrella.

Easy Target
April Fools

After the RiverCats started playing high school baseball, I agreed to coach the GoWags Deacons. I enjoyed coaching and it would allow me to coach my nephew, Cole Wagner. It also allowed me to coach with my son. He was my first base coach. I knew the role of coaching your son is the hardest job in the world (The Second Inning) so I thought my altruistic gesture would be well received by my brother and the other dads on the team. That didn't mean I wasn't going to have some fun at their expense though.

My very first experience coaching the Deacons happened to fall on a Saturday morning. The date: April 1st. This was going to be fun. Dads have a very hard time relinquishing control. They believe they know their son better than anyone (they do) and they firmly believe they have the necessary tools to create success. Furthermore, I was their trusted friend. The unsaid expectation was I would FIRST, DO NO HARM.

The GoWags Deacons were the home team by coin flip. This was a break for me. To pull off my ruse I wanted to take the field first.

Before the game, I sat the boys down and I said something like this.

Ok Guys, Listen Up. This is our first go around together and I couldn't be more excited. We're going to compete like crazy and we're going to have a blast doing it. I'm a very competitive guy. The opportunities you get, you have to earn. I realize each and every one of you would rather play than sit the bench. I'll do my best to make sure you're all getting opportunities to play but never at the expense of winning the game. Winning is a big deal. You guys need to know that teams aren't formed to pick strawberries. Teams are formed to win. That will always be a goal. Hopefully, each and every one of you will find a role that you can embrace and feel a part of. If you can't, we can talk about what you need to do to improve your role. Having said all of that, this first game we're going to have some fun at your parents' expense. I know many of your parents are anxiously awaiting where each of you take the field. Let's play an April Fool's joke on them. THEIR EYES LIT UP WITH EXCITEMENT. Here's what I'm thinking. Let's take the field like this. CRAZY LINEUP FOLLOWED.

The kids loved it. The parents' reactions bordered between curiosity and rage. Bret and the other dads skewed more to the rage side. Mission accomplished.

After the pitcher's (the pitcher wasn't an April Fool's joke) warmup pitches, the real defense took the field. My joke was met with laughter and applause. I had taken the expectations of a survival system game like baseball and inserted some levity into the situation. The anger the parents displayed could be laughed off quickly when the ruse was unveiled. But, make no mistake that anger exists in parents. Sometimes, the anger is allowed to bubble to the top. Sometimes, it's kept under wraps. Regardless, the anger exists.

No evidence of, does not mean evidence of none.

Far too often, coaches only address issues that reach the surface level. When a parent complains, they address it. In other words, coaches live in a world where they demand evidence before acting. This isn't how great teams' function. Great teams recognize that there is so much more that lies below the surface. Just because you don't see it or don't hear about it doesn't mean it doesn't exist. When my April Fools team took the field, I knew the reactions would be palpable. Yet, every time I sent a team on the field with the RiverCats I knew smaller, unseen reactions also existed. Maintaining the pulse of the team meant knowing that just because they were smiling didn't necessarily mean they were happy.

There is a term in psychology called the Fundamental Attribution Error. As a coach, or anyone for that matter that deals with other human beings, it's essential to understand. The fancy name simply means "I was joking. You're a jerk." When actions and intent are considered, most people allow their intentions to determine appropriateness. Yet, when actions and intentions are considered for others, they allow the actions to determine appropriateness.

Here are some specific examples to clarify one of the most important rules to understanding our fellow Homo sapiens.

The Event: Forgetting to clean up the bathroom.

Explaining Me: I had a lot on my mind. I just forgot.
Explaining Him: He's lazy.

The Event: Walking the leadoff hitter.

Explaining Me: I relaxed after getting those two runs.
Explaining Him: He's weak minded.

The Event: Not doing a field job after the game.

Explaining Me: My parents were in town. I asked a buddy to pick me up.

Explaining Him: He's selfish.

The Fundamental Attribution Error accounts for so much discord between coach and player. The coach that assumes the actions are all there is misses the underlying intent. There is always underlying intent. Just because a parent or an athlete displays the courage not to voice it or the discipline to wait until the next day doesn't mean it's still not there. For every unselfish act committed by an athlete wearing a "teammate" hat, there is a selfish itch wanting to be scratched.

I've created a model that helps me to see how individuals are motivated. It's a model based upon three doors. It gives me clarity and understanding for the motivations of all athletes.

Actual Door   Attentional Door   Intentional Door

The Actual Door is the practice field door. Everyone has to show up. This is easy to evaluate. You're either present or your absent. Getting through the first door is essential but often neglected. They need to want to show up. The Attentional Door is the eyeball test. Once they're in your company, have they given you their eyeballs. In today's smart-phone era, the second door is becoming harder and harder to walk through. The last door is the hardest of all. The last door is the Intentional Door. This is the ear test. Just because I'm staring at you doesn't mean I'm listening to you. The Intentional Door is impossible for a coach to control. The only hope he has for getting his athletes to walk through the last door is to use influence instead of power. Winning over an athlete's imagination will get him to gladly open that last door and walk through. But, if you want to win over his imagination, you better recognize his individual goals. A player can only sacrifice so long until he'll stop short of the third door.

The Artist Sets the Bar (Defines Success)
Stop Painting. It's Good Enough

I was good at school. Not because I cared about the content of what was being taught. Rather, I was competitive. You could have replaced Biology with Kite Flying and I would have been just as focused on getting A's. This isn't healthy. As we already discussed, learning things for the sake of winning a prize is a very flawed model. I was good at it. But, not as good as some. I was not as good as Erik Goodhart.

Erik Goodhart was a childhood buddy that was better at school than me. I loved him for it. He was the kid that could calculate the square root of 7 to three decimal places because he cared enough to know it. I loved Erik. But Erik would get frustrated when tests were returned, and he got a 99%. The rest of us would chime in with some childish taunts like "Why are you begging for 1 point?" We were making him feel guilty for wanting a 100%. The reality was, Erik was allowed to demand whatever Erik wanted. If Erik wanted a 100%, he was allowed to ask that of himself. The same kid calling Erik selfish might be selfish under the hood of a car. Maybe Erik could retaliate with "Why do you need a perfect flow with that intake valve?" (I have absolutely no idea how engines work and that question might make zero sense but I'm not changing it.) The artist performing the task is the only one that must live with falling short of expectations. When someone else assigns the level of expectation they are violating the Code of Ethics. They are in fact, FIRST DOING HARM.

Wait a second. What about the coach that sees more in me than I see in myself? What about that guy? Not everyone believes they can achieve. The expert coach sees the potential in the athlete. The coach must be allowed to demand even when the player doesn't quite see it himself. I agree. But only if the athlete has walked through the Intentional Door. If the athlete has given the coach full intention and has committed to the task at hand, physically, mentally and emotionally then by all means, DEMAND MORE OF HIM. But, far too often in the game of baseball, school and life, we allow others to set the bar for us. This is a recipe for frustration at best and extreme anxiety at worst.

I demand my best in the following areas: Husband, Dad, Coach, Teacher, Friend. If I fall short of doing my best, I tend to be hard on myself.

I demand less than my best in the following areas: Cleaning the bathroom, my wardrobe, my engine knowledge and my navigation skills. If I fall short, I lose zero sleep. I'm perfectly content not wanting to be great at these things.

The quest for perfection is a noble cause, in some areas of your life. The quest for perfection in all areas of your life is a very dangerous proposition. You must be allowed to find balance and only the artist can set those levels of expectation. I laugh thinking about someone telling Michelangelo "Hey, that Sistine Chapel, it is good enough. Let's go home." Or, how about the alternative. Can you picture someone telling Ty Cobb "Your behavior today was subpar. I believe an apology is in order."

We might not be comfortable when others set the bar higher than we do or lower than we do but it's for them to choose. If you're tasked with coaching the bar setters, your first order of business is recognizing what it is they care deeply about (The Intentional Door) and then find a way to influence them to raise the bar and get over the bar. As a coach, the bar takes on many different shapes, sizes and forms. It could be your swing. It could be your defense. It could be as specific as your 0-2 breaking ball. But each athlete creates their own level of expectation. Each athlete is allowed to chase their own goals under a team model. Some coaches recognize this after Mom and Dad confront them at the concession stand. Other coaches know it exists even though Mom and Dad don't mention a word.

"Hey Kyle. What did you just say?"
Every action has an underlying intent. Recognizing that only the athlete controls his intent is a very important skill for a coach.

Launch Angle
Justin Williams

I've played for a lot of coaches that demanded "hit the ball on the ground." They obviously believed the best chance for success was a lower ball flight rather than a higher ball flight. In 2019, that idea is now met with a ton resistance. To even suggest a ground ball focus with certain baseball people is the equivalent of "the earth is flat argument." The data is in. The data suggests hitting the ball in the air leads to more success. The key question becomes, how do we define success?

For me, I laugh at the argument. The reality is both the "hit the ball on the ground" coach and "hit the ball in the air" coach (launch angle) are right. They simply define success differently. Let's look at the debate through a Poker lens. The "hit the ball on the ground" coach realizes that a winning hand is any hand that beats his opponent. He doesn't need to have the best cards; he just needs his opponent with the best cards to fold. He needs his opponent to make an error in judgment. The "hit the ball on the ground" coach knows that winning baseball doesn't always require hits. Winning baseball often takes advantage of errors. What positions make the most errors? Why the infielders of course. So, by hitting the ball on the ground, that team gains the opportunity of a base hit but also the increased probability of winning by opponent's error.

The launch angle coach has data on his side. But the data is skewed to the selfish hitter. All hitters are selfish, and all hitters should be selfish. If I reach base on 4 infield errors, I'm still 0-4. So, although the team might benefit from an opponent's error, the selfish hitter is left taking the collar.[15] The best chance for success lies with hitting the ball in the air. Furthermore, the longer you play the game, the less errors the defense makes. You can't rely on errors to win forever. The launch angle coach knows you can only bluff your way to success so long at the poker table. Eventually, you need to have good cards to keep playing the game.

Justin Williams had "good cards" as a 12-yr. old. Justin Williams was producing appropriate launch angles. Specifically, he launched 19 balls at Cooperstown, NY. As I mentioned in The Eighth Inning, the Cooperstown experience is incredible. The RiverCats finished 2nd to the Texas Gladiators. We fell short of our ultimate goal, but we did make it to the championship game and along the way we hit 69 home runs in 13 games. Justin Williams hit 19 of them. Justin hit 3 in the championship game. Granted, it was a 200' fence with very powerful bats but let me say it again. Justin Williams hit 19 home runs in 13 games.

---

[15] Going hitless.

In the fall following that magical 12u season the RiverCats played 13u baseball. 13u baseball is like visiting Abilene, TX (I've never been to Abilene. It sounds dusty and barren.) after returning from the Bahamas. It's something to do but there's no way you're going to really enjoy it. Here's what I remember about a specific tournament in Hershey, PA. We played a good team and we played on a field without a fence. When Justin came up the outfielders backed up; more than you just pictured. They REALLY backed up.

I'm at my normal perch in the third base coaching box. I notice the outfielder's depth, but I shrug it off. It seemed more likely that Justin would get a single in front of them rather than actually hit it to them. Justin worked the count full when he unloaded in typical Justin Williams fashion. He destroyed the baseball. For a strong 13-yr. old with a -5 (5 ounces lighter than the length) bat, that probably meant he hit the ball 325-350 feet. It was hit very far. It was caught.

Justin touched 2nd base and quickly diverted himself back to the dugout. To add insult to injury for Justin the dugout was uncovered. Justin was on the bench for everyone to see. He had nowhere to hide his emotions. Justin cried. I didn't know it at the time. I was still finishing out the inning in the third base box. Only when I returned to the dugout did I see the commotion on the bench. Justin's teammates were looking at him incredulously. I'm sure they were thinking to themselves "Dude, I've never hit a ball that far. Who cares that it was caught?" He cared. Only Justin is allowed to set Justin's bar.

Justin Williams dedicated himself to becoming a very talented baseball player. Justin was always the strong kid with a very high ceiling. He's becoming a man that's approaching that ceiling. Justin played his last season with the RiverCats following that 13u season. Justin is a freshman at Penn State University. He'll be competing for the starting job at 3B. If he doesn't win the job, most would say "It's ok. He's just a freshman." That might be ok for them, but it might not sit well with Justin. The athlete sets the bar. He must then learn to live with the outcome. I see ya workin' Justin.

The Fourth Inning
Why Travels

As a math teacher, you hope your students show up with questions to explore the potential that exist in numbers. You show them how things work. You show them how to apply it. You try and connect things they already know to the possibility of what could be. As you're teaching a new concept, you're imagining all the ways your students are making their own connections. You're hopeful for a question. A question is that small spark that suggests "What if." A hand goes up in the sea of humanity and they ask, "When am I ever going to need this?"

For many teachers, my former self included, this was always a point of contention. I'd clamor about with all the fields that use quadratics or all the fields that require factoring. There are posters that are made justifying the value of algebra. Believe it or not, algebra has value. But, that's beside the point. The question the student was asking was "Why is this important?"

The question reveals the mindset of the student. The student that demands "time" be valuable needs to know that he's not wasting his time. If I'm going to sit here and you want me to walk through that Intentional Door, you have to give me a reason to do so. Otherwise, I'm checking out. The student that allows for uncertainty and recognizes that "time" is an opportunity to add more tools to the tool belt for a very unpredictable future considers what it is the teacher is saying. The student that allows for an unpredictable world, listens. The student that sees the world in predictable terms does not listen.

I was a student of the game of baseball. I always allowed for the unpredictable future. I was always scared that a situation might arise, and I wouldn't be prepared for it. I studied rule books. I watched how pitchers sequenced their pitches. I watched how coaches organized their practices. I listened to every nugget of every story told hoping I could extract something of value. Maybe, it would benefit me someday. Someday would be an August doubleheader in Birmingham, AL.

Being a twin has its downfalls. People aren't always as friendly as you'd like them to be because people don't want to be wrong with who they're talking to. I found this out my senior year at Wake Forest after Bret had signed and went the professional baseball route. People actually looked at me and said, "Hi Kyle." Up until that point it was often a glance and a head nod. Sometimes, I'd get a "Hey, Wags." But, being a twin has some very cool advantages as well. One summer weekend, Bret and I took advantage of being a twin.

Bret was playing for the Huntsville Stars in the Southern League. He was a starting pitcher. The life of a starting pitcher is basically wait, wait, wait, wait, pitch. You observe your teammates for 4 days and then you pitch on the fifth day. The wait days allow your body to heal so you're ready to pitch again on your fifth day. This particular story involves the pitch day followed by the first wait day.

Jes Kaercher, a childhood buddy, and I took a road trip to see Bret play for the Stars. Bret was scheduled to pitch against the White Sox affiliate on a Friday evening. A double header was scheduled the following Saturday. In other words, Bret's wait day would consist of two games in one day. That makes for a very long day.

Friday evening wasn't much fun for me in the stands. I'm sure Jes would say we had "fun," but the reality was I probably wasn't much company. When Bret pitches, I focus. I watched him pitch scrutinizing every last detail. *Did he command his fastball? Was he showing his changeup enough? Was he predictable in the counts he threw his changeup? Which breaking ball was he using? Was he controlling the running game? Did he lose "stuff" when he pitched out of the stretch?* Make no mistake, I wasn't in attendance to have fun. I was in attendance to monitor Bret's progress. Bret pitched. I observed.

The following day was a much better experience for me as a fan. Without the pressure of Bret pitching, I could relax. Until, the first game of the doubleheader ended. That's when I'd come to take advantage of the unpredictable nature that a student always allows for.

Birmingham, AL in August is hot. Between games of the doubleheader Jes and I went down to talk to Bret behind home plate. Bret was accompanied by a teammate. While we were talking the teammate couldn't stop staring at me. I'm sure he had seen twins before, but this experience was really taking him for a ride. He was fascinated that Bret had a twin. So, he suggested something. "You two should switch positions just for the fun of it." I said, "I'm in."

I don't think he thought I was serious but when I made it as far as the clubhouse dressing room, I think Bret's teammate realized this was going to happen. Kyle Wagner was about to become Bret Wagner in a professional baseball game. It's August. It's hot. It's Double A baseball. I was willing to provide some novelty to the team and the game.

As I dressed into Bret's uniform, Bret was restricted to the clubhouse. After dressing, I made my way into the dugout and eventually into left field. The pranks we were playing were minor ruses designed to get a chuckle or two. We'd ask about bus departures and we'd ask about dinner plans. It wasn't anything too spectacular. But it was different, and it was appreciated by the baseball players in the dog days of August. Eventually the game started, and I was a Hunstville Star. Thankfully, I didn't have much of a role other than watching the game. I was good at watching games. I could do this. My role of spectator wouldn't last long.

Glenn Abbott had a Big League career. He was the pitching coach of the Stars. If you've pitched in the Big Leagues, I'd guess you have an expectation of what sort of behavior is required of you.

Sitting in the clubhouse in your underwear is probably frowned upon as appropriate behavior while the game is being played. That's exactly how Glenn Abbott found Bret Wagner on a Saturday afternoon in Birmingham. "Bret, what the...."

I knew something was up when Glenn Abbott walked into the dugout scanning the team looking for something. We made eye contact and he smiled. Apparently, Glenn Abbott is a good sport and he wasn't about to let this opportunity get away from him. August must be hard on professional coaches as well as the players. As Glenn approached, he made a hand gesture to the guys beside me to spread out. The inquisition was about to begin.

"Bret let's talk about the game yesterday. I want to know some of your thoughts with how you pitched certain guys." In his mind, I'm sure he thought *you're not the only guy that's allowed to have some fun with this.* In my mind, I was thinking *you have no idea what you're walking into.* He grilled me about innings and counts and strategy. Every question was answered not only with accuracy of the situation but with insight into why I did it. The last question he asked was in reference to Pete Rose Jr.[16] "Why the 0-2 fastball to Rose?"[17] I replied, "Well, it was the first inning and I didn't have great cutter command yet. I didn't want to risk the dirt ball with 1 out and a man on 2nd. So, I figured why not stay with a hard fastball on his hands. So, I tried to tie him up and see if I could jam him." With that, Glenn stood up and started to walk away. As he neared the clubhouse entrance he turned around and gave me a sideways glance. I'm left to think he thought something to the effect of *How did he remember that?*

The student must allow for the unpredictable future. By admitting that tomorrow has the potential to be something entirely different

---

[16] You may have heard of his dad. It is why I can recall the at bat 25 years later.
[17] Rose singled on the 0-2 fastball.

than today you're driven by the need to add as many skills as possible. If the world is dangerous, I better protect myself. With Bret and me, it was simple. We were twins. Bret was and is my best friend. I wanted to help him succeed. In order to do that, I needed to know why he was doing what he was doing. It had to be deeper than "what pitches." It had to be deeper than "how did you pitch?" It had to be WHY DID YOU DO IT?

What we do from moment to moment makes up the events of our lives. It's the plot to the story we each write. The how we do it gives our story flavor and makes it unique to us. The how is why we laugh and why we cry when we hear the stories. But the why is what we remember. The why embeds itself so deep into our being that it's impossible to forget. The why attaches itself to a greater purpose. Its underlying message resonates for years after accepting its true nature. In other words, the WHAT changes from team to team, year to year. The WHO changes from team to team, year to year. The HOW changes from team to team, year to year. The only steady influence in the life of a player, the only opportunity the aspiring athlete has to stay curious and full of energy is if he can remember his WHY.

Now, when a student asks me "Mr. Wagner when am I ever going to need this?" I answer matter of factly, "I have no idea. The future is impossible to predict. But, maybe, consider the possibility that someday you just might." It's not every day that a former Big Leaguer asks you questions on how you went about executing pitches. It's even more remote when you consider I wasn't even a pitcher. But he did ask me questions. And, I was prepared when the time came.

"Hey Kyle. What did you just say?"
Our WHY is critical for long term growth because the WHAT, HOW and WHO are always subject to change. The WHY is the foundation that allows us to experience much of life's twists and turns without the constraints of certainty.

Great Competitors are Great Entertainers
Jared Payne

I often question the value of practice. Time and time again, I see players succeed in a practice setting only to fail in a game setting. Then, I see someone who takes the worst batting practice simply rake in the game. It doesn't translate well enough for me to know it adds value. I believe the missing ingredient for most practice settings is the environment.

Sometimes I think athletes would be better served giving public speeches than taking batting practice. It's not that their skills don't need honing, but rather the honing is happening in a non-threatening environment. In order for practice to translate to games there must exist a threatening environment in which to practice.

I don't mean threatening as in dangerous. I mean threatening as judgmental. The number of critics in the audience can make comfortable very uncomfortable rather quickly. Many people are willing to sing in the shower. Few people are willing to sing on stage. But there are those few that are willing to get up on stage at a very early age and say, "look at me."

Jared Payne has always been an entertainer. Jared Payne never cringed when the crowds grew. In fact, in Jared's mind, the more people in attendance, the more people Jared could impress. This personality characteristic was obvious when Jared was a 10-yr. old competing at Sports at The Beach. Sports at the Beach is a very big venue for tournament baseball in the Northeast. It's located in Georgetown, DE and it attracts some of the best youth travel teams in the region to compete every weekend. On this particular weekend, the GoWags RiverCats would face the Tri-State Arsenal in the Finals. Jared would be our championship game pitcher.

The Arsenal had developed a well-earned reputation throughout our region. They were the travel team Mike Trout had played on. For the most part, they presented themselves as the bully on the block. Their success on the field allowed them to carry that monicher proudly. The Arsenal had an incredible championship game pitcher as well. Stephen Restuccio[18] vs. Jared Payne. It seems disingenuous to pit a couple of 10-yr. old's against each other like this. But, at the time, our travel baseball lives revolved around playing late in the day on Sunday and watching two good teams compete for a championship. If the RiverCats could best Restuccio, it would be a well-earned championship.

Stephen Restuccio threw very hard. It was obvious from the first pitch. The RiverCats were Green Light Hitting trained. What this meant wasn't always apparent to casual fans. But there was a very real method to my madness in why I trained young hitters to hit in a Green Light mentality. Green Light Hitting recognized that the biggest hurdle young hitters' face is fear. This psychological hurdle gets mitigated as you move from The Imagination Game to The Precision Game, but the hitter always has a smidgeon of fear when competing against hard throwers. Most hitting programs address precision well before baseball players learn to truly protect themselves in the batter's box. On this day, Stephen Restuccio would be facing a lineup trained to protect themselves with aggression. Restuccio was the hardest thrower we had faced to date. I'd like to think we were the toughest lineup Restuccio had faced to date.

---

[18] Stephen Restuccio is the son of a former teammate of mine, Ross Restuccio. At the time of the game, I didn't know he was coaching for the other team. Only when we shook hands at the end of the game did we realize our sons were on the same field. Stephen will be attending Virginia Tech in the fall of 2019.

Whereas many young hitters' step in the batter's box with cues like "get a good pitch to hit" and "make it be a strike," the RiverCats stepped in the batter's box with cues like "turn it loose" and "let it fly." To beat an elite 10-yr. old pitcher, you can generally take one of two strategies. The first strategy is the only strategy that works if you place precision ahead of imagination. That strategy is "wait em out." In other words, since you haven't trained their brain to work fast enough to hit the elite velocity, we might as well take his pitches to see if he'll walk us or elevate a pitch count. The second strategy was the one the RiverCats employed. Attack his pitches. In order to hit elite velocity, you must be willing to swing and miss at bad pitches. You simply don't have enough reaction time and enough experience to draw from to do it any differently. Thankfully for us, Stephen Restuccio threw strikes.

The Arsenal took the other approach. As Jared Payne took the mound, he had his own formidable fastball. Jared Payne has become a great catcher. He'll be taking his talents to the University of Kentucky in the spring of 2020. As a 10-yr. old, however, Jared was our staff ace. Jared pounded the strike zone pitch after pitch. It almost appeared as if the Arsenal were in take mode right from the beginning. I even remember our players on the bench asking me "Coach, why don't they ever swing?"

The RiverCats won the championship that weekend. It was early in the season. We would play in many more championship games afterwards. Jared Payne's role would change as he grew. More and more he crouched behind the plate. But when Jared Payne was young, he loved to throw towards that plate. Although Jared's position changed his love of competing never did. Very early, the RiverCats knew that Jared Payne would entertain us, entertain those that came to watch him and frustrate those that came to play against him.

Romance Before Marriage
Efficiency and Optimization Sabotage the Journey

In my mind, I'm a romantic. At least, I think I am. Then, I get
distracted and time slips away from me and I revert back to
ordinary. But my imagination allows me to believe that if I had
more time and if I had more opportunities, I could woo someone
with the best of 'em. My wife, I'm sure, would beg to differ.
Before Heather and I married, we dated since we were 16. We are
high school sweethearts. But the road wasn't always easy, and it
certainly wasn't without a ton of failure on this guy's end. One
story that will never get old, on her end, is my Valentine's Day
debacle sometime in the 90's. Here's how I remember it.

I was walking through Strawberry Square in Harrisburg with Bret.
As we were leaving, I noticed the Hallmark store on the first level.
I noticed there were more displays on the outside than normal. It
peaked my interest. Upon closer examination, it appeared to be
Valentine's Day. Apparently, it was February. The 14th to be
exact. Wow, I had almost forgotten this most sacred of couple's
days. It's a good thing I didn't miss this, otherwise I couldn't
imagine the wrath that Heather would rain down on me. So, with
time on my side, I walked into the Hallmark store and bought her
the most romantic gift any young, vivacious female would adore. I
bought her a Precious Moments coffee mug with her name on it.

Look, I know it was bad. If there's a worse present, I'd love to
know what it is. A coffee mug with your name on it, at best, says
"You're cool." I was hoping to buy a gift that screamed from the
highest mountain "I love you always and forever." I fell a wee bit
short of that goal. It makes for a great story. We laugh about it
now that we have two awesome kids and lifetime full of memories
that we share. At the time, it was terribly cold and callous.

Imagine how much she must have loved me to even accept the gift?[19]

Must every date end in marriage? Are we even allowed to enjoy the process of dating anymore? Or, must every interaction prove beneficial? Must there be "evidence" to justify that the time we spent was in fact, worthy of the time we dedicated to it? Is there time allowed anymore for coffee cups to be purchased? Does every event need to be scripted for perfect execution? Does every misstep need to be guarded for fear of damaging one's fastest track to success?

Heather and I eventually got married. I proposed. She accepted. July of 2020 will mark 20 years together. But I have to think, those moments of failure and tears and the struggle to overcome my ineptness have to count for something. I have to think that without allowing for the rudeness and the subsequent anger that followed, our relationship today wouldn't be nearly as strong.

Careful attention must always be paid to whether we're busy chasing the prize or busy living our life as we move in the direction of the prize. In the back of my mind, I think I always knew someday Heather and I would get married. Maybe that thought created a complacent mindset for Kyle Wagner circa 1995. At the time, Heather Wagner cared more about the journey than the destination. We'd all be well served to evaluate from time to time, the journey isn't to be taken for granted. We'd all be well served to remember WHY we're wooing our loved one instead of WHAT we're chasing.

---

[19] She smashed it upon my departure.

Playing the "Long Game"
Who Benefits by Winning the Prize

The goal of many teams at the beginning of a year is to win a championship. The New England Patriots don't start preseason camp hoping to win a couple of games. They set out to win the whole thing. In order to win the whole thing, they have to win a lot of things (games) along the way. The games are great when they are won but the games are simply a part to a whole. Playing the "long game" allows for winning the Super Bowl as its primary objective. Some, me being one of them, would argue that the "long game" extends well past winning the Super Bowl. The true "long game" means growing men for life.

Not every system has a Super Bowl at the end of it. But, growing people for life is an opportunity that every system could choose if they could remember the WHY along the way. In the Eighth Inning I discussed the "hard middle." Another way to frame the hard middle is we simply forget our WHY as we chase other people's WHAT'S and HOW'S. It's critical that we can stay focused on the WHY. When organizations and teams can also stay focused on the WHY that's called a good culture. It would be nice if one persons WHY matched the company or teams WHY. That would be a great place to spend a day.

What causes teams and organizations to create environments where people don't like to spend a day? Goals. It's really that simple. Goals are powerful motivators when properly set and properly aligned to the "long game." Goals are destructive forces when they're not properly aligned with the "long game" and they're set by people with the illusion of control. Let's consider a student and talk about the "long game" since I have an Inside View (The Second Inning) on this particular subject.

The Super Bowl for a student is graduation day. This is the end of the journey. Unlike the survival system of NFL football, graduation day recognizes multiple graduates. Some graduate with distinction but many people graduate. Along the way, classes were passed (wins) and grades were received (awards). Over time, these wins and awards are remembered as incidental to the big prize, graduating. Yes, these memories are important. Success is in fact a journey. But without the WHY at the end of the journey, the journey loses its motivation.

When the "wins" and the "awards" of a system become so important to people along the journey, the WHY gets buried underneath. WHY do we enter a school system wanting a better education? To improve the world in which we live. WHY do we have children? To love them and give them an opportunity to experience the awesomeness of life. WHY do we play sports? To experience competition and develop powerful relationships that will sustain us throughout life. These WHY'S are noble and generally accepted when you take a very MACRO view of things. But life is lived in the MICRO and so often the big picture MACRO perspective only comes into view when the journey is over (In the end, there's only love) or when something tragic happens forcing you to retract your lens.

Goals are very dangerous because goals create a micro perspective. They are designed to eliminate distraction and create a laser focus on achievement. Achievement is so satisfying. Therein lies the danger. If the danger were something to avoid, we'd find resolution quickly. But achievement is satisfying in the MICRO but often extremely dangerous in the MACRO as it tends to bury our WHY.

Ed Catmull, in his book *Creativity, Inc.*, writes, *"The Holy Grail is to find a way so that we can teach others how to make the best movie possible with whoever they've got on their crew, because it's just logic that someday we won't be here....As leaders, we should think of ourselves as teachers and try to create companies in which teaching is seen as a valued way to contribute to the success of the whole."*

Not only does a MICRO perspective prevent you from seeing the danger of setting goals, it can also create a very false sense of growth. If I were choosing from the graph below who I would want on my team, I'd pick Mr. Enthusiasm of course. Mr. Enthusiasm is going to help my team win the "Long Game." Although his present-day evaluation might suffer, his potential for long term growth is much better. Far too often, the evaluations we make assign more weight to the present-day position than the potential for next year's position. Maybe Mr. Enthusiasm has more purpose and a better vision than Mr. Complacent? Maybe Mr. Status Quo is comfortable? He might certainly be content. Good for him. Life isn't all about achievement. But teams aren't formed to pick strawberries.

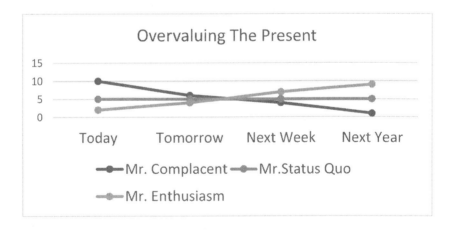

Life is meant to be lived and wins are meant to be celebrated. But they are not meant to be celebrated if they don't contribute to the success of the whole. If they're handing out A's I want as many as I can get. But, should I celebrate the A if along the way I chose to ignore other students that were asking for my help? Recognizing that empathy is a skill for the "long game" allows you to avoid the risks that goals sometimes present. Goals are meant to be set and meant to be conquered. Victory is meant to be embraced with teammates and a job well done is meant to be celebrated. But, playing the "long game" requires all of us to step back and determine after every win, after every A, after every job well done, DO WE STILL REMEMBER OUR WHY?

The true meaning of life is to plant trees, under whose shade you do not expect to sit.
- Nelson Henderson

"Hey Kyle. What did you just say?"

Remembering our WHY is so important to long term health. The primary reason we forget our WHY is we achieve and subsequently find satisfaction in those "wins" and "awards." Maintaining a flexible perspective is critical if we want to win the "long game."

Twin Imposters
Passion and Heteronomy

Daniel Pink recognizes three deeply rooted motivations for all behavior in his book *Drive*. They are *Purpose, Mastery and Autonomy*. I believe there are three imposters that masquerade as the Big Three. They are *Passion, Achievement and Heteronomy*. I've discussed The Achievement Trap already, so I'd like to devote some time to the dangers of passion and heteronomy (definition forthcoming).

Moving in the direction of a goal, either a short-term goal or a long-term goal, often requires people to assist that cause. It's impossible to achieve without recruiting some help along the way. What if the "help" actually "hurts?" As was discussed in The Fifth

Inning, unintended consequences rear their ugly head from time to time. When errors do occur, the people that have committed the error don't always like to hear about it. As Douglas Stone and Sheila Heen discuss in *Thanks for the Feedback,* there are generally 3 triggers that people aren't always gracious to hear about. These three triggers pop up when …

1. Your perspective falls under attack (TRUTH TRIGGERS):

2. Trust falls under attack (RELATIONSHIP TRIGGERS)

3. What you do falls under attack (IDENTITY TRIGGERS)

In other words, if you want to offend someone, tell them they're wrong, overstep your bounds in the relationship, or question someone's values. That'll do it every time. I've come up with an alliterative way to remember for me. We're prejudiced on our point of view. We're passionate about our "teams." We're proud of our work. It's tough to get an unbiased view on any of the above.

The danger of passion is it's optimally focused. Passion doesn't allow for much wiggle room. What I've come to realize is purpose is a much more appealing and noble cause than passion. Purpose is flexible. Purpose finds value where passion tends to get frustrated. This is true in all career choices. Knowing your WHY isn't about identifying what to be passionate about. Knowing your WHY is identifying what to be purposeful about.

Passion lives in the MICRO.
Purpose lives in the MACRO.

Passion for a team needs wins. Purpose for a team needs success. Passion for a job is working hard. Purpose for a job is serving a cause.
Passion speaks in specifics. Purpose allows for generalities.

143

Here's an example of a teacher I had in High School that taught with passion. He was passionate about doing a good job.

Bret Wagner, Kyle Wagner and Tom Peifer[20] all had the same gym class. We had earned a reputation in the building that teachers could trust us. One gym class, Kyle, Bret and Tom decided to put that trust to the test. We had a substitute teacher. Rather than follow the script the substitute offered us, we decided to go play basketball instead. The following day, the teacher called us out in class. Were we wrong? I suppose we were. We didn't follow orders. Had we committed a major felony? Of course not. Do rules need to be followed? In a survival system, absolutely. The regular teacher had a class full of kids and allowing the three of us access to anything we wanted could prove to be eventual anarchy if others followed our lead. I'm not certain but I'm willing to bet the Principal addressed the teacher about his recalcitrant students. The regular teacher had his identity triggered. He responded by embarrassing his students prior to asking them why they did what they did. He was passionate about doing a good job.

Here's an example of a teacher I had in High School that taught with purpose. She was purposeful about doing a good job.

I forgot a paper was due. I was competitive and the idea of a bad grade wasn't something that I was interested in. It wasn't that I cared about producing a masterpiece or a great work of art. I needed that grade. What was so essential about the due date? Well, it was Wednesday, and Thursday would mean it was late. Wednesday and Thursday hold no significance other than that's when the teacher needed to see the work produced. So, I cheated to get the grade. Except, I didn't cheat well. This English teacher

---

[20] Tom Peifer is a childhood friend. In today's vernacular, he'd be considered an OG.

caught me. The following day she called me up to her desk and said something like this.

Kyle, I know you plagiarized some of your paper. You've never done this before, but you need to know how serious of an offense this is. Authors go to great lengths to create their work. Stealing their words is like stealing money from you or me. They care deeply about what it is they produce. I know you've got so many dreams and goals out of ahead of you. The last thing I want to do is punish you when I think you made a poor choice. Was there a reason you plagiarized some of your paper? HEAD NOD. I WAS RUSHED FOR TIME. Ok, look, take an additional day or two and get me something that is your work. Let's chalk this up as a learning experience. I'd hate for you to plagiarize something in college and really get burned.

The true meaning of life is to plant trees, under whose shade you do not expect to sit.
- Nelson Henderson

On graduation day, this purposeful teacher gave me a huge hug. The passionate teacher was probably there but I don't remember.

There comes a point in every person's life where you look at your mom and dad and realize, "I think they're wrong about this." It's not a very difficult concept to grasp that two people that reside on Planet Earth are wrong about something. It's much harder to grasp when those two people are mom and dad and have essentially been my compass from birth. Mom and dad do more for us than just provide us our DNA. Mom and dad provide us with what to believe and so long as the team is good, who to cheer for.

Heteronomy is defined by Wikipedia as an action that is influenced by a force outside the individual, in other words the state or condition of being ruled, governed, or under the sway of another.

Our parents tell us what we should believe in. It's how they keep us alive. Don't run on the wet sidewalk. We're led to believe that slippery surfaces are dangerous. Don't hit your brother. We're led to believe that brothers have feelings and don't like being punched. Don't let someone bully you. We're led to believe that our rights are important and shouldn't be infringed upon. Most people that aren't successful in life aren't successful because they're lazy.

Gary and Linda Wagner never shared that belief with me. But what they did share is "hard work" is something to be proud of. I guess I may have inferred the opposite of hard work is something to be ashamed of. If we allow ourselves to be influenced by that thought without observing how the world sometimes works, that could be one dangerous set of circumstances. Autonomy is choice using one's free will. Autonomy and heteronomy often get confused. Have I chosen to be a Penn State football fan because of autonomy or heteronomy? Have I chosen to like country music because of autonomy or heteronomy? The choices we make aren't always our own. It takes an extremely insightful person to challenge the beliefs of the people that he identifies with. Most people can't get past the Identity Trigger.

One year for Mother's Day, Heather Wagner and Colleen Wagner decided Linda Wagner deserved a heartfelt gift from her twin sons. The idea that was born was for Kyle and Bret to spend an hour or more crafting a beautiful piece of art from *Color Me Mine*. This is a pottery store. Bret and Kyle were baseball players by trade. We were not artists. But we loved our mom, so we were willing to try. We were both married with small children at the time. Upon entering the store, Colleen and Heather found our pottery guides and entrusted these two adult males with them and their expertise. The wives were to be summoned upon completion of the masterpiece.

We placed our call an hour or so later. Bret and I put extreme effort into this piece of art. Every brush stroke was made with extreme precision and every minute was dedicated to honoring our

146

mother on Mother's Day. When Colleen and Heather arrived, our art was hiding behind our back. We wanted to surprise them with what it was we created. The anticipation that Bret and I felt was a cross between horror and relief. We were horrified that our wives wouldn't think we had put our best effort into this task. We were relieved that our ordeal would soon be over. In many respects it was exactly like taking a test you didn't study for from a teacher you respected. The fact that you didn't study meant you weren't putting much value into the class (Bret and I never put much value into artwork) but the fact that you liked the teacher meant you didn't want to disappoint her (our wives were important to us). With bated breath we unveiled our masterpiece.

"Bret, Kyle we told you two to take this seriously. This looks like a 3rd graders work. What do you think your Mom is going to think? Stop laughing. Get serious. This is unacceptable. You can't possibly think we're actually going to give this to your Mom, do you? Here, take the kids and we'll finish what you two started. Jeez boys."

If pain is the greatest teacher, laughter might be a close second. Let me assure you, Bret and I were not lazy. Bret and I were incompetent. Sometimes, people aren't successful because they're disadvantaged. Bret and I were not blessed with the art gene. Colleen and Heather had not yet come to realize that "hard work" alone doesn't always guarantee success. After witnessing this Mother's Day debacle I'm sure their perspective changed. Using their own free will they could now decide that YES, IN FACT, THERE ARE PEOPLE THAT SHOULD NEVER CREATE ART.

"Hey Kyle. What did you just say?"

When we're not sensitive to our own thoughts were often led astray to the passions and the perspectives that we hold. In order to take a big picture perspective, it's essential to question the overall importance of my job and whether my beliefs are subject to influences from other people.

The Big Picture
Jared Payne

Jared Payne is the son of Rick and Julie Payne. Some people find their purpose on this planet in achievement. Others find their purpose on making a difference. Rick and Julie Payne painted their life's picture with very broad strokes of compassion and empathy. While we're all tempted to tend to our own selfish needs, eventually we all come to realize we're in this thing together. Rick and Julie came to this realization before most.

Whether it was offering up their home, their vehicle, their time, the Payne's were generous people. The Payne's hosted countless RiverCats' parties and both Rick and Julie had key roles with the RiverCats and their success. Julie acted as our "social director." Her energy and enthusiasm were a necessary and healthy balance to the coaches' competitive spirit. Julie Payne was the mom that would congratulate the other pitcher for striking out her son. She was kind.[21]

Rick was a different kind of kind. Whereas Julie was kind with her heart, Rick was kind with his time. Many facets of the GoWags facility was the result of Rick Payne's sweat equity. Rick was generous in every aspect of making the RiverCats experience as memorable as possible. It even included a Harlem Globetrotters appearance.[22]

---

[21] Her kindness overstepped the bounds of baseball protocol one game at Cal Ripken's complex. As Jimmy Losh was stepping into the batter's box, Julie was passing out grapes and cheese in the dugout. I said "Julie. Not now."
[22] Rick recruited Chris "Handles" Franklin to provide a very big picture perspective on what talent looks like at a RiverCats event.

Jared Payne would inherit this big picture mentality from Rick and Julie. When it comes to learning the game of baseball, it is imperative to do so with a MACRO perspective. The MICRO perspective is dangerous if you simply find yourself running the habit loops of execution. You can execute the play but if you don't know why you're doing it, you'll never really own it. I had coached Jared Payne since he was 8-yrs. old in the New Cumberland Pony League. Jared had heard my "WHY'S" for a very long time.

When Jared was 14, he double rostered[23] with US Elite. Making more baseball contacts is never a bad thing when you're trying to network yourself for a college scholarship. On one Sunday afternoon in Camp Hill, PA, US Elite played the GoWags RiverCats. Jared Payne was in the 3rd base dugout. The RiverCats were in the 1st base dugout. It was an awkward experience for everyone in attendance. But once the game started it was simply baseball as usual. The game was a slugfest. I honestly believe the final score was 21-18 in 8 innings. It was one for the ages.

In around the 4th or 5th inning, US Elite had a 1st and 3rd situation. Jared was on third base. I forgot Jared was on third base. I need to digress and discuss how it is we teach some 1st and 3rd offensive situations with the RiverCats.

With a left-handed pitcher on the mound, the offensive team has the opportunity to take advantage of some tough to defend situations. One such play we liked to run was something we called "Double First Lift." On this particular play, when the left-handed pitcher lifts his leg both runners take off sprinting towards 2nd base and home plate respectively. It's imperative that both runners keep their eyes on the pitcher. How they react depends on where

---

[23] Playing for more than one team is a popular strategy to get more baseball.

the pitcher throws the ball. If the pitcher throws home, the runner on 3rd base immediately slams on the brakes and retreats back towards 3rd base. The result of this play is a steal of 2nd base. This is the most common result when calling for a "Double First Lift." The more uncommon result is a steal of home. In order to execute this play, the pitcher must throw towards first base. When the pitcher lifts his leg and both runners begin sprinting, the runner at 3rd never breaks stride as the ball goes in the direction of the 1st baseman. By the time the 1b catches the ball, the hope is the runner will have such a head start that it won't matter. SAFE. Run scores. Runner on 2nd base. In all my years of coaching the RiverCats, no one had ever executed this play against us. We were the only team that had pulled off this feat. Except this one particular Sunday in Camp Hill, PA.

Sitting on my bucket, signaling signs to the catcher, I called for a pickoff attempt at 1B. Unbeknownst to me, Jared Payne was staring directly at me. Essentially, I invited him to run a "Double First Lift." As Aleksei Guzman lifted his leg to pick the runner off at 1B, Jared anticipated the move and sprinted home. I had forgotten who the runner was. As the throw went in the direction of 1B, I knew there was no way we could prevent the run from scoring. As Jared crossed the plate, I put my head down in disgust. "I should have known better. I can't believe they beat us at our own game." My Asst. Coach, Kyle Nornhold, elbowed me in the ribs and said, "You do know that was Jared, right?" I replied, "I do now."

Playing the game of baseball at a very high level takes a precision focus on the details of the game. Baseball players must be meticulous in their swing, their pitches, their base running and their attention to every little detail. But the coaches they play for change. The WHAT to do can change from year to year. The HOW to do it can change from year to year. When you understand WHY you do something it stands the test of time. It's impervious to the environmental changes and the daily adjustments each coach makes with HOW the scripts are taught.

Jared Payne scored a run against the RiverCats on that particular Sunday, but I had won. Jared was one of my early RiverCats and I had obviously taught him something that he could use to his advantage. Coaches are servants to their players. Playing the "long game" requires us coaches to not just take satisfaction in the wins and the awards of today but also invest in a holistic approach to the player's long-term health and his long-term goals. After realizing that Jared merely scored a run against me, I shot him a glance across the field. He was grinning from ear to ear. In all likelihood, I probably extended my arms in his direction and applauded good baseball. Jared Payne had remembered WHY we run the play and because he knew the WHY, he also knew the WHEN (and he could see my signs).

The true meaning of life is to plant trees, under whose shade you do not expect to sit.
- Nelson Henderson

As I mentioned earlier, Jared will be attending the University of Kentucky in the fall of 2019. I see ya workin' Jared.

152

The Third Inning
Throw the Kitchen Sink at 'Em

I was the RiverCats Head Coach. I had information that I wanted them to know. Rather, I had information I needed them to apply. In the book *Make it Stick,* they describe three types of intelligence. They are Creative Intelligence, Practical Intelligence and Analytical Intelligence. I was more interested in the first two types of intelligences for the RiverCats. I wanted the 'Cats to think creatively (The Imagination Game) and I wanted them to apply what they learned practically. I was tasked with taking my analytical intelligence and producing great art on the baseball field. The ability to turn my information into their intelligence is what basic coaching consists of. I had a model how to do that.

Some time ago, me and some buddies opened up a bin of baseball cards from the 1980's. I'm sure there were some from the late 70's and 90's interspersed but mostly they were from the 80's. Soon, after finding the cards a game developed. My friends would hide the name of the player and I would have to identify the player. It's important to understand the context of the game being played. I hadn't looked at these baseball cards since I left home for college. And, in all likelihood, that's being very generous with the time gap. It was more likely since I was a sophomore in high school. To be safe, let's assume a gap of 20 years passed. I wasn't perfect but I was good at the game. The names and the faces came pouring back to me. I don't know how I did it, but I could literally see the name that was attached to the face after 20+ years.

If playing the "long game" was essential for being a coach, I was going to need a model that would hold up over time. I was going to need a model that would be precise enough to execute inning to inning but broad enough to stand up over time and from one coach to another coach. The baseball card model would do the trick. Of course, I didn't know it at the time but the baseball card learning model can be summarized with some basic ideas.

The Baseball Card Model
How to Remember Names After 20 Years

1. Do not presort the cards.
Baseball cards come in packs. They used to have bubble gum in the packs. My buddies liked the bubble gum more than me. I could handle, maybe, one stick at a time. The opening of the packs was "instant learning." You eagerly browsed through the cards hoping you'd find an Oriole (when I was 6-10) or an elite player when I began selling the cards. Facial recognition was the first act of turning information into intelligence.

2. Sort the cards in whatever manner works for you.
I liked to arrange my cards team by team when I was younger. I'd sit on the floor and I'd put the Phillies with the Phillies, the Padres with the Padres. I'd do this for every team. As I got older, I sorted by value. The "commons" were the cards that didn't carry any value. They didn't get a protective covering. The stars were placed in an album. They received their own pages. The elite players got their own protective covering. The sorting of the cards was the second act of turning information into intelligence. Each card collector was entitled to sort in whatever manner he preferred. Adaptable over optimal.

3. Protect the cards.
It's important to realize that not every card needed to have value. I was a young kid and I loved collecting baseball cards. But I had to be willing to prioritize certain cards over other cards. The protecting of the cards was the first step in a value system. By placing a protective sheath over the card, I was declaring it to be an investment I needed to protect. This valuing of certain predetermined cards was the third step in turning information into intelligence.

4. Play with the cards often.

"Playing" with the cards isn't the right term. It's mostly just ogling them. Playing with them would devalue them. So, interacting with the cards was the fourth step in turning information into intelligence.

5. Sell the cards on occasion.

The selling of the cards was just to make money. The "on occasion" part is the operative phrase here. Allowing time to pass between when a card was first purchased, played with and later sold allowed for more mental retrieval strategies to identify with the card. In order for something to be retained for over 20 years, you must create lots of space between the times you interact with the card. The fifth step in turning information into intelligence is create time between interactions.

6. Recognize the difference between price and value.

Baseball cards are purchased for a variety of reasons. The most valuable of my cards are not for sale. The most valuable of my cards aren't the cards that would bring the most money at auction. I enjoyed collecting money when I sold cards. But some cards I wasn't willing to sell. Struggling between selling it and holding it was the last step in anchoring the intelligence.

I met many of the RiverCats when they were very young. Many of them still liked The Wiggles or Thomas the Train. When I became their coach, I knew the game of baseball was theirs to explore. I wanted them to experience the game like I was opening a pack of baseball cards for the first time. There would be many things I would show them that they weren't ready for. But their dads appreciated my willingness to share rather than guarding the information as if I held the key to the vault. The Third Inning is my journey with the RiverCats turning information into intelligence.

"Hey Kyle. What did you just say?"
Learning fails for many reasons. The teacher must identify those reasons and avoid them. Here's how I believe learning occurs best. Allow for imagination, allow for sorting, create consequences, practice with intention, wrestle with ideas and distinguish value among the ideas.

The Imagination Game
Do Not Presort the Cards

I have coached by a saying for years now. "Great players have great imaginations." To be a good player you don't necessarily need a great imagination. Good players can execute the tasks they have been trained to do. The great players have the ability to see beyond the daily occurrences. The great players see things that others don't see, possibly even their coach. To develop a great imagination, you have to be willing to take risks and you must be big picture oriented.

GoWags was located in Camp Hill, PA. That meant our winters were wet, cold and often miserable for baseball. But we wanted to concede nothing to our warm weather competitors. To do that, I needed the RiverCats to use their imagination. In fact, every Saturday night the RiverCats would open our winter practices with a drill called the Imagination Drill. It became a favorite for all our teams.

Essentially, what I would ask our guys to do is make the greatest plays they could see themselves making. I would do this from every conceivable defensive position I could think of. Without the constraints of a ball and a runner to throw out, the player was free to dream and create. Anthony Volpe and Jimmy Losh were two of our most creative. Not only were they reckless with their bodies but they were insanely creative with how they made plays. They'd assume elite footspeed when it wasn't required. They'd often dream of miraculous where others would simply see acceptable. It was insight into a player's MACRO perspective. It was beautiful. They were simply opening up the baseball cards and looking for great players.

RiverCats practices were an exercise in efficiency, intent and fun! They were what practice should be, we wanted MORE! - Mike Williams, RiverCats Coach and Dad

Planning is More Important than the Plan
Adaptable Over Optimal (Sort the Cards in Whatever Manner Works for You)

The best way to communicate information is in a question and answer setting. Most people never entertain this method because the person with the information needs to stick to the script, otherwise he looks vulnerable if he doesn't know the answer. The other reason this method is often overlooked is the people wanting the information don't know what questions to ask. Without the courage to go off script and without the curiosity to ask appropriate questions were often left with a model that manipulates the learner into learning what the instructor demands he learns.

The manner in which the RiverCats held practice was an adaptable model as close to a Question and Answer session as possible. A practice plan would be developed based upon what I thought everyone should know or practice on that particular day. As the practice unfolded, I would adjust quickly, and act accordingly based upon what I saw.

This requires enough knowledge of situations where adaptability becomes a much better teaching tool than optimization. Optimization is a strategy designed around things going according to plan. It's a strategy that can never account for hiccups in the plan or shifts in the climate of the environment. Adaptability is always the preferred method when playing the "Long Game." The biggest advantage to adaptability is it allows the instructor to tie into the desires and the emotions of the learner. Here's an example of adaptable over optimal.

I never liked to talk too much prior to practice. Time is valuable and kids are excited to move. I wanted to use my early practice time to have them attack the practice with fun exciting things. The beginning of practice is time to explore and test boundaries, not listen to the plan that is to be executed. On this particular practice, maybe the plan looked like this...

6:00-6:25 Warm Up/ Hit Targets
6:25-6:35 INFIELD/OUTFIELD POP UP COMMUNICATION
"Discuss" / DRINK
6:45-7:05 PFP[24]/ FIGURE 8'S IN THE MIDDLE[25]/ SDPT WORK
IN OUTFIELD[26]
"Discuss" / DRINK
7:15-8:00 SITUATIONAL BATTING PRACTICE

Every practice there'd be an optimal plan I'd want to execute. Very often, my plan would fall apart at the mercy of the player's emotion. For instance, the batting practice routine at the end of practice was a 45-minute activity. Everyone likes to hit. Typically, this might be a runner at 3rd < 2 outs situation. But

---

[24] Pitchers Fielding Practice
[25] 2nd Baseman and shortstop work around the second base bag
[26] Sure double possible triple.

maybe the middle infielders were rushing the double play balls. In their quest to get 2 outs, they often missed the first out. So, I adjust and create an immediate soft toss drill at home plate with all batted balls being hit up the middle. The middle infielders are forced to turn two with the authentic consequence of getting one before two. This adjustment eats into the 45-minute block of hitting at the end. The kids want swings. I'll cater to their whims by adopting a NO FOUL BALL BP where everyone hits at the same time and if they foul a ball off, they run and retrieve 5-8 balls each. We hit until I run out of balls and we do it again. They get as many swings as the original plan allowed, we just eliminate the base running.

Adaptable beats optimal because you can craft a message that applies to the NOW.
Adaptable beats optimal because time is so important, not just to Coach Wagner but to the family's you coach. Practice should end at 8:00. When bumps in the road occur, it's not fair to the other people in their lives to steal from their time.

Pain Is the Greatest Teacher
We Must Compete (Protect the Cards)

Losing hurts. Winning affirms. The outcome of a game is so finite. It's not a 77% that allows for subjectivity and dialogue. A game produces outcomes that are black and white. A game creates certainty in the end. That's why they're so rewarding. That's why they're so painful. That's why every coach must compete if he wants to turn information into intelligence.

As a coach, if I tell you that we need to work on your fastball command you might nod your head, but I doubt you're ready to walk through the Intentional Door. However, if I sit down beside you after you gave up two home runs, I'm willing to bet the

Intentional Door would be wide open. I'd expect you to answer, "Absolutely Coach."

Real world authentic consequences teach us faster than anything else. Real world authentic consequences that you can't recover from (a 55% on your report card) teach us to quit.[27]

That's a huge component of the competition game for making learning stick. There must be risk involved (the opportunity to lose) but there must exist an opportunity to recover. This is true whether baseball is being taught to 10-yr. olds or calculus to high school seniors. Risk without recovery becomes anxiety.

Competing as a tool for learning is like placing the protective sheath over the baseball cards. Competition is such a valuable tool for learning that it protects our knowledge securely from outside influences. As a pitcher, once you forget to cover 1st base on a ground ball to the 1B and lose the game because of it, I'm guessing you might finally remember to COOOOOOOVER!!!!

A specific example of competing is generally how we conducted batting practice for the RiverCats. Two of my favorite methods were two completely different strategies. The first method was while we were still playing The Imagination Game. The second method was more The Precision Game. I'll detail both here.

As a baseball coach, you need to play H-O-R-S-E. At GoWags we'd run H-O-R-S-E tournaments. It was so much fun. I used it more when the 'Cats were younger, but the game transcends time. It's copied from the basketball version, but we create it as a team

---

[27]Education needs to decide if they are in the education business or the judgment business. The current structure for grading punishes more than it provides feedback. If learning is to occur, recovery from risk is non-negotiable. Of course, when teachers are rewarded for "yearly" outcomes produced its obvious education isn't playing the "Long Game."

game. Split the team in half. If you're outside, one side goes to the first base side, one side to the third base side. Allow one team to hit first. We'll call this Team A! Team B is allowed to see the lineup that Team A has created. Team B is then allowed to match Team A's lineup. The hitting sequence goes like this.

A B A B A B A B A B A B

As in the basketball version of H-O-R-S-E you must match the preceding result, or you assume a letter. If the first batter of the game hits a double (real or imagined), the next batter is required to hit a double or better. If he fails to do so a letter is attached. The first team to get all 5 letters loses. The RiverCats and all GoWags teams begged to play H-O-R-S-E.

As the RiverCats got older and I wanted to induce more learning into the equation we would play a game where runs, not letters, determined the winning team. We often did RUNNER ON 2ND, 2 OUT BP

followed by RUNNER ON 3RD, 1 OUT BP. We would usually split the team up into 2 or 3 teams depending on our volume (we'd often have over 20 guys show up from all different teams because our practices we're generally a blast). The team that scored the most often would win. The team that scored the least often would lose.

Coaches should have a huge portfolio of games that they can use to whatever situation arises. Be creative. Adjust to the time constraints. Adjust to the emotion of the team. Give the kids what they want. But, be unwavering in your expectations of turning information into intelligence.

> *Then we started coming on Saturdays and Anthony would talk*
> *about it all week. Your practices were amazing to say the least,*
> *and it's not like Anthony just started playing... In your relatively*
> *small space, you had every kid involved and doing something, and*
> *you had them all compete with each other in everything - which I*
> *think is what Anthony loved the best.*
> *- Mike Volpe, RiverCats Dad*

Deliberate Practice
Play with the Cards Often

Anders Ericsson's work is now famous among coaches and
instructors searching for expert performance. Ericsson's research
revealed the 10,000 hour rule. Of course, 10,000 hours is merely a
number and 10,000 vs. 9,913 would be a trivial argument to
engage in. Nonetheless, Ericsson has identified the need for
deliberate practice to create an expert performer. It is critical to
note that Ericsson did not say 10,000 hours of practice. He said
10,000 hours of DELIBERATE practice.

What constitutes deliberate practice for an aspiring baseball
player? For me it's simple. Did they walk through the Intentional
Door? If the answer is yes, it's deliberate practice. Far too many
coaches confuse "stressful practice" as deliberate practice. If the
athlete hasn't walked through the Intentional Door, you're
confusing busy with productive.

A reminder is in order. Only the athlete chooses when he walks
through the Intentional Door. Talking louder won't do it. Being
more precise with your language won't do it. Bringing Reese's
Peanut Butter Cups won't do it. Actually, that might. The point
is, it's very difficult to know whether the athlete is fully committed
to the task at hand.

When the student is ready, the teacher will appear.

The above quote doesn't read, when the teacher is ready the student will listen. It just doesn't work that way. Students, for all time, have learned to give the teacher their eyeballs but not their ears. The coach must understand in order for practice to be deliberate he must have influence over the player so when he speaks, he'll gladly walk through the Intentional Door. What's the best way to carry influence? Be a person of high character. Be a coach with high competence. That'll usually do the trick.

The WHAT you teach will take care of itself once you become competent.

Being a RiverCat taught him (Carter Christopher) how to practice with a purpose, how to compete and how to be a good teammate. For that we are eternally grateful.
- Judson Christopher, RiverCats Dad

Struggle with Best Practices
Sell the Cards on Occasion

In order for ideas to stick around for a very long time you must wrestle with them. Tasks are meant to be finished and forgotten. Ideas are meant to be held onto, thought about, wrestled with, and thought about some more. Too often we treat things we care about like tasks on a "to do" list. No one ever finds the Jiffy peanut butter in aisle 6 and continues to think about Jiffy peanut butter. It's over. I found it. Movin' on. Lost forever among the millions of other things I've finished.

One of the greatest tragedies I see in our schools daily is the extreme amount of work and effort that gets put into tasks that are allowed to be forgotten upon completion. It breaks my heart. The task completion tragedy stems from the "evidence of growth" model that is dumped down our professional throats as teachers. Teachers and students are on the Theatrical Level of team chemistry (The Seventh Inning). We're the WHO in the giant scheme of how information becomes intelligence. Well, above the Theatrical Level sits the Strategic Level. Those folks that aren't on the front lines of education have deemed it important to see evidence that learning is occurring. Trust erodes when the people on the front lines aren't allowed to DO, OBSERVE, CORRECT. Many teachers are being paid, trained and encouraged to DO, GRADE, MOVE ON.

But I had full authority to do as I pleased with the RiverCats. I could allow the kids to wrestle with ideas and struggle with what works best and what to part with. The only limitations on what they struggled with was their own imagination. It was great to see the 'Cats ask questions about what technique they preferred. It was great to see the epiphany of "That's why you don't want us to pick up the 3rd base coach when we're rounding 2nd base." Yes. Thank you for seeing that.

Ideas trump tasks when it comes to learning. Ideas don't have deadlines. Ideas don't have artificial finish lines for completion. Ideas can grow into new ideas so long as the teacher allows the student some freedom to run with those ideas. Ideas, when finally congealed, often take the form of a mental model in one's head. This mental model becomes a framework where nuances are allowed to sit until they too can attach to the picture in one's head. Here's a specific example with the RiverCats that sheds some light on the idea of struggling with best practices.

One day at the end of practice the RiverCats and I were talking about "Why left-handed catchers don't exist." They threw around the idea that there are more right-handed batters and such. I said, "I don't think that's it. It's probably the orientation of the field. Second base is dead center. It probably has more to do with throwing to 3rd base than throwing to 2nd base." I don't remember now but I'm sure Carter Christopher was knee deep in the discussion. Before long we had Luke Wagner and Jayson Kramer (our two lefties) throwing runners out at 3rd base on the stopwatch vs. two right handed non catchers. The results were inconclusive. We'll continue to wrestle with the idea of why lefties can't catch.

"Everything I know about baseball developed from things I learned as a RiverCat. From when to be aggressive on the bases, to aligning your defensive position according to the pitch, to what your job is during a rundown (after getting chewed out for going back to 2nd!)."
- Bobby Whalen, RiverCats player

Coordinating Imagination and Precision
Recognize the Difference Between Price and Value

Not everything that came out of my mouth was worthy of remembering. There was this one story I told the 'Cats sitting in the dugout in Hershey, PA that Bret and I pulled off this amazing feat. Bret thought of a number between 1 and 500. I guessed it. We went nuts running around the house thinking we were blessed with the power of ESP. The folks in the room with us, the Jubanowsky's,[28] weren't impressed. They thought this is their act. They do this all the time. Bret and I were aghast. Our reaction should have been enough to convince them it was authentic. They

---

[28] An incredible host family to Bret while he played for the New Jersey Cardinals. We miss you guys.

demanded we do it again but this time they picked the range of numbers. They picked something like 400-800. We nailed it again. This time I think we ran around the outside of the house. This time, they were running around behind us.

I'm sure the RiverCats actually remember this story. Nick Embleton even thought he could do it with me. Although that story was fun and engaging, I didn't really care if they remembered it. The RiverCats greatest challenge would be turning the MICRO lessons I would teach them into MACRO lessons that could travel with them. It was important for me that a 10-yr. old knew how to execute a bunt, but it was more important for me to know that he could eventually execute the bunt in a high stakes game in high school or college. Imagine the physical differences that undoubtedly exist in a person when they begin their 10,000 hour trek and when they finish. It could easily span over 10-20 years. The information learned is interpreted by a completely different human being every single day of that journey. The intelligence displayed by the expert is the end product of information received over countless hours of training. The information that was shared wasn't the precious work of art that was eventually produced. The information entered the person as a vague mental model of what could be. The expert, over time, turned that imagination into precision.

The beauty of the art produced betrays the struggle that took place along the way. For every idea that was accepted as true and worthy of retention there were hundreds of others that were discarded as ancillary and irrelevant. In other words, some ideas have value, and some have a mere price tag. The precision of the expert was once the imagination of the beginner. Most of the human beings on the planet are neither an expert nor a beginner. We're stuck somewhere in the middle. Allowing for discrepancies of thought is what life is all about. I'm not where I want to be but I'm further along than yesterday.

All of us have creative thoughts. Some we discard out of irrelevance. Some we discard out of fear. Those of us that can hold onto those ideas, those of us that can share those ideas knowing that creative sometimes gets ridiculed, have a chance to become an "expert." I'm of the opinion that our ultimate goal shouldn't be to achieve "expert" status. However, I do believe that we all should aspire to produce great art and render masterpieces in our life. The only way this is ever achieved is having the courage, on occasion, to share your art.

If it were easy, everyone would share their art. The reason it's so difficult is everyone's art is different. Everyone has an opinion on what art looks like in their particular field. The art the RiverCats were sharing was a work in progress. We liked how it looked but, on many occasions, it took great courage to share it.

"Hey Kyle. What did you just say?"

Learning must start out as fun, develop at its own pace and under its own terms. Learning at the highest of levels requires intentional learning; best created through consequences, spaced out struggle and placing value on those ideas. Retention often involves forming ideas into pictures.

Think Like a Scientist, Train Like an Artist
The Curse of Knowledge

I have over 10,000 followers on Instagram. I think it's a combination of two things really. The first is a tip of the hat to my nephew that had great success on a national stage in the summer of

2015.[29] The second is a much deeper, broader idea that permeated much of the GoWags family's lives. The GoWags family consisted of many teams, many families, more sons than daughters, but one common swing. Our swing brought attention to it. Regardless of where you stood with your opinion, it was hard not to have an opinion.

I wrote a book in 2012 called Green Light Hitting. It's how we at GoWags taught hitting. It was based on INTENT. We wanted our swing artists to worry less about technique and more about swinging with purpose. Our belief system fell under considerable scrutiny from the precision level coaches. They had an extremely high Anchoring Quotient and they weren't afraid to share their thoughts.

> *"A few years back I came across a post on a former Mlb/Milb retired players Facebook page. A video was posted of you or your brother doing hitting with some guys. Someone posted the video and the group started tearing you guys limb from limb saying nasty awful things. Not about you personally as I don't believe names were mentioned, more to the fact that the drill was atrocious. You were stealing money and were a hack."*
> *-Eugene Bleecker, Founder/Director of Player Development*
> *108 Performance*

The coaches and players that played the game at the highest of levels knew our swing looked different. They knew our swing would eventually succumb to the demands the high-level game dictates. They weren't wrong. Eventually, the GoWags swing

---

[29] In 2015, Pennsylvania won the United States Championship in the Little League World Series. Most of the boys on the team were Green Light Hitting trained. Many of the boys tagged me in some of their posts as they experienced that incredible success. You can follow me @rcatscoach on Instagram and @GowagsKyle on Twitter.

would need to find precision and discipline. But our swing produced great results in The Imagination Game.

Every word spoken has an opportunity cost. If I tell a swing artist "Do it this way," I prevent him from interpreting feedback for himself. This can have serious consequences on learning. Most coaches that employ the "Do it this way model" are under time constraints to get it right. I understand that. I do that too. This needs to be learned by tomorrow's game. I, the coach, can't risk letting you learn on your terms, so I'll just tell you and show you. Yep, that's sometimes necessary. When we're merging with traffic, we don't always have time for a civilized discussion. But, if you're playing the "long game," and if you know time isn't of the essence, the spoken word often interrupts progress.

The GoWags RiverCats and all of our teams for that matter, were very young. The oldest teams we had were 14U. Our boys weren't playing The Precision Game yet. Time was on our side. We could allow the boys to grow at their pace, on their terms, on their conditions. If you allow boys to choose how they want to swing a bat, they'll choose CRUSH BASEBALLS every time. So, that's what we set out to teach them. Green Light Hitting was about creating an aggressive, bold, fearless hitter. The precision would come later.

One of my favorite memories of coaching the RiverCats involved pre game batting practice. Many of these fields would have batting cages lined up in succession so multiple teams could get practice prior to the games. My memory recalls the Ripken complex in Aberdeen, MD. RiverCats BP always took on the same feel. We had a reputation for hitting baseballs. We had a reputation for hitting baseballs very hard. Our BP was more CRUSH and less TALK. I would take a knee 30' away and throw baseballs in their direction. I offered no suggestions. I offered very little advice. It was their time. They were getting ready to do their thing. Their thing had become crushing baseballs. On game day, I was often a mere spectator to the demolition. The other teams? They were sadly playing The Precision Game. They were looking for the optimal swing among young swing artists. They were being paralyzed by their unknowing coaches. I would often look over into the other cages and I'd think to myself "What could that kid be if they let him be himself?" It wasn't my place to speak up or intervene. Many of the coaches wouldn't listen to me even if I offered my services. As far as they were concerned, the GoWags swing produced results but it was the wrong path for long term success. The path they were on wasn't producing the same results, but it was built for long term success. In their mind, the path the GoWags teams were on would eventually crumble at the mercy of The Precision Game. It was actually a great argument. It was just the answer to the wrong question.

Most coaches when they train their swing artists ask, "What swing is needed at the highest level?"

The appropriate question to ask is "What swing does THAT KID need to REACH the highest level?"

If you dropped in on this planet and the first thing you observed was an NBA game, you'd think these humans are tall. The sample size affects your view of things. This is called survivorship bias. The survivors of the NBA survival system happen to be taller than normal human beings. Every survival system, at its end, requires precision to exist. When it comes to the sample of NBA players, height is an obvious differentiator. It might even be a reason why some people assume they couldn't play in the NBA. Yet, the survivors of the basketball survival system have acquired incredible skills along their journey. Besides the precision of shooting, dribbling and passing they've developed an incredible imagination on the MACRO level. Coupled with their MICRO precision skills they recognize floor spacing, angles and general patterns for movement. Developing precision skills without playing the game of basketball wouldn't make a basketball player at all. It might make a great H-O-R-S-E player but not a basketball player. When it comes to the sample of Major League Baseball, the differentiators aren't as obvious. Yet, they exist.

What is true about every player playing Major League baseball. They had enough success along the way to deserve a roster spot. The success precedes the roster spot. How and where was success defined? On a baseball field in a competitive environment. Major League baseball swing artists have honed their skills by incorporating the MICRO skills associated with a good swing with the MACRO skills of which there are many. Attempting to match a swing without using on field success as your guide is very dangerous. In attempting to consider all the variables that go into on field success for a Major League swing artist I came up with this list of MACRO skills.

1. Anticipating ball speed trajectory
2. Anticipating ball spin trajectory
3. Anticipating ball location trajectory
4. The count associated with the pitch
5. The consequences associated with failing (loss aversion)
6. Authority figure watching (coach)
7. Loved Ones watching (family)
8. The act of running after hitting
9. Situational hitting. i,e Runner on 3rd < 2 outs
10. Umpire decisions (not all strike zones are created equally)
11. Learning from pitch to pitch, at bat to at bat
12. Psychological factors (i.e doubt, life concerns, competitive grit, familiarity with pitcher)
13. Physiological factors (heart rate)

I'm not suggesting that coaches shouldn't recognize an elite swing and attempt to chase it. That would minimize the MICRO skills required to play at the highest of levels. Great ball handlers don't become great by not practicing their dribbling. But great ball handlers sometimes don't make great point guards because they lack the MACRO skills that a great point guard possesses. The same is true with an obsession on the MICRO skills of a swing.

When you constantly obsess over the swing, you're stealing much of a great swing artists MACRO skills.

Todd Rose in his book *The End of Average* sites a great example for trying to match the behavior of elite performers without also having the success that led to that elite level. Rose says imagine trying to mimic the typing speed of an elite typist because that typist is more precise than you. She's become elite over years of practice. By observing her, you'd be led to believe typing faster would produce less errors. This, of course, would be a critical mistake. Attempting to match the behavior of elite performers without using success as a guide is a dangerous proposition.

The sport of baseball is a survival system sport. The coaches that coach the sport are tasked with turning the information that they have into intelligence for the athlete. In order to do so, they must recognize the extreme balance between the MICRO precision skills and the MACRO imagination skills.

My daughter and I have copies of our signatures below. In many ways, our signature is our art. My awful signature has evolved as my age sees signing my name as more obligation than art. I've lost the imagination. What exists is a very hurried yet precise representation of my name. Grace's signature lacks precision yet the patience which she demonstrated in creating her signature screams imagination.

"Hey Kyle. What did you just say?"
Every learner is somewhere on a continuum between imagination and precision. Forcing The Precision Game too early on learners ignores the fact that experience cannot be rushed. Imitating great artists at the top of their field often neglects the innate characteristics that these artists possess, honed through survival.

Teaching for Precision
Recruiting Help and Creating Dialogue

The truth is, at the beginning of any survival system, commitment to the message is more important than the message. The competition isn't great and practicing something, anything might produce extraordinary results. I'm not naive to that point of view. Eventually, the small field became bigger and the pool of players playing the game of baseball got much smaller. The talent improved. In order to survive, precision was going to be required.

The value of Twitter cannot be overstated. It's an incredible resource for turning information into intelligence. The danger of Twitter cannot be overstated. It's an incredible cesspool of insults and posturing. Our swing artists need Twitter. Thankfully, they don't need to navigate through all of the bickering and debating. Their coaches can do that. But their coaches must navigate Twitter because there are amazing minds out there with information to share. The coaches on Twitter must have the courage of competence to fight through the confirmation bias that we all come to have from time to time. No one person has this thing figured out. Some are precision biased. Some are imagination biased. They all have information that can help our swing artists improve.

If you want to move a mountain, it's critical you recruit the same type of people as you.

If you want to climb the mountain, it's critical you recruit different people than you.

Our swing artists are climbing the mountain. They're trying to survive and make that next step on their journey towards success. It's critical that the coaches in their lives demonstrate the courage to listen instead of the confidence to speak. It's not a matter of who is right and who is wrong all the time (although sometimes it is). Many times, the argument simply exists somewhere between imagination and precision.

The RiverCats are now on their way to college or at college. The survival system has become rather difficult to navigate. My advice to them, acting more as a consultant than a coach, is protect yourself with as much knowledge as possible. Why travels! When a coach attempts to turn his information into your intelligence you must have a filter that protects you. As is true with anything in life, there are good coaches and there are bad coaches. The truth of the matter is you're probably going to play for each at some point in the journey. Being labeled uncoachable, even by a bad coach, is not a good character trait. Respecting a bad coach is more important than defending your perspective. Yet, it's your career and your results that ultimately determine your success in the survival system of baseball.

I've never met a coach that turned his back on good results. Most coaches would allow you to hit by standing on your head if you were a Double Machine. Coaches are well intentioned. Sometimes, they just practice Iatrogenesis (The Fifth Inning). As a player traveling the survival system of baseball, you must use the greatest weapon you have to protect yourself, your voice. Never disrespect a coach in practice in front of the team. But, after practice, walk up to him and ask for a conversation. Be specific with what you know and how the information just shared may contradict what you currently believe. Hopefully, the conversation is productive, and resolution can be found. If not, have another conversation. If that doesn't lead to results, the player has a decision to make.

Baseball is a game. I call these games we play survival systems. They're important to us while we're in them. In the game of life (I call this a thriving system), there are 15,312 things more important than how you're handling the fastball away. Yet, when you're in the survival system, compete and do your best always. That's the love growth cycle of life (The Ninth Inning).

The Second Inning

You See the World through the Eyes
of Your Son

The Wagner Family would take the same vacation every summer.
We loved it. We looked forward to it. Some families like to
explore and do new things. Our family treated a week's time
together in the middle of the summer as a sacred time. Doing
something new and different would have to come at another time.
The summer was for Myrtle Beach, South Carolina. Specifically,
it was North Myrtle Beach and the Mar Vista hotel. It was our
thing.

The memories I have of those vacations revolve around swimming
in the pool during the day and eating seafood at night. Every now
and again a more specific memory might surface like diving for
pennies in the pool or riding bike scooters on the beach but by in
large we would wake up, swim and eat. It was a magic time and a
time that I cherish.

But there is something else that I vividly remember about those
vacations. I remember watching the Chicago Cubs in the
afternoon. What a treat that was for me and Bret. While Linda
and Gary Wagner would relax poolside, Kyle and Bret were in no
mood for "relaxing" as young boys. So, between swimming in the
pool and eating dinner in the evenings we'd often break up the day
by running into the air-conditioned room and watching the
Chicago Cubs.

In the 1980's, the Chicago Cubs didn't have lights at Wrigley
Field. That meant, if the Cubs were at home, they were playing a
day game. That also meant, Bret and I watched a lot of Cubs
baseball games on TV during our childhood vacations. We got
attached to the team and the players. Now that I think about it,
what a privilege it was to listen to Harry Carey call many of those
games. One of those players was Bill Buckner. He played first
base for the Chicago Cubs.

Bill Buckner hit .289 over a 22-yr. professional baseball career.
Buckner hit 174 home runs. Bill Buckner was the National League

batting champion in 1980. In 1981, Bill Buckner represented the National League in the All-Star game. Most people only know Bill Buckner by one thing and one thing only. Bill Buckner made an error at the most unfortunate of times.

Buckner would eventually leave the "Friendly Confines" of Wrigley Field and play for another one of Major League Baseball's storied franchises, the Boston Red Sox. It was here, and not as a Cub, that Buckner would forever be remembered.

History recognizes the play as an E-3. Many first baseman have committed the same error before and since. Buckner's error had slightly more significance because it came at the end of Game 6 in the 1986 World Series. The 21st Century has been very kind to Boston fans. The 20th Century, not so much. So, although recent baseball fans might chalk Buckner's error up as a "lost opportunity," the 1986 Boston fan literally wanted to strangle Buckner. The team hadn't won a World Series since 1918 and Buckner's error prevented the team from making the final out for what would have been the 4th and final win in the Series.[30]

The Boston Red Sox fans have recently made amends with Buckner. Time has eased the pain of 1986. More likely, World Series Championships have made the Boston fan base more magnanimous. Buckner has taken on a nostalgic persona. He symbolizes an era that was snake bitten for success. Buckner's gaffe has been covered over by tears of joy and celebrations of success. That's the way the world often works for those that commit those "one moment in time" errors or highlights. Despite a game consisting of a hundred micro plays, the brain immortalizes only one.

---

[30] There are many people that believe the New York Mets Mookie Wilson would have beat the ball to 1st base even if it was fielded cleanly.

Bill Buckner, Bill Mazeroski, Fred Merkle,[31] Kirk Gibson, Bobby Thomson, Joe Carter, Carlton Fisk, Willie Mays and even Babe Ruth have all been linked with one moment in time that encapsulates a career. Each of those moments affected the World Series. Each of those moments received more attention than it probably deserved for the outcome of the game. Yet, each of those moments absolutely determined the fate of the game.

It seems sports fans take on two roles as they choose to dole out their blame. One role is the benevolent minimalist. "It's never just one thing" is their mantra. A game consists of a thousand micro events that leads to an outcome. The benevolent minimalist recognizes that it's only through our recency bias that we can highlight and recall the last outcome. Certainly, there are a thousand other micro outcomes that affected the result prior to the most spectacular of outcomes. The second role is practical judge. "He choked" is their mantra. The practical judge knows that although those thousand micro events count, they always lead to an ending. Despite the fact that all plays in a game are a percentage to a whole, the plays at the end of the game carry with it more significance. How an athlete reacts to this added significance determines his competitive ilk.

I subscribe to the theory that the truth lies somewhere in the middle. The "it's never just one thing" crowd would be well served to realize success can come down to one moment in time. The "he choked" crowd needs to know that sports are hard. Regardless of which side you find yourself on, not all moments in time are created equal.

---

[31] Merkle's blunder has eroded over time but it might be the biggest blunder of all. It wasn't committed during the World Series, but it affected the World Series.

Micro Expectations
Luke Wagner

Grace Evelyn Wagner was born October 2004. Like many fathers of daughters, I held my baby girl and looked into her eyes thinking "I pray I never disappoint you." Us Dad's that are lucky enough to have daughters, envision a future open to a thousand possibilities. The future is only limited to one's imagination.

What would Grace be? Where would she find her passion? Would she be introverted? Would she be outgoing? Would she look like her Mom? What I know I didn't ask myself was "Will she play baseball?" Grace was born without an expectation of any kind. As long as Grace was healthy, I was willing to go down any road Grace wanted to lead me. It's still that way to this day. When it comes to my daughter, she can do no wrong. I'm sure that's not entirely healthy and I probably need to help my wife with the finer points to raising Grace but it's very hard for me. I'm not female. I don't know their emotions. I don't know their desires. I don't know much of anything. When it comes to raising my daughter, I'm the guy at the movies eating a bucket of popcorn waiting for the next event. It's pure entertainment. I love every second of being Grace's father.

Luke Ashley Wagner was born September 2001. He was Kyle and Heather Wagner's first born. When Kyle Wagner held Luke Wagner in his arms for the first time, he was a 28-yr. old man. 28-yr. old men are very competitive. 28-yr. old men still have mountains to climb and goals to achieve. When I held my son for the first time, I want to say I looked at him through the exact same lens through which I viewed my daughter. That would be unrealistic. I looked at Luke through an entirely different lens.

Baseball wasn't always kind to me. Baseball hit me with some body blows that I still feel to this very day. The pain the game caused me wasn't something I would wish on someone that I loved. If Luke didn't want to play baseball, I wouldn't begrudge him. But baseball gave me so many of life's great moments too. I know baseball didn't have the market cornered on great experiences. I'm sure if Luke wanted to play football or basketball or wrestling those same bonding experiences are in every competitive field. But baseball was the field the Wagner's knew. I'd give him a nudge and see where it would lead.

If I were being honest with Luke, I'd tell him that I love both my children equally, but I always had different expectations for him than for Grace. From a macro level the expectations were exactly the same. I hope they find their purpose in life. I hope they find someone they can love and have a great life growing old with. I hope they can find great friendships that sustain them. In the end, there's only love. That was true for both of my children. But, from a micro level, it was entirely different.

When I held Luke in my arms for the first time my thoughts weren't centered on disappointing him. My thoughts centered on all that he could achieve. A 28-yr. old father knows what it's like to be a son. The circumstances are entirely different, of course, but he's traveled down that road before. Men and women are wired differently. Whereas I didn't know what made women tick, I had an idea what made men tick. I looked at my son and thought "Whatever it is you want to accomplish, I'll help you."

The nudge became a push by the age of 2 or 3. It was quickly apparent to me and my "thin slicing" that Luke had some qualities that would play. What I mean by "would play" is he had great hand eye coordination and his arm moved fast. If he liked the game of baseball, I thought he could be very good at the game of baseball. I had enough tools in my tool belt that I could help him.

182

When Luke Wagner was born my life changed. Children change all adults. I don't mean to state the obvious. Luke Wagner's birth was one moment in time that would alter my life's trajectory forever. Granted, it took some time to see the tangible effects but without Luke there would be no RiverCats. Without Luke there would have been no GoWags. Kyle Wagner took an INSIDE VIEW when it came to Luke's growth in the game. When someone adopts an INSIDE VIEW of things, the lens can be awfully narrow. It wouldn't always be an easy go of it for Kyle and Luke. But it was always paved with love and growth at its core.

Inside View vs. Outside View
Why People Think We're Nuts

When I would show up to youth baseball tournaments, I would sometimes play a game with myself. My game was "Can you find his son?" Most teams that spend considerable hours together during a weekend aren't coached by someone not associated with the boys. In other words, Dads coach youth teams. It makes all the sense in the world. Who would find considerable value in working with very young baseball players more so than the men who have skin in the game? Find people that care deeply about the development of the young baseball players. Let them coach the team. Perfect.

The perfect coach is credible enough to be competent but humble enough to have doubts. They have gained experience after experience that have solidified their perspective. They can identify right from wrong. They have the necessary information that can turn information into intelligence. Yet, they also leave room for doubt. This doubt is context centered. Human beings, specifically very young human beings, are learning this information. It's important to allow these young people to experience things for themselves. Interpreting feedback is essential for learning to occur. Doubt allows for young people to interpret on their own terms and their own timeframe. Doubt in the perfect coach isn't doubt in what he's teaching, rather it's doubt that others see it like he does.

The men that wear the "Dad Hat" and the "Coach Hat" simultaneously have the most difficult job I can imagine. Ostensibly, it's no different than coaching the other boys on the team. Realistically, it's coaching 11 boys whose growth you care about while coaching one boy whose growth is a necessity. These men are usually very easy to find at a baseball game. The exceptions to this rule are generally the men that have experienced so much pain in the game that they have learned to not say as much. But, when Dads become Coaches without the pain of experience, their INSIDE VIEW of things creates a dynamic that can be very easy to spot. When certain environments threaten our optimal view of things, we can get very defensive. These are the episodes that tend to end up on the nightly news if cooler heads can't intervene.

When Moms and spectators see this, they tend to see us dads as certifiably insane. What would compel an adult to behave in this manner? How could he allow his emotions to get the best of him? He's actually a really nice guy.

When competition meets optimal it becomes combustible.

The INSIDE VIEW is what I call the perspective when you care about the process. Dads have an INSIDE VIEW on their sons because it's very important to them that they see progress. They want assurances that they're on the right track. Moms have an INSIDE VIEW on things too but it's often not at competitive sporting events. When Bret and I were growing up, we'd always get frustrated when someone would give us something and before Bret and I could reply we'd hear, "What do you say?" Our Mom, and many other Moms on this planet, demand behavior that is optimal. This is an INSIDE VIEW. If perfect is available, that's what we want. Teachers tend to have an INSIDE VIEW of their curriculum. Doctors have an INSIDE VIEW of their specific field. Lawyers have an INSIDE VIEW of how law gets interpreted. As we acquire specific knowledge about things, the process becomes very important. Optimal is often all there is. A high level of expectation is born and anything short of that is grounds for unacceptable.

The INSIDE VIEW is completely understandable when you realize you're in a system that demands optimal. Bill Belichek has won 6 Super Bowls maintaining an INSIDE VIEW on football. Try showing up for a team meeting late with Nick Saban and see if he has an optimal position on promptness. In order to be successful in a survival system you must require optimal. The competition is entirely too challenging to allow for any deviations to perfect.

The INSIDE VIEW is completely incompatible when you realize the system that you're competing in is actually in a much larger system in a game called life. It's this systematic mismatch that causes so much of the incongruency with our viewpoints. The football coach that demands optimal effort during practice is excoriated when that young man collapses and is later taken to the hospital for dehydration. The teacher that demands full attention for all 50 minutes is later reprimanded for not realizing that the student's grandfather passed away earlier that morning. The employer who demands the deadline be met only to realize that the employee's daughter was taken to the emergency room with a ruptured appendix. The INSIDE VIEW is narrow and demanding. It must be to have success in a survival system. Yet, the OUTSIDE VIEW realizes that context and a broad perspective is always essential.

I am not and never will be a perfect Dad. I recognize that I have an INSIDE VIEW when it comes to my son. I prefer the

OUTSIDE VIEW when at all possible. I prefer to take a broad view of my son's progress and growth. I prefer to allow for exceptions to rules and circuitous routes to achieving goals. But I fail and I fail often. When I fail, it usually comes down to the fact that there is a prize to be won and I'm a competitive human being. I have an INSIDE VIEW and I'm in a survival system.

When competition meets optimal it becomes combustible.

The INSIDE VIEW isn't reserved only for Dads with sons. The INSIDE VIEW is adopted the minute you place extreme value on the process you're using. Most people adopt an INSIDE VIEW on their children, their jobs, their hobbies, their teams, their politics, their religion. The more they learn, the more they demand an optimal level of process. When success is measured by winning the prize, it's not always an acceptable perspective but at least it's understandable. When Mitch Kauffman[32] mocks me for not knowing how to use a nail gun, I get it. He's got an INSIDE VIEW of all things nail guns. But the fact that my nail went into that piece of wood at all seems like an acceptable outcome from my OUTSIDE VIEW.

Over the years, Kyle Wagner has been told to "relax" more than my fair share. That's code for "Kyle, it's not a big deal. You need to calm down and chill out." I've come to realize that Kyle Wagner took an INSIDE VIEW on all thing's competition. That time I cried in 8th grade when I didn't think our football team was ready? INSIDE VIEW! That time I yelled at our 8th grade basketball team at halftime because I didn't think they were giving their best effort? INSIDE VIEW! That time I punched the dashboard of my car because I didn't think Luke was hustling on defense? INSIDE VIEW! That time Bret wasn't catching the

---

[32] Mitch Kauffman is a childhood friend. In today's vernacular, he'd also be considered an OG.

baseballs I threw him correctly. INSIDE VIEW! That time I got 3 technical fouls in 8 seconds coaching a middle school basketball game. INSIDE VIEW! There is a time and a place for an INSIDE VIEW. It's when championships are at stake and goals are in view. Those are the times when an INSIDE VIEW is desperately appreciated. Those also happen to be the same times when people on the OUTSIDE think you're slightly off your rocker.

And this is what I was counting on when I showed up at youth baseball tournaments to play my game "Can you find his son?" I was counting on some "off his rocker" behavior to clue me in when Dad was talking as opposed to Coach. Often, it's a dead giveaway. They root harder, they cheer louder, they coach more aggressively. Other times, it's more subtle. The arms cross after a pop up. The feet kick dirt slightly more assertively. Sometimes, the Dad shoots son a look in the dugout hoping for the son to reciprocate that stare back. Son often does. I'm pretty good at playing the game "Can you find his son?"

Inside View vs. Outside View
Life's competitive but it's not a competition

Event	Inside View (process based)	Outside View (outcome based)
Luke takes strike 3 on the outside corner.	Striking out looking is a part of the game. Striking out looking on the outside corner is an awful approach. You got yourself out. Unacceptable.	Everyone strikes out from time to time.

Event	Inside View (process based)	Outside View (outcome based)
Luke throws the 0-2 pitch above the batter's head.	The 0-2 pitch is a great time for the fastball up in the zone. Missing that high never invites a swing. You must be "less high." Unacceptable.	He missed his spot.
Student fails to factor a polynomial correctly. She didn't recognize a difference of squares.	Factoring a difference of squares correctly is essential for solving higher level problems in calculus. Unacceptable.	She missed a question.
Patient's cholesterol level is high.	Cholesterol is a serious health condition that if unattended could lead to long term consequences and even death. Doctor prescribes medication. Unacceptable.	He should probably improve his health with exercise and diet.
A hunter is talking on the way to a tree stand.	We're not going to see any deer if you can't be quiet. If you can't sit still and shut up, you can't hunt. Unacceptable.	I was just talking.
Athlete chooses to specialize and play only one sport.	Competition is becoming more and more precise. Specialization is required to keep pace. Can't get behind.	Kids should play more sports. They'll only be young once. Never dismiss the value of competition.

"Hey Kyle. What did you just say?"

We all take an INSIDE VIEW or an OUTSIDE VIEW when we make observations. The INSIDE VIEW is taken when the process demands optimal results. This is usually required in survival systems. The OUTSIDE VIEW allows for flexibility in the process. Knowing what system, you're operating under can guide your thinking.

188

Taking an Outside View
From The Inside
Undercover Dad

The hardest part about being a Dad and a Coach is hiding the emotion that comes with being a Dad. I took my role as Head Coach of the RiverCats seriously. There was a general culture I wanted to create. That culture meant a safe place to test boundaries. That culture meant a willingness to make bold mistakes. That culture also meant accountability to their actions and immediate feedback when outcomes didn't match with best baseball practices. In order to be the best Head Coach possible, I needed an OUTSIDE VIEW. Having an outside view allows for perspective. It allows for patience. It allows for contextual understanding. It's a big picture mentality. But this is the exact opposite perspective that a Dad often takes when his son's behavior generally requires optimal.

I have an idea of what it must be like to be an undercover cop. From a macro level your job is to gather information so you can later incriminate the bad guys. On a micro level you must engender trust among the people that you live amongst. In many respects, that's the task of the Head Coach that also plays the role of Dad. The OUTSIDE VIEW must treat all 12 players equally while the INSIDE VIEW always has an eye on the one kid, your kid.

I'd like to say I played the Undercover Dad fairly well. But, that's not for me to decide. The parents and the players are really the only ones capable of assessing my performance. What I am capable of assessing is how I tried to perform the two roles in a practice environment and a game environment.

189

The practice environment, as I have previously mentioned was mostly about using the player's emotion to adapt to what situations presented themselves. I think being a Dad was enormously valuable in that regard. Driving to the field, Luke would always ask "What are we doing today Dad?" I'd give him a broad picture of what I had in mind and he'd nod his head. One particular car ride he gave me the greatest compliment any son could give an Undercover Dad. He said "The best thing about your practices is they are always fun. Whatever we do, we know it'll be fun."

The only metric used to determine the value of a teacher is are they excited to show up.

I don't think Luke would say my practices were always "judgment free." It was encouraging that Luke always thought they were fun, but he and I also knew that with practice came the expectation that we needed to grow. Growth isn't always comfortable. As Undercover Dad, if I needed Luke to grow, I needed the other boys to grow as well. This understanding meant I needed to be consistent with my core coaching values yet handle each player uniquely different. This is very difficult for someone with only an INSIDE VIEW of things. INSIDE VIEW people are rule followers. They demand that everyone gets treated equally. INSIDE VIEW people often have an expectation of performance and any deviation from that performance must be treated equally. As I said, I was playing Undercover Dad. This meant I had an INSIDE VIEW of Luke but an OUTSIDE VIEW of where I wanted the RiverCats to go. I was playing the "long game" with the team but I was playing the "short game" with my son.

At practice settings I was sensitive to the dynamic that everyone deserved my best effort to help them improve. I was also sensitive to the dynamic that for 11 people I was "authority" while one person had seen me in my underwear. This simply meant my message to my son was always framed through his Dad lens. The ability to discern "coaching" vs. "judgment" wasn't an easy task for a young person. Although I wished Luke could parse through the social implications with every message, I realized he probably never could, nor could I. Every coaching cue of "good angles to the baseball" was probably a hidden message of "I'm disappointing Dad." Every coaching cue of "the best defensive team is the most accurate throwing team" was probably a thought of "I wonder if Dad thinks I'm an accurate thrower." If Dad and Son have a loving relationship at home, it's awfully difficult to be Undercover Dad when Undercover Dad requires direct messages from time to time.

As Undercover Dad, I found myself talking in generalities as much as I could. I'd use the mistakes of others to teach Luke. I'd use Luke's mistakes to teach others. The INSIDE VIEW obsession with perfection for Luke always kept my attention heightened in the moment. Yet, the OUTSIDE VIEW of team dynamics allowed me to "try" and coach Luke in broader generalities more so than direct coaching.

I remember one car ride home when Luke said, "You were hard on Shaq today." I said "Luke, was I harder on him than I've ever been on you?" He said "No. You yell at all of us. But today you yelled at him the most." In the eyes of a young player, I suppose that's what an Undercover Dad looks like. I was looking for long term growth from all of them. The practice environment sometimes demanded an INSIDE VIEW and if I needed to coach Luke hard, I'd also need to coach the other boys hard. I certainly wouldn't want someone to be able to play "Can you find his son?" at my practice field.

I can honestly say the games were much easier for me to play Undercover Dad. I'm sure it had a lot to do with the social aspect of playing games. I didn't want to be outed for favoritism. That didn't mean it wasn't especially difficult after the game or on the car ride home. Those moments are private and I'm sure Luke has some vivid memories of the car ride home. But games are sacred times for the players. I still had an INSIDE VIEW of Luke, but I generally realized that true competition requires 100% attention on the task at hand, not on Undercover Dad in uniform.

This can be an extremely difficult task for a young athlete. It was hard for Luke and it's hard for many sons that share a dugout with Undercover Dad. "Luke, stop looking at me." It's just a habit for young people that love one of the adults in the dugout. Competition gets mixed with loving acceptance and it becomes very difficult. Ultimately, this was the reason that me and my son had to part ways. But, in the early stages of helping my son, I needed to be in that dugout. I knew the risks associated with Undercover Dad. I also knew the rewards. I had a lot to offer the boys and I'd have to figure out how to manage the INSIDE VIEW I had of my son with the OUTSIDE VIEW I had of the RiverCats. The last game I coached as a RiverCats Head Coach is now 4 years ago. Playing the role of Undercover Dad was the hardest part of my job.

"Hey Kyle. What did you just say?"

Dads that coach have a difficult task. The INSIDE VIEW that demands optimal processes from your son must be coordinated with the OUTSIDE VIEW that allows for patience and discovery among all learners. Combine that with the social implications of being on a team and it's an extremely difficult if not impossible job to perform well. The best we can often hope for is awareness of the dynamic.

When Plan A Becomes Plan B
What the Inside Looks Like in the End

The hardest part of taking an INSIDE VIEW on anything is learning to live with the outcomes when optimal isn't met. It's rather easy to have an INSIDE VIEW on Optometry. It's much harder to have an INSIDE VIEW on your son. Optometry is a profession. There are optimal processes and optimal courses of action to be taken. Using analytical processing skills is acquired through years of education and experience. Year 15 in Optometry would presumably make you a better Optometrist than Year 1. The information that we gather and collect helps us be a better Optometrist. This isn't true with people. This certainly isn't true with family.

Acquiring information is addictive. It's essentially a scavenger hunt of life. Walk the planet and collect more and more of stuff you can use. In the physical realm, collecting this "stuff" has its obvious advantages. The more stuff I have the better equipped I'll be to defend myself. The more stuff I have the more I can be self-sufficient. This becomes almost a quest in life. Learn more things so I don't need to rely on anyone else. Learning allows us to predict.

People aren't meant to be predicted. They're meant to be celebrated.

The minute I met Luke Wagner I loved him. It's true of Dads. It's true of Family. The flesh and blood of together is a bond that's unbreakable. As I looked into those eyes, I committed to a lifetime of loving and helping that little boy become a man. Such is the role of every father. Turning our information into their intelligence becomes life's great task. How can I share with them everything I know and still let them experience life for themselves? The great conundrum of parenting. I've been down that road. I know where that road leads. It leads to pain, discontent and frustration. Yet, we still let them walk down that road anyway. How can we do that with someone that we love? How can we not do that with someone that we love?

The man I am today is the result of all of my successes and all of my failures. I've met extraordinary people along the way. I've experienced incredible victories and I've cried with incredible pain. It's all been worth it. I believe Garth Brooks says it best in his song *The Dance.*

> *Looking back on the memory of*
> *The dance we shared beneath the stars above*
> *For a moment all the world was right*
> *How could I have known you'd ever say goodbye*
> *And now I'm glad I didn't know*
> *The way it all would end the way it all would go*
> *Our lives are better left to chance I could have missed the pain*
> *But I'd have to miss the dance*
> *Holding you I held everything*
> *For a moment wasn't I the king*
> *But if I'd only known how the king would fall*
> *Hey who's to say you know I might have changed it all*
> *And now I'm glad I didn't know*
> *The way it all would end the way it all would go*
> *Our lives are better left to chance I could have missed the pain*
> *But I'd of had to miss the dance*
> *Yes my life is better left to chance*
> *I could have missed the pain but I'd of had to miss the dance*

So, it is with Father and Son. Kyle Wagner had been down the road where baseball leads. The end isn't always friendly. The end isn't always kind. The end will provide you with a long list of friendships worth cultivating and friendships worth dismissing. The end will demand you ask the question "Was it worth it?" It'll provide heartbreak and sorrow. It'll provide failure after failure enticing you to choose another path. It'll tempt you with alternative life plans that will seem more pleasurable than anything you're currently experiencing. It'll be laced with fear that you're never going to be good enough. It'll be laced with the anxiety that you're disappointing everyone that believes in you and knows you're good enough to make it. It'll end on the edge of hotel bed crying your eyes out that everything you dreamed of and hoped for was for naught. You let your son go down that road anyway! But, you sure as hell give it your best shot so when that day comes, he's ready for those tests.

But, that's the struggle with Father and Son. I know what lies ahead. I know where the end of a baseball survival system leads. I cried those tears already. I lived a life of doubt and fear and constant judgment that I wasn't going to live up to my dreams or others expectations of me. It was a terrifying time. That's the danger of ambition. You simply can't achieve without risking the most dangerous of life's emotions. How do you prepare your son for those obstacles and those pitfalls yet still enjoy him in the present moment? The only way I know how is to take an OUTSIDE VIEW from time to time. The OUTSIDE VIEW is the healthy view. The OUTSIDE VIEW is the practical view when space and time is allowed between incidents and outcomes. The OUTSIDE VIEW begins to understand that although he is your son and your responsibility and your pride and joy, he's also his own man. The OUTSIDE VIEW allows you to be grateful you even had the opportunity at all. Having a son is never guaranteed. The OUTSIDE VIEW is the view that Kyle Wagner began to take as Luke turned 14.

When Luke was a little guy, I knew the best way to experience success in The Imagination Game was to give him the necessary skills to succeed. Success breeds success. If you want to motivate someone, show them what success looks like. Yet, I also knew the end of the survival system requires precision. The Precision Game is ultimately where the road ends. The Precision Game is the game where all the dreams and goals become reality. The Precision Game is where the tears of failure live. If skills are necessary to move past The Imagination Game, it was love that would be required to keep playing The Precision Game. When Luke turned 14, I needed to show him how to love the game of baseball.

195

Baseball is a lousy lover. You can pour your heart and soul into the sport and in return it says, "Thank You." It can be heartless. But, that's the beauty of the sport. Love something with all of your heart knowing the satisfaction isn't in a returned gesture of love but simply the opportunity to experience.

The INSIDE VIEW is so narrow and so exacting and so demanding that at the end, during The Precision Game, you often question "Why did I do this again?" When Luke turned 14, it became obvious to me that he had the skills that might be able to tackle The Precision Game. Luke was a left-handed pitcher that was going to be a 90 mph plus guy. Luke's ball had natural sink. Luke had a nasty little breaking ball and was developing a change-up. Oh, and Luke could hit too. Luke was better than Kyle ever was. There was no doubt in my mind, Luke would wind up in The Precision Game before his baseball career was over. I knew what he needed. He needed me to step away from the dugout.

The RiverCats stopped playing baseball in 2015 because we ran out of pitching. That was my surface level explanation. We simply didn't have enough arms to continue to compete. Most of the 'Cats became position players and it's an unmanageable situation without depth of arms. The real reason the 'Cats stopped playing was I wasn't interested in coaching Luke anymore.

Here's what I believe is true of The Imagination Game and The Precision Game.

To be most successful in The Imagination Game, your skills simply need to be more precise than those you're playing with. To be most successful in The Precision Game, your imagination must be more intact than those you're competing against.

That's very deep but it's merely the LOVE GROWTH CYCLE (The Ninth Inning) at play again. When you first start playing the game of baseball you love the sport. You think about the sport and you dream about the sport. This dreaming allows you to play and the more you play the more you improve. Precision improves.

As you continue into The Precision Game, your precision becomes all there is. Honing your skills and sharpening the tools becomes all there is. The Precision Game naturally requires great precision. But The Precision Game is a game of failure. Success in The Precision Game isn't defined by real world consequences, success in The Precision Game is defined by the imagination of the little boy that started playing baseball at all.

The Precision Game deceives you into relinquishing control to those "experts" that can help you improve your craft. The Precision Game invites you to follow the crowd of knowledge. The Precision Game is lined with scouts, agents, college recruiters, facility experts. Essentially, The Precision Game is lined with a lot of people that will tell you what you need to do and why you need to do it. Without much strain at all, you're lost in a sea of precision. The most successful people in The Precision Game are those people that reclaim the love of the game as simply a game. The most successful people in The Precision Game rent their success, own their failure but know that failure is fleeting and what a pleasure it is to know that failure in the game of baseball is still only failure in a game.

As Luke grew older, I owed him this perspective. As Luke grew older, I needed to make sure he understood that all the sweat, all the energy, all the hard work to become more precise will crumble at the feet of a lost imagination. Luke needed less of "advanced scout" Dad and more of "love and laugh" Dad.

"Hey Kyle. What did you just say?"

The survival system of baseball requires the imagination in the beginning to become precise at the end. In the end, when precision is required, it takes the imagination of the beginning to reframe success and reclaim how you experience the game.

Saying Goodbye to Your Son
Luke Wagner

Luke was always the youngest player on the RiverCats. From an INSIDE VIEW of Luke, I never wanted him to think he was the best player on the team. When you surround him with a team like the RiverCats, that was easy. But, from an OUTSIDE VIEW, I wanted him to know that his Dad thought he was simply one of the most creative, one of the most competitive, one of the most talented dudes I had ever coached. One of the greatest mistakes' coaches make is they place growth ahead of love. For the same reason we were hesitant to create too much failure for the Sampling and Specialized Groups, is the fine line I walked with Luke. On the INSIDE I knew he needed challenged. On the OUTSIDE I knew he needed success.

Thanks to Anthony Volpe and the Volpe family, Luke received a highlight that I'll take with me to my grave. Granted, it was an 11u moment, but it was a very big moment and it was indeed the success that he needed and rightfully deserved. As the RiverCats were preparing for Cooperstown, Mike Volpe mentioned to me that Anthony would be trying out for Team USA and he thought Luke should try out as well. We were hesitant. Without an invite, these events tend to be mere formalities as the team is often pre-determined. We decided as a family it would be a very cool opportunity. We lowered our expectations and flew to Georgia for the one-day Team USA tryout.

The family's nerves were high. It was obvious by watching warm ups that there were a lot of talented kids in attendance. Luke showed well enough in the preliminaries. He beat his guy in their test of foot speed and showed a strong enough arm from the outfield. But it was the stuff that happened after lunch that took my breath away. As the game portion of the event started, Luke said "Dad, I'm hitting first and then I'm pitching." So, Luke would have the opportunity to be the first player to hit in what felt like a pressure cooker of drama. Luke homered on the very first pitch. He hit it way up into the trees. Luke would homer two more times for a total of 3 home runs at the Team USA tryouts. Luke would also double and line out deep to the fence. Luke went 4-5 and also pitched a shutout inning. Luke had himself quite a day. Luke certainly had enough success to validate his position.

But Luke didn't make Team USA. That was a lesson only someone on the INSIDE could appreciate. His teammate, and friend, would make Team USA. Anthony would prove to be one of Team USA's stalwarts over the years. In fact, this past year Anthony was named captain on the 18u team.

I guess all we can ever do is live and learn. The best of us learn before we make mistakes. The rest of us learn after we make mistakes. Maybe, the key is learning from others. One of the best teachers I ever had in life was my Grandfather, Harold Wagner. He taught me so much, but I remember one thing he said that stuck with me when he was an older man and he was watching life take its toll. He said, "Bret and Kyle, I love you guys so much I'd apologize even if I knew I was right."

I suppose that's the mindset I needed to take with Luke. It was no longer important being right. Optimal was no longer required. Luke and Kyle had laid the foundation for success by taking an INSIDE VIEW. The game was very hard at the end and skills are required to survive. But, in the end, Dad is more Dad than Coach.

Luke graduates Red Land High School in 2020. Luke is committed to the University of Georgia. As Harold Wagner used to say, "If the Good Lord's willing and the creek don't rise" Luke should have an opportunity to play professional baseball. When The Precision Game comes, Luke is going to hear coach after coach profess to knowing what skills will lead to more precision. I hope he listens intently to each and every one of them. There are

199

so many people with information that can become intelligence. It's the athlete's responsibility to hear all of it. Yet, not all information is necessary and not all information is good. It's the athlete's job to be knowledgeable and as informed as possible. This knowledge of why we do what we do is the athlete's last line of defense. I think I've prepared Luke for this aspect of The Precision Game.

I have no idea if I've prepared him for how to handle the failure. The failure The Precision Game deals out is ruthless and arbitrary. It discriminates against no one. The only defense someone has against the ruthless nature of The Precision Game is to love the game unconditionally. I could never do that. I could only love the game when it loved me back. I was like thousands and thousands that went before me and came after me. My hope is if I can give Luke back the imagination of the little boy, he's got a chance to defend himself against the attacks The Precision Game throws his way. I look forward to watching, on the OUTSIDE. I see ya workin' Luke.

The First Inning

The Only Difference between Right and Wrong is Time and Perspective

When I first started GoWags I had a grand idea on how to practice and develop baseball players. Time is valuable and, in my opinion, our young players weren't getting the most out of the training opportunities. We were giving our athletes as much deliberate practice as we could throw their way, but we weren't "training ugly."

Training ugly is a term used for retrieval practice or some like to call it random practice. Essentially, don't script the environment for practice. Allow the environment freedom to change and demand that your athletes react appropriately. In many respects, I see deliberate practice as sharpening the tool and I see training ugly as choosing the appropriate tool. It does us no good if you bring the sharpest of knives to a gunfight. Our athletes at GoWags needed more tool choosing practice. They were getting plenty of tool sharpening practice.

I'm not sure where the thought came to me, but I decided to create a Fall Baseball League called the GoWags Developmental League. This league was an invitation only league. That was awfully exclusive, but the fall is a time to develop in Pennsylvania. We don't have the best of weather and September to November was just an incredible time of year in South Central PA. I wanted to make the most of the weather. I also wanted to part ways with the constraints that don't make baseball players better. Anything that was superficial was going to get axed. I got rid of paid umpires. Those weren't necessary if we were just developing. I got rid of teams. Teams need coaches. I didn't want lack of appropriate coaches to be the reason players didn't develop. I got rid of time constraints and age restrictions. Some kids played football and couldn't commit to a full schedule. I didn't want that to be an issue. I also wanted the best players to be able to move up and down based upon their appropriate level of ability. I made the league. I held tryouts so I could assess and place accordingly. I recruited competent people of high character to coach and umpire each game. I made every lineup for each night and I picked positions and picked the pitchers. When you showed up to the field, you had your assignment as to where you were playing and where you were hitting. The entire GoWags Developmental League was extremely selfish in nature. If a kid said his primary position was shortstop, that's where I tried to get him the most reps.

I monitored pitch counts and I monitored innings won. Each of the six innings started with men on base (I realize this isn't training ugly, but I was too impatient to wait for perfect environmental changes). I wanted high stress innings with men on base. As I recall, the 1st inning was a runner on 1st. The second inning was 1st and 2nd. The third inning was 1st and 3rd. The fourth inning was 2nd only. The fifth inning was 2nd and 3rd. The sixth inning was bases loaded. Scores reset after each inning. I wanted each inning to be something to be won or lost. In baseball, the last three outs are the hardest three outs to get. I wanted each inning to have that feel. I wanted the boys to compete for something every time they were on the field. It was an awesome success. The boys ranged in ages from 7 to 12. I had three divisions based upon skill level. The Honus Wagner division was our lowest skill level. The Ty Cobb division were our intermediates and the Lou Gehrig division were for our highest skill level players. After each night I'd collect the results of the innings won. The only standings kept were by each player and they simply identified how many innings you won. It only ran for one year because the following year we coached our travel teams in the fall.

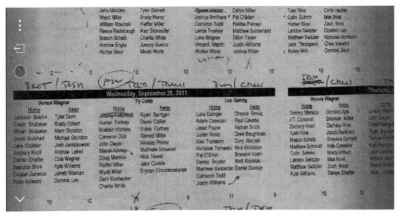

A Weekly Outline of the Developmental League

Looking back on the league it accomplished what it set out to do. It made better baseball players. They were put in situations more often and they had to respond every night. No longer was a 1st and 3rd defensive situation a result of chance.

Every night we knew it was coming at least once in the third inning. There was an unexpected consequence though. There was something missing. Baseball is a team sport. Without the camaraderie of teammates, many evenings rang hollow. Sure, there was the mom and dad celebrating the occasional double and the umpire/coach offering encouragement after a great play but without teammates to get attached to, it wasn't quite what I expected. Yes, shortstops experienced the ground ball with the infield in more than they would have. But I don't think I created an authentic environment that matched the intensity and commitment that being on a team always elicits. I chose the individual over the team model. In hindsight, I may have won the battle for finding the appropriate tool, but I think I lost the war of building competitors.

The parents generally thanked me for running the league. I believe the boys got more at bats than a regular league would have provided. I believe the league provided more beneficial mound time. I believe the league created more situational baseball. I know the league created cousin vs. cousin matchups (I neglected to call Luke out on strike 3 and Cole still holds a grudge towards his Uncle Kyle. It was right down the middle. I choked. Sorry Cole). But I think the parents shared my general sense of malaise with the league. Without friends to compete with and opponents to compete against, it wasn't quite the same experience.

I've never been afraid to try new things. The GoWags Developmental League was an exciting idea that had value in the precision it added to the game of baseball. I challenged convention and was willing to test some tried and true positions. I don't think I'd call that fall a failure, but it certainly didn't meet my level of expectations either. Do, Observe, Correct. If I were doing a developmental league today, I'd do it in a team vs. team format. I'd recruit opposing coaches and run joint practices where every inning had value and every inning provided a result. I'd make sure the innings won were celebrated and I'd make sure there was a prize or trophy awarded to the champion. I think that would look great. I think I knew that training ugly was important. I didn't realize how important the aspect of team was to the environment I was trying to recreate.

I Think You're Missing Someone
Bobby Whalen

Multi-sport athletes are a dying breed. Society's focus on efficiency and optimization have driven this model. If you want to get great fast, specialize! Some say this is a flawed model because you choose the "short game" over the "long game." By focusing on optimal and efficient you fail to pick up the competitive perspective that eventually serves you well at the end of survival systems. Essentially, by focusing on the precision of now you'll lose the imagination that is critical for tomorrow. It's a great argument for many.

Bobby Whalen is the son of Bob and Mandy Whalen. Of all the RiverCats families, the Whalen's were the family that I had known the longest. I had grown up with Bob Whalen. Actually, I had grown up knowing Bob Whalen. Bob was an outstanding local athlete that played for Cedar Cliff High School. His forte was wrestling but I had gotten to know the Whalen family years prior through football. The Whalen's and the Wagner's played youth football at St. Theresas. The Whalen's were football players. The Wagner's played football because we were competitive kids looking to do something in the fall. I'm not sure Bret and Kyle Wagner would have chosen football if they were born in today's specialization climate. In the 1980's we played football and we competed. Football was the first time I felt truly nervous. Standing alone in the batter's box can test your skill. Standing back for the opening kickoff tests your will. I learned to respect the gridiron competitors because they stared fear in the face and tackled it head on, literally and figuratively. Football made me tougher. I'm certain of that.

Bob Whalen and the entire Whalen family (Bob had 3 younger brothers who all played football too) were football players. Bobby Whalen came to be a football player. Bobby Whalen's spirit and will are two of his greatest assets in assessing the athlete Bobby Whalen.

Following the RiverCats inaugural season, Dan Law approached me. Dan was a mutual friend of the Whalen's and the Wagner's. Dan had coached with me and Dan had coached Bobby. Dan was an advocate for local youth sports and Dan had a keen eye for talent. Dan's son Trey would also play for the RiverCats in subsequent years. But it was a conversation that Dan and I had that opened my eyes about Bobby. Casually, Dan and I discussed the RiverCats and the success we had in our first year. We commented briefly on the boys and their skill sets. We talked about the long-term plan for the 'Cats and where the future might lead. Dan calmly said, "If you think you have the best players in the area, you're missing one." Dan, matter of factly, told me I needed Bobby Whalen on my team.

When Bobby Whalen joined the RiverCats he wasn't a great baseball player. He was a good baseball player and certainly acquitted himself very well. Dan Law wasn't wrong. Bobby deserved to be on the team and Bobby made us better. But Bobby wasn't one of our best baseball players. Bobby's glove skills were raw. Bobby's swing was crude. Bobby's baseball acumen was unrefined. But Bobby competed.

I think great competitors become great competitors because they learn that the goal of competition isn't to outperform the opponent it's to beat the opponent. I think in today's era of specialization that message sometimes gets lost. Pitchers are led to believe that throwing harder and executing pitches is how you win games. In reality, throwing harder and executing pitches allows you to take the rubber. Learning how to make pitches after your shortstop boots the ground ball or the umpire doesn't give you the pitch on the corner is how you beat your opponent. Athletes are training more and more in neutered environments. They train and compete without authentic risk. Then, when they're thrown in the cauldron of real competition with real consequences and real heartache they panic and fail to overcome and compete. Despite Bobby's raw baseball skills, Bobby brought with him an ironclad will to compete. The only thing I needed to do was add more tools to his tool belt and sharpen those tools. Bobby would take care of the rest.

Art Isn't About Creating, It's About Revealing
Jayson Kramer

The whole nature vs. nurture debate fascinates me. The argument for nature is something is born into you. The argument for nurture is something is coaxed out of you. As is true with everything, the argument lies in the middle. People have proclivities to be great. These are the genes they are born with. David Epstein highlights this in his book *The Sports Gene*. Yet, the cliché *hard work beats talent when talent doesn't work hard* has merit too. This speaks to the idea of nurture and the value of coaching. Daniel Coyle's *The Talent Code* and Anders Ericsson's research on expert performance detail the importance of deliberate practice.

Succeeding in a game like baseball requires an awful lot of skill but also an awful lot of luck. Some people don't make it because things just didn't break their way. Kyle Wagner didn't possess the offensive skills to "make it." The survival system of professional baseball kicked me out at the Single A level. Bret Wagner didn't "make it" for numerous reasons. Maybe he didn't make it because he was traded to the A's and never found the same nurturing environment he had with the Cardinals. Maybe he didn't make it because the broken leg his senior year of playing football finally caught up to him causing early stage arthritis in his hip. Maybe he lost the imagination required to win at The Precision Game. Bret was kicked out of the survival system at the Double A level. Barry Houser made it all the way to the AAA level before getting kicked out of the survival system of baseball. Barry was a left-handed pitcher in the Pirates organization.

I have a great deal of respect for Barry Houser. Barry was an Assistant Principal at Red Land while Bret and I played at the high school. At the time, I knew Barry used to play baseball, but I was too self-absorbed to understand just how well Barry played baseball. Barry Houser was and still is an imposing man. He carries himself with a dignity of competence. He carries himself with the self-assurance that needs not the affirmation of others and the humility of knowing many people simply don't care. Barry Houser's grandson was on the RiverCats. Barry Houser's daughter Steph was the mother of Jayson Kramer. In my mind, Jayson Kramer had the potential to "make it." In my mind, Jayson Kramer still has the potential to make it.

We seldom called him Jayson. He went by Shaq. The good story is a long story. The short story is Jayson Kramer has the same name as my former Wake Forest teammate Jason Kramer. We named him Shaq because one day Jason Kramer bought an Orlando Magic (Shaquille O'Neal's team at the time) hat. When we met Jayson Kramer, the nickname was inevitable. Barry Houser's grandson would go by the name of Shaq so long as he played for the RiverCats.

I was hard on Shaq. I thought Shaq had and has every tool to play the game at a very high level. I still think it's not out of the realm of possibility that Jayson Kramer could someday be a Big League baseball player. He's a left-handed throwing outfielder. He's a left-handed hitter. He's got great hair (never underestimate the value of great hair for a baseball player). But most importantly Shaq always had a love for the game. As I detailed in The Ninth Inning and later in The Second Inning, the balance between The Imagination Game and The Precision Game is critical for success. When I was coaching Shaq as a young RiverCat, I demanded he be more precise. I was critical of the angles he took on balls in the outfield. I was often critical of his base running reads. He needed to be more precise with some of his decisions. When Steph Kramer responded with a quote for the book, this was offered up as a response.

He mentions all the time how he learned SO MUCH from you....and he immediately said "Angles, Shaq, Angles!" - Steph Kramer

Sometimes, the skills that athletes bring to the table aren't valued in real time. Sometimes, the skills that an athlete brings to the table only reveal themselves as the survival system narrows. I think Jayson Kramer has a chance to "make it" not necessarily because he's proven that his precision skills have eclipsed his peers, rather because at its narrowest I think Jayson will still be able to smile when his peers can't. I still hold out hope that Jayson can demonstrate enough precision skills that allow his wonderful imagination a chance to "make it." I coached Jayson hard when he was a RiverCat. I suppose in my mind I always knew that if I could catch his precision up to his imagination, he could possibly be the best RiverCat of all. He had it in his genes.

Why an Umpire's Job is Impossible
How Reality and Expectation Mesh

The first tournament the RiverCats won occurred in Flemington, NJ. This is home of Diamond Nation. The name embodies the size of the complex. It's a very large complex that facilitates great competition in the Northeast. Diamond Nation has been an incredible asset for baseball development from as far north as Connecticut and as far south as Virginia. Diamond Nation's existence is a function of travel ball's explosion. Baseball's ever-growing need for efficiency (we must get better faster) and optimization (we must play better teams) is the impetus for all such mega complexes. When the 2011 RiverCats arrived at Diamond Nation for the first time, we had yet to win a tournament. We were rained out in Maryland. We were runner ups in

Delaware. The RiverCats' expectations of winning our first tournament were rather high.

The 'Cats found themselves in a semi-final game with Justin Williams on the mound and 3 more outs needed for an opportunity to play in the championship game. Justin was your classic big kid, big arm pitcher. If he could throw three (strikes) before four (balls) it was going to be a successful day. On this day Justin was flirting with 4 balls quite often but he was averting the dreaded walk. Justin was mowing them down and the 'Cats had the lead with 3 outs to go. But it was 3 outs we still needed.

I believe as the game nears its conclusion, the mind plays a trick on itself. The mind, knowing only 3 more outs are needed, claims the victory before the victory itself is claimed. In other words, the closer we get to the end of the game, the more likely we are to own the outcome before the outcome is determined. I believe this is where "choking" comes from. Psychology knows how powerful *loss aversion* is. We hate to lose things twice as much as we enjoy winning things. When you effectively "win the game" in your mind before winning the game on the field, relinquishing the result of the actual game becomes a very distinct possibility. The mind is a very powerful tool. It takes incredible fortitude to deny yourself the victory before victory itself is won.

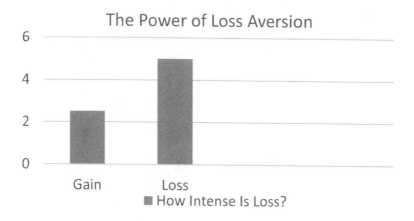

The Power of Loss Aversion

So, it was on this fateful Sunday game where Kyle Wagner's loss aversion spiked. With 3 outs to go, a ground ball was hit to Carter Christopher at 3rd base. It was a routine play and Carter made the play. He fielded it. He threw it. Nick Tomasko caught it well before the runner arrived. The runner was ruled safe.

Without having seen the actual play itself, readers are left with some possibilities to consider. 1) The umpire got the call right and my bias towards avoiding loss skewed my perspective. 2) The umpire got the call wrong and my bias towards avoiding loss was the reason I was ejected 10 seconds later. Option 2 is the reality of the situation. Of course, the reality of the situation was he may have gotten the call right (no chance) but I was definitely ejected. As the Second Inning detailed, I had an INSIDE VIEW of the situation.

The RiverCats deserved to win this game. We were the better team. We had been rained out the first weekend and had taken a runner-up the next weekend. This weekend was to be ours. I won the game in my mind before we won the game on the field. This umpire was taking what was rightfully ours. I needed to have my say when this injustice was revealed. I opened the gate by the first base dugout, and I ran onto the field. I may or may not have said to Kevin Arnold, "I'm not coming back." As I ran onto the field the first mental jab that came into my head was *How can you miss that play? These kids are 10 years old. It's not like they're running fast.* So, what came out of my mouth was "Is the 10U game too fast for you?" GONE! Apparently, umpires are offended by such comments.

The umpire of record was actually a very good umpire. He had done a nice job all game long and he was in position to make the call. I am certain this umpire didn't hold a grudge towards the RiverCats. I'm convinced that he wasn't out to get us. He simply made a bad decision. He called the runner safe when he was clearly out. This "injustice" that occurs is the reason instant replay exists. We have decided, as a society, to recruit a more optimal position with how games are being adjudicated. We have recruited technology to slow the game down. With the benefit of slow motion and even distance (off site command centers to observe emotionally unattached) we can make an accurate call. The games we love demand this. Optimal trumped efficient in our quest for the perfect game.

And so, it was on this late Sunday afternoon game. Without the ability to slow down the game, without the ability to distance myself from the emotion of the game, I attacked an umpire for merely doing his job. Of course, I was in the wrong. Of course, I make mistakes every day just like he does. Of course, my athletes messed up during the course of the game too. That is to say, none of us are perfect and mistakes are inevitable. But, the umpire will never, never, never avoid the wrath of judgment because the umpire's decision is demanded of him…**NOW**.

For most of us humans that don't wear pinstripes, the urgency of a decision isn't made among a thousand spectators. It doesn't mean these decisions are any less hard. It just means that we're not afforded the immediate feedback from the crowd or from an unforgiving coach. The rest of us humans find our feedback in the form of guilt and regret.

With the passing of time, we come to understand that mistakes were made. With the passing of time, you begin to realize that in the **NOW** I saw it one way. Later, I saw it a different way. Of course, **NOW** and later is relative. Later could be 10 minutes after getting tossed and sitting down the right field line hearing sane people talk about your incivility. Later could be 30 years from now looking back and realizing the emotion of **NOW** is what life is all about. Correcting errors is comforting because we can right our wrongs. But maybe every wrong isn't to be righted. Maybe the wrong is what makes life so right. Maybe the wrong is where our character gets tested and our ability to forgive grows. Maybe in a world designed on becoming more and more optimal in the

NOW, we'll look back in 30 years with regret and guilt that we didn't have more stories about young ambitious coaches getting tossed because he said, "Is the 10U game too fast for you?"

Life is a mystery to be enjoyed, not a riddle to be solved.

"Hey Kyle. What did you just say?"

How we experience life is never viewed in isolation. Our reality is always framed through our level of expectation. Expectation is a dynamic often influenced by events that fall below our conscious level of experience.

As Our Experiences Grow and Our Expectations Narrow
The Explore/Exploit Phenomenon

Imagine traveling to an island you've never been to before. You show up and you're in awe of your surroundings. Imagine the possibilities. I wonder what's beyond that curve in the road? I wonder what food the restaurants will serve? I wonder what the water is like? I wonder what language they speak?

Now, consider being a native on the island and this crew shows up to tour the island. You've been here for 25 years. You know through experience what most people enjoy and what has caused the most excitement. How do you communicate this? Do you tell them what to do and where to go? Or do you allow them to experience the pleasure for themselves? It's probably a combination of both but most assuredly you can't dismiss their imagination for the possibilities.

Coaching an athletic team is like being a tour guide on an exotic island. The coaches with the experience must allow the player's with high expectations to experience on their own timeline. The sole responsibility of each coach is to make sure the players love the island so much they keep coming back. The coach must adopt an island tour guide mentality. He must embrace the dream of each athlete, but he must shape each experience in the present so that it's productive.

The secret to coaching is simple. Make them dream of a better tomorrow AND train them like today is all that matters.

It's that simple. As long as the future me has a chance to be better than the present me I can tolerate today. As long as the future me has a hope for a brighter tomorrow, the sacrifice and pain of today will be worth it. The bigger, brighter you must continue to stay out of reach. The best version of yourself must remain elusive. It's the role of the coach to perpetuate this mindset. The minute the coach forgets that this is the primary objective of the coach, is the minute the present begins to grow too large at the expense of the future. This MUST be avoided at all costs for the athlete, the dreamer!

But hope is not a plan. Eventually the dreamer needs to awake from his slumber and get after it. When the time moves from thinker to doer the coach must have the ability to

1. At worst, get the athlete's attention. At best, get the athlete's intention. AND

2. Give the athlete directions to explore the island on his own (train ugly). OR

3. Build on a current experience (deliberate practice).

Not understanding how our perspectives change over time is a critical misstep for teachers and coaches alike. In fact, I would argue it is the single biggest reason that old people and young people have such a difficult time seeing eye to eye.

216

The children now love luxury; they have bad manners, contempt for authority; they show disrespect for elders and love chatter in place of exercise. Children are now tyrants, not the servants of their households. They no longer rise when elders enter the room.
- Socrates

It seems the issue of young people and old people having a different view of the world has been going on for quite some time. If seeking to understand someone else's opinion is of value, it would seem we'd all be well served to understand the idea of exploring vs. exploiting.

The other day I went to the Maple Donuts. We here that live in South Central Pennsylvania are blessed with Maple Donuts. The donuts are incredibly tasty and they're huge. Well, I walked in and a young boy and his dad stood at the counter and the worker asked the obligatory question. "Can I help you?" The Dad said, "I'll take a glazed donut and a large coffee black." The dad looked down at his son and the son was paralyzed with the choices. It really is an incredible display of amazingness. I couldn't help but think "If I was 5, this choice would be impossible." The Dad seemed incredulous that his son couldn't make a decision. "Jack, you gotta pick one." Jack's reply, although it went unnoticed by anyone else, signified the human condition that apparently has existed for all time. "How do I know which ones I won't like if I've never tried them?"

The idea of human relationships is never as simple as "fellow human being" to "fellow human being." This would be too easy. Every interaction involves some level of authority. Dads tend to outrank sons. Professors tend to outrank students. Doctors tend to outrank patients. The person with the knowledge outranks the person without the knowledge. This incompatibility of equal footing places a strain on many relationships. I suppose that's the beauty of friendship. Friends stand on equal footing. The playing field is level. I also suppose that may be the reason this quote exists in the Bible.

Now Jesus himself had pointed out that a prophet has no honor in his own country (John 4:44)

Authority in relationships cedes power to the one claiming higher ground. Without higher ground, authority can never be granted. The person on higher ground tends to know what is best because he, of course, has the knowledge the person on lower ground doesn't have. Knowledge gained becomes the undeniable variable that separates two people in the human relationship. The question that I believe is worth asking is *When is authority required?*

I believe authority is required in survival systems when risk is high.

When you need to take the beach or people die it's important to know who has authority.

When you need to make a decision, or you lose market share it's important to know who has authority.

When you need to decide when to call the timeout with 2 minutes to go in the game it's important to know who has authority.

When your plane might land in the Hudson it's important to know who has authority.

On Jan. 15, 2009, Capt. Chesley "Sully" Sullenberger became a national hero. US Airways Flight 1549 hit a flock of geese and Sully's authority and expertise allowed him to save 155 passengers. His incredible bravery and clarity of focus in the most stressful of situations became a major motion picture. Everyone loves a hero. In hindsight, every passenger on board that plane was grateful for Sully's years of training. I'm sure they were eternally grateful they had an experienced pilot and not a rookie pilot. Authority and experience can save lives. Authority and experience are invaluable when survival is at stake and risk becomes imminent.

Unfortunately, the pace of life that we're living creates artificial survival systems and it imposes unnecessary risk. Between the months of September and June, I live this all too real existence. I used to be the authority figure that believed the prize was worth competing for. I've since realized that's no longer my role to decide. Most days it breaks my heart. Some days are tolerable.

Learning (exploring) is a lifelong opportunity. The ability to learn something is never restricted so long as you have your mental faculties about you. You don't reach the age of 71 and aren't permitted to Google something. "Sorry, the googling is for anyone under the age of 42. Your googling time has expired." Learning is the primary mission of education. It's the primary reason thousands and thousands of buildings exist nationwide. They exist to help the future of our country learn something. Learning something implies that someone else has something of value for me. One person immediately takes higher ground. That person is known as the teacher. Whether that teacher exists in a survival system or a thriving system will ultimately determine the relationship that teacher has with the students. When the teacher exists in a survival system, he often is forced to become the exploiter.

Characteristic	Survival System	Thriving System
Target to hit	YES	NO
Winners/Losers	YES	NO
Time constraints	YES	NO
Narrowing of opportunity	YES	NO
Optimal path	YES	NO

When a person of authority checks any of those 5 characteristic boxes as YES, you're imposing a survival system on the people in the system. There is a time and a place for survival systems. But, many times the people in authority get distracted and exhausted and confuse a thriving system for a survival system. Here are the most common ways teachers get exhausted and distracted.

1. Grades are due Friday (Time constraints)
2. Test is Tuesday (Target to hit)
3. 100% is the goal (Optimal path)
4. Gold star for those that do well (Winner)
5. When the bell rings (Narrowing of opportunity)

In a thriving system, the person of authority would simply share the information because the person wanting the information cared enough to ask. That's the beauty of learning. When "learning" has survival system characteristics imposed upon it, it loses its most basic fundamental attributes. Rather than learning for the sake of the learner, it becomes authority's prescribed plan. There is a time for Dad to pick the right donut for the son. That time happens to be when the donuts start disappearing faster than the son can think. But, so long as the donuts aren't being threatened, the son deserves the right to make his own choice, on his own terms and experience the donut for himself.[33]

But experience has to count for something even in a thriving system. It's completely unrealistic to suggest that those without the knowledge should be able to blindly choose whatever it is they want to experience. If I've been on the island for 25 years, it's completely natural to suggest which island spots are the best places to visit. I don't think the exploring tourists would begrudge the

---

[33] Jack picked a Glazed, Chocolate Frosted

older native if he simply recommended where the best waves are found, or which restaurant served the best banana daiquiris. The strain exists when the recommendations are ignored. Any suggestion made without an opportunity to ignore, isn't a suggestion, it's a demand. Demands don't exist in thriving systems. Authority easily gets offended in thriving systems.

What's a yes mean if you can't say no?

"Hey Kyle. What did you just say?"

People with experience can be an incredible resource for those without the same experience. We can learn from those people, so long as the relationship exists under thriving system rules. The minute the system reverts to a survival system the relationship becomes hierarchical in nature. The strain on the relationship generally prevents learning from occurring.

Trust vs. Truth
The Battle Rages On

The first glove I ever received was a catcher's mitt. Harold Wagner was a catcher and my future position was inevitable. I was playing tee-ball at the time. Give some thought to the implications of that gift. When a 6-yr. old (this was back before organized baseball started at 2 years of age) receives a catcher's mitt, he doesn't consider the beauty the future position holds. He sees a reality of squatting behind a still ball and absolutely no action. It was painful at the time. But, the gift of becoming a catcher was one I wouldn't trade for the world. Constant action.

Today, the trade of catcher has become a watered-down version of the one played before the information age demanded truth. Before every pitch was scrutinized and every pitch was charted for its precision and accuracy, catchers were trusted with calling a game.

Now, the coaches that happen to have all the answers often choose "truth" over "trust." I'm actually of the position that this process is best done collaboratively between catcher and coach. The coach does have resources available to him that the catcher doesn't have. The catcher has incredible perspective that the coach doesn't have. The coach is able to distance himself from the emotion of failed at bats. There are so many "what if's" that I think the best course of action for calling a game is a fluid relationship between coach and catcher.

When I was an 18-yr. old cocky catcher, I thought I knew how to call a game. I didn't of course. I was more confident than competent. But, when Bret and I were being recruited for colleges, one of the reasons we chose Wake Forest was because they allowed their catcher to call the pitches. At the time, I preferred a coaching style of trust over truth. I was impressed that George Greer realized that allowing his catchers to develop that skill was also a responsibility of a college coach. Coach Greer placed value on trust.

Many relationships are exactly like coach and catcher. To me, it seems all of us are on a pendulum of back and forth perspectives between trust and truth. Do I interject my view of the truth? I know right from wrong and allowing for misinformation is unacceptable. Do I trust the other person to find the answer on his own time? What if he never finds the answer? What if he isn't curious enough to know what questions to ask? How will he ever navigate the rough and tumble waters of the dangerous world?

As I mentioned in The Second Inning, it often is simply one person's "Who Cares?" vs. another person's "It's a Big Deal!" More and more it seems we have less "who cares" and more "it's a big deal." When everywhere you turn, someone is telling you what to believe and what is the truth, of course trust takes a hit. Trusting other people to find the information out on their terms and their timeline takes incredible patience and perspective. If sharing the truth becomes more important than trusting another human being, it probably means you're in a survival system (real or imagined) and the stakes are high (real or imagined).

"Thanks Wags"
Bobby Whalen and Jayson Kramer

Rivalry is what makes sports so compelling. Without Duke, what's North Carolina? Without Ohio St, what's Michigan? In South Central Pennsylvania, Cedar Cliff and Cumberland Valley are rivals to Red Land. All 3 schools compete in the Mid Penn Commonwealth Division. It's one of the better baseball conferences in the state of Pennsylvania. In 2018, Red Land won the Commonwealth Division. In 2018, Cedar Cliff beat Red Land 2 out of 3 games played. In 2018, Red Land swept Cumberland Valley, yet Cumberland Valley won the District Championship. All of that to say all 3 teams were really good at baseball. Bobby Whalen hit leadoff for Cedar Cliff. Jayson Kramer hit leadoff for Cumberland Valley.

As I mentioned in the GoWags Developmental League, teammates are a powerful force. Teammates can motivate and teammates give meaning to competition. If it wasn't for the fact that Bobby and Shaq wore different colored uniforms, I'd want to hug them when I saw them. The fact that they had Colts and Eagles splashed across their chest made me want to beat them, of course. That's the nature of every survival system. Survival systems aren't designed for empathy and curiosity. Survival systems are designed for imposing your will on the competition. And that's the way it was in 2018 for a bunch of former RiverCats. They wanted to beat Red Land as badly as Red Land wanted to beat them. If Bobby or Shaq even admitted that Kyle Wagner in the other dugout was extra motivation, I would have agreed with them.

Luke Wagner was Red Land's ace. He won The Patriot News Player of the Year in 2018. He had an incredibly good year and Red Land's hopes generally rested on the back of Luke. In the district semi-finals Red Land and Cedar Cliff would face off in round 3 of their yearly backyard brawl. Red Land held a 2-0 lead when Bobby Whalen laced a triple down into the left field corner off of Luke. Aaron Walter (Red Land Assistant Coach) could only muster these words, "Thanks Wags," implying I had some role in the triple.

Luke had great success against the Cumberland Valley lineup ever since he was a Freshman. As a matter of fact, I believe Luke is 4-0 against the Eagles. The 4 wins were against a very deep and talented lineup. Drew Baughman (a former GoWags player and current Liberty University standout) and Justin Williams comprised the heart of that order. Luke didn't do too badly against those guys. But Shaq? Shaq was like 14-16 with 13 doubles. Needless to say, Jayson Kramer owned Luke and he owned Red Land. Aaron Walter would calmly say "Thanks Wags."

Competitive grit is a characteristic of all great athletes. When the stakes get higher, the pressure produces a heightened focus that produces clarity. While lesser competitors succumb to the fog of tension and pressure, the great competitors allow the tension to narrow their focus on the things that really matter. Results get lost and process remains. The great competitors find incredible satisfaction in the meticulous nature of their execution. They see distraction where others see value. The great competitors are incredible minimalists. They find a way to see what only matters.

When Bobby Whalen's legacy is written it'll be written in ink. His indelible legacy will be remembered as Dan Law envisioned years ago. Bobby Whalen competes. He's competed on the gridiron, on the basketball court, on the wrestling mat, in the hallways of Cedar Cliff, on the baseball field and in life. Bobby always finds a way to win. It's what I love about Bobby. It's what made the RiverCats whole when he joined our team. To beat Bobby, you had to match his clarity of focus. This wasn't an easy task. Bobby beat you more than you beat him. I loved him as a RiverCat, not so much as a Cedar Cliff Colt. Bobby Whalen will be attending and competing for the University of Louisville in the spring of 2020. I'll be extremely grateful that my relationship can again resume the role of admirer. Competing against Bobby has been gratifying, but it's been exhausting.

Jayson Kramer will be attending Patrick Henry Junior College in Martinsville, Va. Far too many athletes live and die with the prestige that Division 1 baseball presents. It's often an illusion offered up by people that gain control in The Precision Game. Baseball isn't owned by anyone. There is incredible baseball played at the Division III level, the Division II level and certainly Junior College baseball. Jayson's best baseball, as I've mentioned before, lies in front of him. My hope is he continues to play for coaches that can coax The Precision Game out of him. Shaq can swing it and he's always had a penchant for seeing the game from a beginner's mindset. Time will tell how and when Shaq says goodbye to the game. If he's anything like Barry Houser, he'll leave the game with grace and dignity. If he's anything like Barry Houser he'll be playing the game for a very long time.

Bobby and Shaq have challenged me. For five years they were regulars in my outfield. For the last four years they've been regulars in someone else's outfield. I always trained them to hope for a better tomorrow. I guess when you play the "long game," tomorrow might end up in the other dugout. Bobby and Shaq always saw me as authority. Never once did Bobby question the manner in which I coached him. Never once did Shaq fire back at me during one of my precision tirades. Bobby and Shaq knew that the game narrowed as you survived. They trusted me to help them navigate the narrows. I trusted that they'd listen, and they'd learn on their terms, on their time. I see ya workin' Bobby and Shaq.

Bobby Whalen

Jayson Kramer

In the Clubhouse
Culture Starts at Home

The idea of family is unrealistic in survival systems. Whenever a goal exists, even a superficial goal like winning baseball games, people are often a casualty of ambition. The political level of WHY always trumps the theatrical level of WHO. Teams aren't formed to pick strawberries. This is why the role of the Head Coach is never an envious position. The Head Coach in a travel organization acts from a political position. He must always keep the mission in perspective and make decisions in accordance with the mission. In a business, this means sometimes people lose their job. In a school, this means sometimes students get expelled. On a travel baseball team, this means sometimes players don't get to play. Families are supposed to love unconditionally. Families don't just exist during prosperous times; they support each other during difficult times. Survival systems and family are completely incompatible. Yet, the fact remains that on the outside and even on the inside The RiverCats felt like a family.

Just something different about the RiverCats that you couldn't really find many other places. How the coaches coached, how the players not only played but how they came together as a team. The RiverCats weren't just a national caliber travel team they were a family. Growing up in the Northeast you didn't really see a lot of talented teams like the RiverCats, playing against them was always a welcome pleasure whatever the outcome would be because it was real baseball. - Karen Singh (Gallagher Travel Baseball)

Ambition is such a dangerous notion. The need to achieve can feel so rewarding. The allure of finishing a task. The pleasure of finishing a book. The need to finish a conversation (get the last word in). Ambition is certainly pleasurable, but ambition without gratitude often makes for a lonely life. As a I reflect on the RiverCats and the years we spent together the best I can make of our time together was a mutual understanding of ambitious gratitude. The respect that the coaches had for the personal goals of each family. The respect the families had for the role of Coach in communicating an authentic message necessary in a survival system.

Culture Eats Strategy for Breakfast. - Peter Drucker

The RiverCats family didn't exist without some struggle and tension. That's true of all families. Painting the RiverCats story solely through a rose-colored lens would be disingenuous. I certainly wasn't privy to the conversations that took place behind closed doors. I could be completely off base here but I'm willing to bet the RiverCats parents supported and echoed the messages offered up through the lessons learned by being a RiverCat. This tug-o-war that often exists in the lives of athletes can be the single biggest reason true growth never occurs. There's a coaching cliché' that speaks to this idea. *Many games are lost at the dining room table.* Rather than face the doubt and uncertainty that comes with growth, many families jump to denial and blame that lives with comfort and certainty. Parents sabotage the team goals by creating false hope in the eyes of their athlete. For the RiverCats, it was clear to me that parent and coach were pulling the same direction on the rope.[34]

Some of the relationships that I appreciated the most were ones that ended too early. The RiverCats were designed for the "long game." As Head Coach I had one eye on developing our guys to the best of their abilities and one eye on the future model of the 'Cats. I realized the likelihood of all our original 10U players wanting to play college baseball was remote. Nonetheless, I threw the kitchen sink at all of them. I wanted my guys to sort what information was relevant and what wasn't relevant. Some of the

---

[34] If I was being completely honest, the most important parent is probably mom. Whereas dads tend to understand competition with their son, moms tend to be nurturing, caring and often protective. The RiverCat moms never once protected their sons from my message. At least, from what I can tell.

'Cats that might not play college baseball might have coaching in their future. The game of baseball offers opportunities when you sometimes least expect it.

Kevin Arnold was an assistant coach on the early RiverCats teams. He was a smart baseball man. His son, Avery, would find his future on the ice. He went by the name of "Scooter." Scooter could have been a very good baseball player. I don't think the game was fast enough for him. Scooter can....scoot on the ice. Scooter's time on the 'Cats was short lived but his time in the GoWags organization extended into the Expos and the LumberKings. Scooter was actually an age younger than many of the 'Cats. His baseball would end in the Imagination Game.

Tommy Reilly would find his future on the links and in the classroom. His Dad had a smooth golf swing and Tommy's baseball swing always had a golf look to it. My fondest memory of Tommy was his display at Myrtle Beach when he displaced some very talented baseball players to claim the #2 spot in the lineup, for the entire week. Tommy was a fierce competitor that always accepted and appreciated the kitchen sink that was thrown at him.

Nick Tomasko would find his future in many athletic arenas but ultimately the classroom. Nick Tomasko had the ability to play for the 'Cats longer than I probably permitted. I had a hard time saying good-bye to the Tomasko family. The need for pitching and weekend expenses forced me into the hard reality that Nick's future with the RiverCats would be short lived. If the Tomasko's thought they were wronged, I never heard them voice their discontent.

Chris Dare was a very good baseball player. Chris Dare was also a very good football player. Chris' love for football eventually won out. But the kid we called "Smooth" could have been a very smooth, slick fielding shortstop if he was interested in playing the "long game." Chris' "long game" will end up on the sidelines of Bloomsburg University where he'll be playing football.

Joseph Matter was one funny kid. If I ever wanted to smile, Joseph was my guy. I can't look at that face without thinking "stir fry Luke Wagner."[35] Like Scooter, Joseph was actually an age younger than the RiverCats. His time with the GoWags organization would eventually be spent more with the Expos and LumberKings. Joseph's charming personality will most assuredly serve him well in his Long Game.

Winning baseball games in the lives of 10-15 yr. old boys was a very big deal. It created authentic pride in their lives. Posting the obligatory championship team photo was a gesture all young baseball players make. It was validating. It said *I'm a part of something bigger than me.* The boys loved the championship photos. The families loved the hope and promise that their son was moving in the direction of their goals. But, more important than the goals, was always the understanding that a RiverCat was a boy first and foremost. The playing component was important. It's satisfying knowing you're a winner. But what I found so heart-warming was the development the 'Cats had off the field too.

Cancer sucks. Many of the RiverCats were dealt this slap in the face reality because they played with Tayven Kelley. Tayven was on our original team. He was a member of the 10U GoWags RiverCats. Tayven's sister Heaven developed brain cancer that first year while Tayven played with the RiverCats. Cancer not only strips families of their hopes and dreams, but it strains relationships too. You'd have to ask the Kelley family if having the RiverCats in their lives made their suffering any easier. Only they could answer that. But, on the outside it was simply awe

---

[35] In the barracks at Cooperstown, NY, Joseph went into a hilarious monologue about the flexibility that stir fry presents.

inspiring to watch Julie Payne, Rick Payne, Lisa Maring, Glenda Arnold, Mandy Whalen, Heather Wagner, Kyle Nornhold and all the RiverCats embrace the Kelley family. In times of great despair, people join forces to do whatever they can. I remember observing Haircuts for Heaven[36] and Hits for Heaven[37] with a detached wonder almost. I couldn't believe the depth of care and compassion these families were showing for Heaven and the Kelley's. Still to this day, the Hits for Heaven event is one of my all-time favorite gatherings of people. I hope Heaven knew how many people showed up to honor her and love her.

Little boys aren't meant to deal with big life problems. They're supposed to spend their days playing baseball. Their biggest worries are supposed to be why they're not playing as much as they'd like. Unfortunately, that wasn't the life Tayven Kelley was dealt. Tayven was born with

ability but Tayven Kelley was a raw baseball player. In order for Tayven to improve, he needed to practice and play with good players as often as possible. Cancer prevented that from happening. Tayven's first year with the RiverCats would be cut short but it provided one memory I'll never forget.

The Payne's and the Kelley's developed a great relationship through this awful life experience. Tayven Kelley and Jared Payne spent a lot of time together at the Payne house. One such interaction gifted Tayven with a baseball glove called "Shoeless Joe Jackson." It was a glove Jared had but it wasn't a glove Jared used. It was probably something Jared received at one point, but it took a back seat to the premier gloves Rawlings or Wilson carried in their line. Tayven fell in love with the novelty of the glove. It

---

[36] A fundraiser and show of support for Heaven as she began her chemotherapy.
[37] A fundraiser and birthday party to say "we love you" as Heaven's condition worsened.

wasn't a bad glove, it just wasn't "game ready." But, 10-yr. old Tayven loved his new glove.

The Ripken Complex in Aberdeen, MD is awe inspiring. The first time you walk on that complex you can't help but develop a sense of wonder about the love that the Ripken's must have for youth baseball to build such a complex. The jewel of the complex is dedicated to Cal Ripken, Sr. In his memory, this field represents the beauty of the game. This field is where they play the championship games at the Ripken Complex.

The RiverCats played Piedmont in a semi-final game at Cal Sr's field. Finals were becoming a common occurrence for the 'Cats. The semi-finals were supposed to be a formality. Let's hurry up and get this game over with so we can win our prize. Piedmont wasn't so accommodating.

Luke Wagner is an incredible pitcher. 9-yr. old Luke was a very good pitcher. 9-yr. old Luke got eaten alive by the 10u Piedmont team. Luke didn't make it out of the first inning. Jimmy Losh came in to pitch as it seemed very unlikely that we would need his services for the championship game. The score was 6-0 Piedmont after 1. In the dugout after I pulled him, Luke said "Dad, if we make the championship game, can I pitch?" Ever, the RiverCat optimist.

The score would grow to 10-3 after 5. The outcome seemed inevitable. With only 3 more outs to play on defense, in what I thought would be a meaningless bottom of the 5th, I told Tayven, "go play left." He and Shoeless Joe went sprinting to left field.

In the bottom of the 5th, wouldn't you know it, but a line shot was hit in Tayven's direction. We were losing 10-3 and it appeared Piedmont would be adding to that lead as the ball was rocketed down the left field line. At this point in the game, I had resigned myself to the fact that we would lose the game. The score was the only question to be answered. Tayven dove and caught the ball. He caught the ball with the Shoeless Joe Jackson glove. In a game!! I laughed out loud. I remember thinking. "Good for him. At least, that's something we can smile about." The RiverCats had 3 more outs to play with and then Piedmont would take our place in the finals.

The reality of a comeback is you never want to get your hopes up. The loss is painful to bear but when you're down by 7 runs with only 3 outs to go, you begin to settle on the reality of the early ride home. Mentally, you check out and learn to live with the new reality. Allowing for a comeback can be unsettling. Is it worth it to raise your expectations? When we cut the lead to 5, I was thinking "Nice. Our kids aren't going quietly." When we cut it to 3, Piedmont started to panic. That's when I thought, "This is going to get very interesting." When Chris Dare stepped to the plate with the go ahead run on 1st base I said, "Ah, what the heck Smooth, you might as well give us the lead." Triple down the line! The comeback was complete. The RiverCats would win bigger games down the road. The RiverCats would never overcome a bigger deficit with so little time.[38]

We Call Him "Magic"
Adam Maring

We call him "Magic." He wore #32. The connection to Magic Johnson for me was easy. The RiverCats simply followed suit. Adam Maring would be called Magic. It was a fitting name for a player of Adam's ability.

---

[38] Luke started the championship game.

235

Adam wasn't an original RiverCat. I found him at a GoWags
Christmas camp. Adam could do the "ball drop"[39] drill better than
anyone at the camp. Adam ran the fastest time at the camp.
Adam's glove skills were off the charts. Adam would play for the
RiverCats as an 11u player. As a 12u player, Adam was arguably
our most valuable player.

The RiverCats played an early tournament in Richmond, VA.
Driving 4 hours south was a convenient excuse to get away from
the brutal Pennsylvania early spring weather. This tournament was
a unique format. The format wasn't a typical play your Saturday
games and compete for something on Sunday. This tournament
demanded you play well from the beginning. The entire field was
strong. On Saturday night, we drew the local favorite. We had
won our pool, but we faced a very strong Tidewater Drillers team.
I knew they were every bit our equal when we tossed the coin to
see who the home team would be. They won the toss and called
"Visitors." That was our thing.

Calling "visitors" guaranteed you that 5th at bat if you mercy ruled
the other team. If you thought the other team would play you
tough, choosing the home side is always the preferred option.
They called "visitors" and I remember thinking *Here We Go!!!*
I'm sure I huddled the 'Cats together and offered up something to
the effect of "We're the home team because they didn't respect us
enough to choose home. We're playing in their backyard with
their umpires. Now listen to me. Emotion won't win this game.
Execution will. Adam's got the ball. They're gonna have a heck
of a time with Adam under these lights. It'll be equally as hard on
us. Play great defense and let's compete. Full reps on 3."[40] Adam
struck out the side.

---

[39] The ball drop drill allows gravity to simulate velocity. It's become a popular
way to measure a hitter's reactive ability.
[40] Full reps is a phrase coined by Bob Gorinski in describing my nephew
through marriage, Kyle Ford. Kyle died unexpectedly New Year's Eve when he

The only problem was, their guy was every bit Adam's equal. This would be one for the ages. In the third inning, Anthony Volpe left the game with a suspected broken arm. A collision at second base got tensions a little high. Anthony would be fine, but Coach Kyle started playing the emotion game despite urging the boys not to. Despite no hits being allowed through 5 innings, we held a 1-0 lead thanks to great base running by Luke.[41] He made a great read on a dirtball to put us up 1-0. We were hoping it would stand.

In the bottom of the 5th, still with no hits allowed, a lead-off walk brought Luke Wagner to the plate. Luke smoked the first hit of the game into the right center gap. Nick Embleton followed with his own triple. When the dust cleared the Cats beat the Drillers 8-0 by mercy rule. Adam Maring threw a no hitter.

Adam Maring was a special piece to the RiverCats. The Maring family was a special piece to the RiverCat family. Adam Maring doesn't have aspirations to play baseball in college. Such is life. Make no mistake, for 2 or 3 years, the RiverCats were as special of a team that existed in the Northeast, maybe even the entire East Coast. Adam Maring hit 3rd on the team. Adam Maring was a special baseball player.

Sharing My Art

was only 15. Bob said "He didn't know him well but he always gave full reps when he lifted." Our teams all broke the huddle with full reps.

[41] Earlier that day, I had really let Luke have it when he demonstrated some lousy base running. Luke was a runner at 1st with the bases loaded. He took off to second on an anticipated passed ball. The lead runners never moved. His head was down and it took us completely out of the inning. We ended up losing that game but won our pool.

Make Bold Mistakes

I was 28 years old when Heather gave birth to Luke. Luke is closing in on 18. That means he's closer to being a dad than when he started playing baseball. That thought shakes me to the core. Writing this book was an unselfish act in that I wanted the stories of those that meant so much to me to be written. I hope I portrayed them in a good light. Yet, writing this book was a selfish act as well. I have some beliefs about how our world falls short in serving our youth. If I made some of my points articulately, I will have challenged some pre-existing viewpoints. I haven't always believed what I currently believe. My current position has evolved through lots and lots of reading and even more reflecting. If pain is the greatest teacher, I've been shaped through the pain of coaching and teaching.

Coaching baseball is such a rewarding vocation because, for the most part, the kids want to be there. They show up with an excitement and a spirit of wanting to get better. The coach is entrusted to help them improve. My greatest desire for my players is they enjoy the game in the present. Playing the game of baseball is such a fleeting opportunity. I fear in today's obsessed specialization and precision culture the game is moving towards less imagination and less dreaming. That's the foundation of the game. Great players have great imaginations. I know the game is hard. I know the game narrows in a survival system. I know that very few baseball players exit the survival system on their own terms. I realize that. That's where precision is required.

The game of baseball isn't owned by anyone and the game of baseball doesn't owe anyone.

I see baseball player after baseball player honing their craft. I commend them for their detailed manner in which they're acquiring precision. My hope is they're doing this for all the right reasons. No one owns the "truth." The game of baseball has been around since the 1800's. Smart people have been on this planet long before the current crop of smart people. Of course, we've made technological advances and we know more now than we've ever known. My point is everyone claiming the "truth" is going to claim it from an INSIDE VIEW, not the athletes view. No one will ever discover the "truth" because the truth of the matter is the game of baseball is a game. Games, by their very nature, are meant to be played not perfected. Games are meant to be explored and the nature of the exploration is meant to be seen from an artist's perspective, not a scientist.

Money can influence our perspective on things. Earning money is addictive. There are a lot of people that have a self-serving perspective in this game because their INSIDE VIEW makes them money. That's the beauty of capitalism. If you can get someone's attention enough to buy what it is your selling than have at it. There are consequences though to giving yourself entirely to someone else's product. Dreaming and imagination often disappear in the face of execution and precision. It's a dangerous path. It's a dangerous path because achievement feels so good. Execution and precision often trump dreaming and imagination in the short game. If you have bought into execution and precision, I sincerely hope you haven't entirely lost your imagination. You'll need it when the game beats you down and the precision of 0-25 is staring you in the face. Imagination's greatest gift might not be in imagining the greatness that is yet to be. Its greatest gift might be in imagining the greatness that once was.

The beginner's mindset isn't a mindset to be lost through years and years of experience and knowledge. The beginner's mindset is the mindset that doubts all that it has learned because it knows the limitations of experience. One man's opinion, albeit your personal opinion, is still just one man. Maybe wisdom comes when one man can distance what it is, he experiences with what is reality... I actually said this one time to Luke.

We were training for a tournament in Jupiter, Florida. Jupiter is home to the largest amateur baseball event I have ever seen. Golf carts line the perimeter watching the next wave of prospects. Luke and I were training for velocity. I was throwing him balls at a fairly quick pace from close range. They were light baseballs and they were "rising" a little. That's the path I wanted. I didn't want the ball to fall as fast as a normal 5 oz. baseball falls. Luke, like every hitter, was missing under the ball. No one ever misses elite velocity above the ball. I told him, "Luke, you have to doubt your eyes. You have to hit with the mistrust that everything you have seen to this point has been a deception. The ball will be traveling faster than you have yet to experience. Where your brain thinks it will end up isn't where it actually will end up. You have to betray your eyes and set your sights higher." Holy smokes. I literally stopped like I tend to do now. I said "Luke, did you hear that? That might be life's greatest lesson. Betray your eyes." He said "Here we go again dad. Can you just throw me the ball?"

The pain of coaching has taught me that Danny Kahneman, author of *Thinking Fast and Thinking Slow,* is exactly right when he said *what you see is all there is.* But it doesn't have to be if you can keep your imagination alive and active. The survival system of baseball cuts people up in the end because the players are led to believe it's a Precision Game owned by those that have the "truth." They don't have the "truth." They just have experience on their side from an INSIDE VIEW.

When I was 23 years old there was nothing, I wanted more than to be a Major League baseball player. That's not true. At 23, I wanted nothing more than to not be attached to the game of baseball. I had experienced entirely too much pain from the game. At the age of 7, 11, 14, and 19 there was nothing I wanted more. As I aged, I lost my beginner's mindset in the face of precision. I couldn't hit enough. My belief was I needed to improve my swing. Maybe the answer was there all along. Maybe Mike Martin gave me the answer and I hadn't realized it yet. Maybe he was giving me a similar life lesson like I gave Luke. Maybe his message was simply "Stop spending so much time on what's not right about your game and start appreciating what is right about your game." I don't know if Kyle Wagner, circa 1994, could have made the life altering perspective change. I see it now though. I hope I can relay that message to the players I coach.

My perspective has changed in more than just the game I love and coach. It's changed in the profession I've chosen. I've been the authority (teacher) in public education since 2000. This is year number 19. For the most part, the people that show up in my presence don't want to be there. I've taught ambitious students. I've taught apathetic students. I've taught competitive students. I've taught disconnected students. I've taught them all. The Intentional student is a very rare exception. Maybe it's because I haven't been a good enough teacher to get their full and complete buy in. Maybe others in the profession have had better luck than me. My instinct is very few teachers have been able to get students to walk through that Intentional Door.

The system of school has led us to believe that learning takes place between the hours of 7:30am and 3pm. The system of school has led us to believe that learning takes place between the months of September and June. That's when learning happens. Those are times when students ask me questions. I have never had a student see me in July and say "Mr. Wagner, the idea of hypotheses testing. I've been thinking. Do you think you and I could test the hypothesis that ice cream in a donut would be a huge success? How large a sample would we need?" The only time I get sincere learning questions is when we assign a number to the answer. That's the equivalent of a hitter suggesting, I don't want to take any swings unless it affects my batting average. Otherwise, I'm not interested in the reps.

I haven't always thought this way. For the longest time, I trusted my eyes. I believed that students needed the information that I possessed. They might not need it now, but they needed it to play the "long game." I'm not even sure that was ever true. The truth was, they needed the information to play "my game." I was in control. I had the knowledge and therefore I was the authority. I had the higher ground and I was going to motivate them by managing the grade book.

What's a Yes Mean if You Can't Say No?

2019 is a great time to be alive. It's never been easier to learn something. The barriers for learning have been removed. Time is frictionless. Distance is merely a computer screen, smart phone away. If you want to turn information into intelligence you can do that whenever you want. You can even do it in July if you'd like. 2019 is the easiest it's ever been to learn something but it's the hardest time to be a student.

The quality of one's life is often judged by the amount of time that you claim as your own. In many respects, it is why adults hate working for someone else. If our time on earth here is precious, many people are entitled to claim that time as their own. It reminds me of a parable of the Mexican fisherman.

An American businessman was standing at the pier of a small coastal Mexican village when a small boat with just one fisherman docked. Inside the small boat were several large yellowfin tuna. The American complimented the Mexican on the quality of his fish. "How long did it take you to catch them?" The American asked. "Only a little while." The Mexican replied. "Why don't you stay out longer and catch more fish?" The American then asked. "I have enough to support my family's immediate needs." The Mexican said. "But," The American then asked, "What do you do with the rest of your time?" The Mexican fisherman said, "I sleep late, fish a little, play with my children, take a siesta with my wife, Maria, stroll into the village each evening where I sip wine and play guitar with my amigos. I have a full and busy life, senor."

*The American scoffed, "I am a Harvard MBA and could help you.
You should spend more time fishing and with the proceeds you
could buy a bigger boat, and with the proceeds from the bigger
boat you could buy several boats, and eventually you would have a
fleet of fishing boats."*
*"Instead of selling your catch to a middleman you would sell
directly to the consumers, eventually opening your own can
factory. You would control the product, processing and
distribution. You would need to leave this small coastal fishing
village and move to Mexico City, then LA and eventually NYC
where you will run your expanding enterprise."*
*The Mexican fisherman asked, "But senor, how long will this all
take?"*
To which the American replied, "15-20 years."
"But what then, senor?"
*The American laughed and said, "That's the best part. When the
time is right you would announce an IPO and sell your company
stock to the public and become very rich, you would make
millions."*
"Millions, senor? Then what?"
*The American said slowly, "Then you would retire. Move to a
small coastal fishing village where you would sleep late, fish a
little, play with your kids, take a siesta with your wife, stroll to the
village in the evenings where you could sip wine and play your
guitar with your amigos…"*

I'm not suggesting this parable is a model school should enlist.
That's actually preposterous. School is designed to provide
opportunities for young people. Opportunities require much
struggle and growth. What I am suggesting, however, is the
incentive of claiming time as your own is born into all of us. What
I am also suggesting is the American in the parable is overstepping
his bounds by imposing his view on the Mexican fisherman.

The world is changing faster than ever. Technology has created
this. Predicting the landscape our High School students will be
working in is impossible. The greatest asset we can give our

students is an intact imagination to challenge convention. The world demands more questions. The answers will be found through technology. Questions live in the world where imagination flourishes. Questions evolve from the tolerance of another perspective, to the curiosity of what might be and eventually into the freedom and courage to challenge the status quo.

Here's where the breakdown lives in the daily interaction of what we see as school. School is a survival system. It checks all the boxes. Moving from Kindergarten to Graduation Day has expectations associated with it. Teams have been formed to assist the student in meeting that goal. As in every team, there exists a political, strategic, theatrical and tactical level of implementation. The disconnect is obvious when you realize the habit loops that each of them run. At each level of the school system, THE INSIDE VIEW has been adopted and the routine of chasing the reward has trickled down into a burden on the students. The glossed over look in the eyes of so many students screams "Is it over yet?"

At the political level, education is seen as achievement. To this end, the best way to assess whether the people in the system have achieved is to measure them. Standardized tests make all the sense in the world when people are seen as products and achievement is seen as success. Quality control demands precision. Minimize errors and test the product.

At the strategic level, education is seen as a process. Develop the necessary skills that will serve them upon graduation. Enlist qualified, trained professionals to teach them these necessary skills. Demand rigor as rigor is what is needed in the real world. The students might not appreciate the value of what they're learning now but over time they'll appreciate the doors that opened because that high standard was set.

At the theatrical level, education is seen through relationships. The teachers and the students interact on a daily basis. Teachers set the pace. Teachers use feedback to evaluate the process the strategic level set in motion. The teachers use a grading method to evaluate correct from incorrect. At the theatrical level, the teacher dispenses the information. Because the theatrical level involves people, opinions are formed emotionally. Teachers that provide equitable pacing and just grading are seen as compassionate. Teachers that provide stricter pacing and unjust grading are seen as oppressive.

At the tactical level, education is seen as a social experience wrapped in competition. The political demands of testing minimize the student's ability to ask more questions and think creatively. The strategic demands of process minimize the student's choice. Optimization and efficiency trump adaptability and struggle. The theatrical level erodes into a power play of giving the person in authority what it is they demand. At the tactical level, the student is left questioning simply "When will I get my time back?"

"Hey Kyle. What did you just say?"

Our eyes deceive us. By solely relying on what it is we see, we're often duped into relying on our experiences and our expectations to guide us.

Strong Opinions Loosely Held
Stick In The Mud

Years ago, when Heather and I were married without children, we went to a place called Rod's Roadhouse. Heather liked to dance. Kevin Troup, a childhood friend and Wake Forest roommate, came up from Florida to visit. I hadn't seen Kevin in a while. It was an opportunity to catch up. Heather, Sarah (Kevin's wife), Kevin and I grabbed a booth and ordered some food and drinks. After dinner,

Heather and Sarah went on the dance floor. Kevin and I weren't
exactly dancers so we begged out so we could catch up and chat.
The girls said they understood. Five minutes later, an older
woman reached over her booth and tapped Kevin and I on the
shoulder. She offered this suggestion. "You two guys need to go
out and dance with those girls." Kevin and I came up with some
excuse about catching up and we're not dancers. She looked at us
in disbelief and replied, "You're a Stick In The Mud."

There's this crazy phenomenon that I notice as I get older and
think about relationships. When someone laughs, I tend to laugh.
When someone cries, I tend to cry. The people in our lives affect
us in ways we can never even imagine. Psychologists call this trait
"mirror neurons." The human condition wants to mirror those it
sees. It learns how to emote through imitation. Imagine how
important the people in your life are if you tend to mirror their
emotions. Imagine how incredible the character trait of tolerance
and curiosity is if you can't control your environment. I'd argue
that curiosity is the one great superpower that anyone can tap into.
It's a game changer. It's not easy to be curious though. It's much
easier to be certain.

One of the reasons people tend to be so certain is they're so
competitive. Survival systems demand certainty. Yes or No.
Optimal or Sub-optimal. The funnel narrows. Time is running
out. This elicits happiness or anger emotions. I see it in myself
every time I enter survival systems. But, going to the grocery store
doesn't have to be a survival system. Going to breakfast with the
family doesn't have to be a survival system. Spending time at
school doesn't have to be a survival system. Survival systems are
very dangerous. Not because they declare a winner, but rather
because they create a winner's mindset when one isn't required.

My favorite time of the year, shocking as it may seem, is
Thanksgiving. The entire country stops and gives thanks. We
slow down. We gather around those that mean so much to us and
for one day we stop competing. The next day we amp our juices

back up again but for one day we let those mirror neurons fire with displays of gratitude and love. To me, it's undeniable how the occasion affects so many subconsciously.

So, it seems we're left with a choice. Dive into a survival system upon waking up and compete with everyone around you. Or, wake up and reflect before diving. Is there a prize worth chasing? Is winning the prize more important than the people I interact with? Is "winning the day" a phrase based upon ambition or gratitude? How you answer those questions matter.

The fact that I remember being called a "stick in the mud" twenty years later means it impacted me. I laughed at the time, but it probably resonated enough to know there was an ounce of truth to her jab. The "stick" component is irrelevant. The "mud" component implies certainty. Certainty scares me now. I try to be certain of less and less. I try and be curious instead. That doesn't mean I like dancing in public, but I've realized that most of my dislikes center mostly around fear of losing. I have competition hardwired into my being. Once I realize there isn't a prize to be won and I'm not competing, the stick isn't so much stuck as it is loosely placed in the mud. That's where I think I am right now. I think I've become a "stick in the sand."

Oh, but Kyle, "If you don't stand for something, you'll fall for anything." Love it. I agree with it. The values we hold dear are meant to be cemented into the fabric of our lives. I hope Luke and Grace someday never stop loving the country that has seen so many patriots give their life to it. I hope Luke and Grace find value in respecting everyone and fearing no one. There are thousands and thousands of values to hold onto with the firmest of grasps. But, far too often we're confusing beliefs and opinions as values. The only thing that does is limit curiosity. I'm not playing that game anymore. The prizes to be won are merely superficial rewards named ego, hubris, power and control. I'd rather entertain the notion that if a better outcome is what I'm after, reflecting curiosity in my position might actually get the other person to reflect curiosity back at me with those mirror neurons.

The Phase Shifts of Life
Balancing Competition and Compassion

I don't always want to be a coach. I don't always want to be a teacher. At some point, I'm sure I'll watch others coach and teach. If I've done my job well, some of those coaches and teachers will be people I've influenced on my journey. When that time comes, I'll no longer have an INSIDE VIEW of competition and education. In writing this book, I felt an urgency while I still maintained my current view. I'm sure my urgency had a lot to do with my son being a Junior and my daughter being an 8th grader. If my window is closing, I owed it to the 'Cats and my students to express some of my perspectives.

How The RiverCats Won is a story told about the people that lived it. *How The RiverCats Won* is a bigger ideal that can be woven into the lives of those that didn't live it. The RiverCat families were special people. But, truly, they're no more special than anyone. Value is placed through a very individual lens. The RiverCat families are special to me. I hope you enjoyed their stories. But I hope you found value in the message that each inning shared.

The people that enter your life can either be seen as an ally or an adversary for achievement. If you're in a survival system, that's called competition. The people in the other dugout aren't there to build your self-esteem. But life isn't always a survival system. When the constraints are removed and there are no longer prizes to be won, the true beauty of life are the people in our lives. The irony of my situation occurred to me about a year ago. Bret and I were talking, and I said, "The funny thing is, it took my insanely competitive nature to realize that the root of most of our problems is competition."

A couple months ago, Heather asked me to run down to the local convenience store to grab a bag of ice. I drove down, walked inside, paid for the bag of ice and left. I never grabbed the ice. I walked in the front door and Heather said, "Thanks for the ice Kyle." "Shoot." I turned around and drove back down to the store to grab the ice I paid for. I walked in the convenience store bought a coffee and left without the ice. I got home and Heather said, "Sorry you had to run again." "Shoot" I drove down and finally grabbed the bag of ice that I had paid for two trips prior. There are times when I think too much. Heather would say "You're always distracted." I reply, "I'm always thinking." It has its advantages and its disadvantages.

Empathy for others is often tyranny for yourself.

I honestly believe one of the greatest gifts we can give ourselves is time alone and time to think. The future belongs to those people that can make connections. You don't always need to come up with a new idea. You simply need to be able to connect ideas others have already shared. But, allowing other's ideas to fester can be painful indeed. The easier play is to fight back. That's where confidence lives. The more noble play is to allow for doubt. That's where competence lives.

I'm not sure what phase will come next. But I do know I'll be on the lookout for those artificial finish lines that deceive us into thinking we've actually achieved something. I'll certainly be on the lookout for the fool's gold that claims itself as a prize worth accepting. And, I'll be hesitant to jump into systems that masquerade as competition at all.

Life is Hard
We Make it Harder

Imagine looking down on all of us. Imagine looking down and seeing us conduct the business of our daily lives. From 20,000 feet above it seems so useless. From 10 feet in front of us it seems so important. The things we face in the NOW are to be experienced. This is life. *Be where your feet are* seems to address the idea that we're always worrying about the future and we're always regretting the past. *Be where your feet are* is a cliché way of saying "if your mind is elsewhere, life is going to pass you by." The people that you interact with on a daily basis give meaning to life. The people that are 10 feet away are your life. Those people cause you pain. Those people give you joy. Those people are the people that occupy your conscious thoughts. Those are the people you dream with and fight with. Those are the people that you call when life breaks your way and those are the people that will break your heart. The people in our lives create intense emotion. The people in our lives motivate us to do great things and the people in our lives can hurt us emotionally to the core. Life is lived 10 feet away.

But, from 20,000 feet above, those same people are faceless inanimate objects hustling around doing what it is they do. They have an agenda to change the world. Each and every person finds great satisfaction in mastering their thing. It's what gives us identity. It's what allows us to find motivation and meaning from 10 feet away. It's addictive. It's transforming. It's also destructive.

Every single one of us is fighting our own fight. The fortunate ones have supportive people 10 feet away. The unfortunate ones often feel alone and detached. The fortunate ones find validation from other people. They're affirmed daily that what it is they hold dear and true to their heart is in fact how the world works. The unfortunate ones move through their day with fear and trepidation wondering if they need to change for the world or if the world will someday change to meet them. The RiverCats found a group of people they never once had to consider changing for. Mike Williams may have said it best.

---

*Last, but certainly not least, is my favorite part of being a RiverCat...the **people** we've had the pleasure to meet, and now call friends. People used to tell me we were "crazy" for playing travel ball (all the travel, time, $$$). They were right, we were crazy...no doubt about it, but it worked really, really well for us. For those of us that experienced it, and still after all these years, the mention of "the RiverCats" is still sacred in these parts and remains the standard for what a group of players, parents and coaches can achieve.*

- Mike Williams, RiverCats Dad

"Hey Kyle. What did you just say?"

If they're keeping score, compete respectfully and dream relentlessly. Competition deserves your best. If you're not competing, live fearlessly and love shamelessly. Everyone is fighting their own battle. In the end, there is only love.

The Good Players That Practiced and Played with the RiverCats

This list can't be exhaustive. It would be too long. There were so many players that impacted our success. Many of them are known. Some are unknown. This list comprises the players that were typically at our local practices and or played with us at tournaments.

Avery Arnold (Cedar Cliff High School) Junior Professional Hockey

Carter Christopher (Bishop McDevitt High School) Princeton University (football)

Donovon Ball (Cedar Cliff High School) Penn State University (wrestling)

Cameron Barto (Lancaster Catholic High School) University of Pittsburgh

Velly Bartow (Trinity High School) TBD

Drew Baughman (Cumberland Valley High School) Liberty University

Nathan Blasick (Halifax High School) West Virginia University

Austin Bradbury (Cedar Cliff High School) University of Miami

Justin Caesar (Archbishop Spalding High School) UMBC

Chris Dare (Cedar Cliff High School) Bloomsburg University (football)

Austin Denlinger (Elizabethtown High School) York College

Dylan Ed (Gettysburg High School) TBD

Nick Embleton (East Pennsboro High School) St. Joseph's University

Aaron Feld (Octarora High School) Millersville University

Tyler Kehoe (Archbishop Carroll High School) University of North Carolina

Tayven Kelley (Cedar Cliff High School) Penn State University

Luke Goodyear (Camp Hill High School) Gardner Webb University

Adam Grintz (Downingtown West) Tulane University

Eric Grintz (Downingtown West) University of North Carolina

Aleksei Guzman (Gilman School Md.) Penn State University

Kyle Hannon (Red Land High School) Penn State University

Austin Hendrick (West Allegheny High School) Mississippi St. University

Jaden Henline (Red Land High School) Penn State University

Reese Kauffman (Red Land High School) TBD

Braden Kolmansberger (Red Land High School) TBD

Jayson Kramer (Cumberland Valley High School) Patrick Henry Junior College

Ryan Kutz (Lower Dauphin High School) Davidson College

Trey Law (Cedar Cliff High School) Youngstown State University

Jimmy Losh (Cedar Cliff High School) Millersville University

Garrett Lowe (Kennard Dale High School) Millersville University

Caden Malone (Cedar Cliff High School) Penn State University (student)

Adam Maring (Shippensburg High School) Mt. Saint Mary's (golf)

Joseph Matter (Cedar Cliff High School) TBD

Scotty McManamon (Central Dauphin High School) TBD

Hunter Merritt (Red Land High School) Penn State Harrisburg

Benny Montgomery (Red Land High School) University of Virginia

Drew Mummau (Manheim Central High School) Liberty University

Lillo Paxia (Gloucester Catholic, NJ) Florida St. University

Jared Payne (Red Land High School) University of Kentucky

Kaden Peifer (Red Land High School) TBD

Tommy Reilly (Cedar Cliff High School) University of Alabama (student)

Justin Resto (Cedar Cliff High School) Bloomsburg University (football)

Trent Rowland (Dallastown High School) TBD

Troy Schreffler (Central Dauphin High School) University of Maryland

Zeb Stough (Red Land High School) High Point University

Tyler Thompson (Cumberland Valley High School) TBD

Nick Tomasko (Mechanicsburg High School) TBD

Anthony Volpe (Delbarton High School, NJ) Vanderbilt University

Cole Wagner (Red Land High School) University of Georgia

Luke Wagner (Red Land High School) University of Georgia

Mason Walker (Red Land High School) University of Pittsburgh

Matt Warrington (Sussex Tech, DE) Wilmington University

Bobby Whalen (Cedar Cliff High School) University of Louisville

Justin Williams (Cumberland Valley High School) Penn State University

Corey Wise (Central York High School) TBD

Tyler Young (Central Bucks East) TBD

RiverCats

Adam Maring "Magic"

Early RiverCats

| Avery | Tommy | Nick | Chris | Joseph |
| Arnold | Reilly | Tomasko | Dare | Matter |

Tayven Kelley

Epilogue
Can Education Model the RiverCats?

Here are my current beliefs from THE INSIDE of a classroom.
Here are my current beliefs from THE INSIDE as a parent.
Here are my current beliefs from THE INSIDE of a public high school.
Here are my current beliefs from THE INSIDE of students at the end of a survival system.
Here are my current beliefs from THE INSIDE on a team of professional teachers.
Here are my current beliefs from THE OUTSIDE of the political (I'm not on a school board) and strategic (I'm not a principal) level of education.
Here are my current beliefs from THE INSIDE of the theatrical level of education.

The secret to coaching (teaching) is simple. Make them dream of a better tomorrow AND train them like today is all that matters.

What the Ninth Inning can teach us about education:
In the end there is only love. Teachers are servants to their students. The end is relative. The end shouldn't mean the end of a marking period or the end of a school year. The end for a student is a time that the teacher won't see. The teachers in the lives of our students need to begin with the end in mind. We need to see the student as someone that is asked to struggle for growth's sake. But we also need to see the student as someone to appreciate and love for his sake. Overcoaching and over-teaching 101 is placing growth ahead of love. It's so easy to do when

you see the student as an isolated part to a whole. The students that sit in our classrooms aren't people that produce work. The students that sit in our classrooms are people with dreams and goals to pursue. Great students must have great imaginations. We can't expect them to dream and think when every adult in their life treats the educational process as a sprint with no time to rest. Cover as much ground as possible and produce the necessary work by the necessary date. This is bad practice if you want to create "winners." This is an acceptable practice if all you care about is your world or your classroom.

What the Eighth Inning can teach us about education:
Grades sort students. Grades cede power to the people that do the sorting. Grades are biased to the present. Grades distract from learnings true purpose. Grades are external motivators. Grades are an outdated form of motivation and grades are used so arbitrarily that a grade on a transcript signifies less and less. Extra credit is given for bringing in a box of tissues. Grades are used against a student for missed school. Grades are used to motivate and punish students who don't demonstrate "appropriate" behavior. Grades undermine the learning process as it moves learning from imagination to precision. Grades turn the adults in their lives from someone that can influence and mentor into someone that judges.

What the Seventh Inning can teach us about education:
Being a part of something bigger than yourself is motivating. It requires incredible sacrifice. It is one of life's great lessons. To accomplish incredible things, we need to dream selfishly and participate unselfishly. Yet, our students never are asked to sacrifice as their entire journey is selfish in nature. The rewards they receive are selfish awards demonstrated by the work they produce. The accelerated pace and artificial finish lines promote selfish behavior in a social system. As the political, strategic, theatrical levels of education focus solely on content, the tactical level of education sees the people in their lives as competition, not people to sacrifice for. The daily interaction of student and adults can often be psychological warfare. "Winning and losing" are

accepted forms of achievement. Learning for learning's sake erodes in the face of artificial incentives and artificial deadlines. Furthermore, the adults in the lives of students often see themselves as part of a teaching team. Every model of team that is formed must be formed with the student in mind. Teachers are not teammates to serve their purpose of "teaching." Teachers are teammates to the students they serve. If you can't please everyone all the time, many teachers must be prepared to offend their peers to do the right thing for the student.

What the Sixth Inning can teach us about education:
Rewards create confidence. Skill creates competence. In a system predicated on attaching a number to someone's efficacy, we're creating confident students, but competence lies out of our grasp. School is a giant deception game. I'm not suggesting this is what happens with every student. I'm merely suggesting it's an option. And, if it's an option, students will find it in a system that erodes to a social experiment wrapped in competition. A lesson is taught. Homework is assigned. A student cheats on his homework in the morning during homeroom. He didn't have time in the evening between his sport and/or his job. The teacher checks the homework on completion. The student receives credit for the assignment. The student crams for a test the night before. The student does well enough on the exam but forgets the material two days later. Re-tests are not allowed so the grade remains, yet the skills needed remain out of reach. Without the necessary skills, students are left in one of two states. Find other areas where they're competent or exist in a constant state of anxiety knowing the skills they're supposed to have aren't being developed.

What the Fifth Inning can teach us about education:
How does one get educated? Does he attain a level of mastery by earning more and more degrees? Does he become intelligent by applying the information that he has learned? Does he attain competence by contributing to society? Possibly, the greatest failing of education is the fact that the mission of education isn't clearly outlined. Education can be defined a myriad of ways. I

have students that have failed my math classes that I am absolutely convinced will make a major contribution to society. Their social skills are off the charts. I have students that can produce decent enough work and graduate with honors, but I fear won't be able to do anything without being told what to do. Happiness comes in many forms. For those that want to find happiness by shooting for the moon. Have at it. The struggle will be real, and you'll find a lot of frustration along the way. But ambition is a noble endeavor. Go do your thing. For those that want to enjoy life without the burden of achievement. Have at it. There are millions of people in third world countries with little to show for their time on the planet that still enjoy life. Living below your means is a noble endeavor. Education means different things for different people. It's time we recognize this.

What the Fourth Inning can teach us about education:
Moving fast is a lousy way to experience. Becoming a perfectionist in all areas of one's life is a scary proposition. Yet, that seems to be the model we're only considering. Our "best" students are rewarded for arriving first and the entire emphasis seems to be placed on finding the correct answers to the questions that teachers provide. Our students are running scripts in buildings designed for discovery. Here's the problem Johnny. Give me the answer as soon as you can. If the answer is wrong, the teacher provides feedback and marks it incorrect. Many times, the grade is an indication that the answer wasn't found on the first attempt but subsequent attempts at mastery are ignored. We want our students to embrace a growth mindset and tackle the risk associated with solving any problem of value. Yet, when we assign problems, we "punish" them with a grade and often no chance of recovery. Risk with an opportunity to recover should create excitement. Risk without an opportunity to recover creates anxiety.

What the Third Inning can teach us about education:
Competence, self-esteem, fearlessness, adaptability to a changing world hinges on having the skills necessary to accomplish things. Without the necessary skills, people of all ages engage in

deceptive practices attempting to divert one's attention away from the true purpose. This is what is happening in the building at the end of survival systems. As the skills erode over time, the students at the end of survival systems revert to bad behavior to gain the attention of the adults in their lives that they so desperately need. Without the skills to stand out in the crowd, they use other forms of attention seeking behavior. We need to give our students skills for the "long game." The teachers in the lives of students need to stop creating artificial finish lines by pretending "deadlines" have a real world purpose. "Deadlines" are valuable when the real world provides real world consequences. If I don't get my trash out on Thursday, my house will stink. That's a deadline worth meeting. If I don't turn the paper in on Tuesday because Tuesday is the day authority decided it was due, we're teaching compliance instead of allowing for skill acquisition. Authority is offended easily in thriving systems. Learning is a skill that has no finish line. The authority needs to care more about skills learned and less about respect given. Ego is the enemy when it comes to being a servant leader.

What the Second Inning can teach us about education:
All educators care deeply about the content they teach. Surely, it's a big part of their life. You don't spend years acquiring a degree and not have an inside view of the importance of the subject material. But students often don't care about what it is you're teaching. If I taught Probability and Statistics on the streets of Harrisburg, PA. I wouldn't be the least bit offended if nobody stopped to listen to my message. To each his own. If you're not interested, carry on. Yet, when we mandate that people with the same lack of interest show up in the presence of a teacher and that teacher has an inside view of his material, you're setting everyone up for a combustible situation. Students often have anywhere between 4 to 8 teachers at any one time with an inside view of their curriculum. Add to it a coach with an inside view of their sport. Add to it parents that have an inside view of their home. The life of a student is incredibly stressful because the adults in the lives of students are fighting for attention and the student simply

265

doesn't want to stop on the streets of Harrisburg and listen to the presentation. It's not personal. He's often just not interested.

What the First Inning can teach us about education:
I'm a 45-year old teacher. My beliefs are different than when I was a 27-year old teacher. I'm willing to bet my beliefs are different than a 58-year old woman. How could they not be? That's the point. We're all different and we all have different beliefs. The mission behind education should be equipping our future with the necessary skills to be productive, happy or both. Yet, so often the students conducting their daily lives are imposed upon by so many unique adults that they hear conflicting messages daily. That's an awesome thing to experience and one we adults shouldn't run from. We need the students to see all the different perspectives that adults can share. Adaptable is always preferred over optimal. Yet, we must realize that change is true in everything. Students are often explorers and teachers are often exploiters. Students want to tour the island. Teachers want to tell the students what's on the island. The potential that exists in education exists when teacher can suggest, and student can consider without the obligation to perform. What's a yes mean if you can't say no?

What the Clubhouse can teach us about education:
Some years ago, the district I teach in did a presentation on ACE scores. The ACE scores were "adverse childhood experiences." The presentation was awe inspiring. I sat in attendance thinking this is everything with respect to education. Whatever is second among the priority of teachers is open for debate. But this thing here is first. The home lives of our children is EVERYTHING! It's how they view the world. If you don't get breakfast, you won't care about Biology. If you don't sleep at night, you'll steal sleep in the nurse's office by acting out in Spanish class. The fortunate students show up at school knowing their mission for achievement is often met with adults in their lives that are gladly willing to show them there is a world available to them that fits their hopes and dreams. The unfortunate students show up at

266

school labeled as students that don't work hard, are lazy and are unmotivated. Whether they are or are not is not the point. The world will always have lazy and unmotivated. The point is if the adults in the lives of students never ask the question of "are you ok?" we'll never know the answer to the question of "are you lazy?"

What Would a RiverCat School Look Like?

Every game needs these three questions answered before beginning.

1. What are the rules?

2. What are the stakes?

3. When can I quit?

Nothing great is ever accomplished without enthusiasm.

Assuming the political level of team is here to stay, we'll need to demonstrate some proof that we're learning. In a perfect world, trust would have a setting at the dinner table, but ultimately truth gets people elected. Towards that end, this would be the RiverCat model.

Show every single student what's at stake. Here is the end game. Don't protect the information from them. Here's what's out there upon graduating. Give it to them as early as possible and as often as possible. In order to be this, you need these skills. Someone with an inside view of how to acquire those skills should be consulted. Allowing the students to see the prize at the end of the system is extremely motivating. I couldn't imagine coaching the RiverCats without allowing them to dream of someday playing college baseball or professional baseball.

When the student is ready the teacher will appear. Teachers should be "on demand" teachers not "supply" teachers. Given the target and the stakes, people find motivation intrinsically. This intrinsic motivation will hold up even as years change and teachers change. With a supply model of teaching, students are at the mercy of the messenger and his or her tactics. Sometimes these tactics work and sometimes they fail (some people don't get along with other people). With a demand model of teaching, the student will gladly walk through the Intentional Door seeking information from anyone that can assist. They'll move on their own terms without creating artificial grades as carrots and sticks. Competency is measured through performance. Pass or fail would be just fine with me. The teacher CAN NOT also be the critic. This is an unfair expectation of the teacher student relationship. Some other "expert" or peer review should be responsible for assessment. Reteaching and reassessing these skills would be done as appropriate. Teachers need to be able to take advantage of the situations where students lead with the question. That's the ideal relationship between teacher and student. The question must precede the answer. Otherwise, we're just running scripts. Confidence over competence.

Daniel Pink in his book *Drive* cites autonomy, mastery and purpose as the three primary motivators. By showing them the stakes, you're giving them purpose. By allowing them to proceed on their terms and at their pace, you're allowing them to hunt for mastery. The last piece to the Pink's model is autonomy. If you allow students an opportunity to quit, you give them control of their learning. Quitting is a lousy option in a survival system. Quitting is a wonderful option in a thriving system. If someone proves incompetent in a field, why would we ever demand they stay in that field?

The RiverCats were a special team that achieved special things. We didn't do it by sticking to conventional modes of behavior. The RiverCats were great because we challenged boundaries and we coupled imagination and precision. School could be the same. Currently, the model is tragically flawed. You only need to spend some time on the inside at the theatrical level and observe student behavior at the tactical level to come to this understanding. There is a better way but it's going to require an awful lot of risk from someone at the political and strategic levels.

As RiverCats coach I'd often say, "If you're going to make mistakes, make bold mistakes." We need some bold decisions and possibly some bold mistakes. If the tactical level of education is ever going to serve the best interests of the students, the political and strategic level of education needs to wrestle with change. The change we need isn't about the people. The change we need isn't about the tasks. The change we need rests solely on the idea. The idea must be…Education is not a survival system. Yet, we treat it like one. Wrestling with this thought surely will be uncomfortable. It'll be unnerving. But it's necessary and it's needed.

Acknowledgements
To Those Folks 10 Feet Away

Thank You To...

The RiverCat Families....*For trusting me with your pride and joys.*

The RiverCat Players...*For listening to one man's opinion.*

The GoWags Families...*For believing in the message of Bob Gorinksi (Go) and Bret and Kyle (Wags).*

The GoWags Players...*For allowing us to challenge you when you may have preferred love instead. For allowing us to love you when you may have preferred being challenged instead.*

Kyle Nornhold and Scotty Acri...*For making the road trips enjoyable when we had to distance ourselves from the Dads.*

My Students that didn't like math class...*For showing me the danger of achievement.*

My Students that did like math class...*For showing me the value of achievement.*

All of my students....*For showing me a beginner's mindset.*

All of my Red Land colleagues...*For demonstrating the value of both love and growth.*

Shandon Walker...*For creating a cover almost as great as the team.*

Mike and Susan Ryder...*For modeling the belief that the only targets worth hitting are the targets that you set.*

Chuck and Denise Simpson...*For offering to build a pitcher's mound in your backyard. And, expanding your circle to include a new dog owner.*

Matt Moody...*For telling me to stop reading and start writing.*

Jim Young...*For never allowing age to be a boundary for friendship.*

Darryl Ed....*For modeling for me how to love your son from the OUTSIDE.*

Randy Sullivan...*For seeing the value of the Imagination Game in a Precision World.*

Jason Ferber...*For making lit videos of crispy young ballers. And, helping promote this project.*

Billy White...*For teaching me the value of slowing down.*

Mark Knull...*For loving what GoWags stood for shamelessly.*

Bob Gorinski....*For modeling humility.*

Jeff Cucci....*For never granting me higher ground, yet always honoring my opinion.*

Greg Young...*For not telling me to "stay in my lane" with this project.*

Scott Slayton...*For modeling how to handle pain with great character.*

Heather Wolfe...*For always telling your students you love them, even when they challenge you.*

Pat Galuska...*For never compromising the bar for the bar setters.*

Shannon Zimmerman...*For always demonstrating what self-discipline looks like on a daily basis.*

Wrigley*...For allowing me to see fighting for control is an animal instinct.*

Michael Holmes*...For making the HOW we lived our lives so memorable during the precision of college.*

Kevin Troup*...For being a great teammate and friend during The Imagination Game AND The Precision Game.*

Jaimie Beisel*...For knowing a Survival System always allows for great theater.*

Doug Enders*...For knowing the difference between values and beliefs.*

Jes Kaercher*...For becoming more of a "trust" guy than a "truth" guy.*

Brian Willoughby*...For being aware enough to realize competence always requires discipline.*

Aaron Walter*....For playing the "long game" better than any coach I've known.*

Nate Ebbert*....For coaching Luke with an eye on The Precision Game that lies ahead.*

Teed Wertz*....For becoming competent enough to challenge me.*

JK Kolmansberger*...For taking an OUTSIDE VIEW on player development.*

Scott Cubbler*...For creating an environment where friends can be themselves.*

Mitch Kauffman*....For being a minimalist in a cluttered world.*

Tom Peifer*...For ALWAYS putting the team before yourself.*

Melissa Freet*...For demonstrating the courage of competence in all your relationships.*

272

Fred Adams...For helping me write this book when you thought you were just telling me stories about your job.

Sandy Adams...For always prioritizing the idea (love of family) above the task.

Irma Wagner...For maintaining an OUTSIDE perspective when the rest of the family tends to obsess over the INSIDE.

George Harris...*For cheering unabashedly.*

Frances Wagner...For always being honest in love and honest in growth.

Gary Wagner...For letting me learn on my terms always, except that one time I wrestled in gym class.

Linda Wagner...For modeling the belief that "caring" is non-negotiable.

Bret Wagner...For being my best friend.

Luke Wagner...For believing that my once upon a time was pretty good too.

Grace Wagner...For always sharing your art.

Heather Wagner...For being you when I didn't always deserve you. I love you.

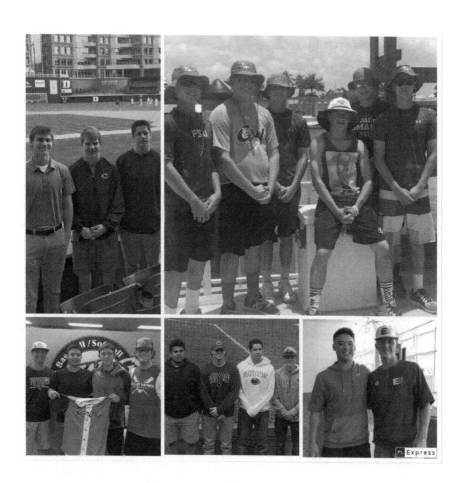

References

Arbesman, Samuel. *The Half-Life Of Facts: Why Everything We Know Has An Expiration Date*. Current, 2013.

Ariely, Dan. *Predictably Irrational*. Harper, 2008.

Ashton, Kevin. *How To Fly A Horse: The Secret History Of Creation, Invention, And Discovery*. Anchor Books, 2015.

Barretta, Jackie. *Primal Teams*. AMACOM, 2014.

Bishop, Bill, and Robert G Cushing. *The Big Sort*. Mariner Books, 2009.

Brown, Brené. *Braving The Wilderness*. Random House, 2017.

Brown, Peter C. *Make It Stick :The Science Of Successful Learning*. Dreamscape Media, 2014.

Burdick, Alan. *Why Time Flies*. Simon & Schuster, 2017.

Carse, James. *Finite And Infinite Games*. Free Press, 2013.

Catmull, Ed. *Creativity, Inc*. Random House, 2014.

Christakis, Nicholas A, and James H Fowler. *Connected*. Back Bay Books, 2009.

Christensen, Clayton M. *The Innovator's Dilemma*. Harpercollins Publishers, 2006.

Coyle, Daniel. *The Talent Code*. Bantam Books, 2013.

Csikszentmihalyi, Mihaly. *Flow*. Harpercollins, 2009.

Deci, Edward L, and Richard Flaste. *Why We Do What We Do*. Penguin Books, 1996.

Dreeke, Robin. *Code Of Trust*. St. Martin's Press, 2019.

Dubner, Stephen J, and Steven D Levitt. *Think Like A Freak*. Harpercollins USA, 2015.

Duckworth, Angela. *Grit*. Simon & Schuster, 2016.

Duhigg, Charles, and Mike Chamberlain. *The Power Of Habit*. Random House, 2012.

Duke, Annie. *Thinking In Bets*. Portfolio Penguin, 2019.

Dweck, Carol S. *Mindset*. Robinson, 2017.

Ellenberg, Jordan. *How Not To Be Wrong (The Power Of Mathematical Thinking)*. Penguin, 2014.

Epstein, David. *The Sports Gene*. Yellow Jersey Press, 2013.

Ericsson, Anders, and Robert Pool. *Peak*. Houghton Mifflin Harcourt, 2016.

Ferrazzi, Keith, and Tahl Raz. *Never Eat Alone, Expanded And Updated*. Crown Publishing Group, 2014.

Fishman, Charles. *The Wal-Mart Effect*. Penguin Books, 2014.

Friedman, Thomas L. *The World Is Flat*. Picador/Farrar, Strauss And Giroux, 2007.

Gaunt, Derek. *Ego Authority Failure*. New Direct Press, 2019.

Gilbert, Daniel Todd. *Stumbling On Happiness*. Vintage Canada, 2009.

Gladwell, Malcolm. *David And Goliath*. Back Bay Books, 2013.

Gladwell, Malcolm. *Blink*. Back Bay Books, 2014.

Gonzales, Laurence. *Deep Survival: Who Lives, Who Dies, And Why*. Norton, 2017.

Grant, Adam. *Originals*. Viking, 2016.

Greene, Joshua David. *Moral Tribes*. Penguin, 2013.

Groopman, Jerome E, and Michael Prichard. *How Doctors Think*. Tantor, 2007.

Hacker, Andrew. *The Math Myth*. The New Press, 2016.

Harford, Tim. *Messy*. Riverhead Books, 2016.

Heath, Chip, and Dan Heath. *Made To Stick*. Random House Books, 2010.

Hoffman, Morris B. *The Punisher's Brain*. Cambridge, 2014.

Holiday, Ryan. *Ego Is The Enemy*. Penguin, 2016.

Jensen, Frances E., and Amy Ellis Nutt. *The Teenage Brain*. Harpercollins, 2015.

Kahneman, Daniel, and Patrick Egan. *Thinking, Fast And Thinking Slow*. Random House Audio, 2011.

Kelly, Matthew. *The Culture Solution*. Blue Sparrow, 2018.

Keltner, Dacher. *The Power Paradox*. Penguin Books, 2017.

Klawans, Harold L. *Why Michael Couldn't Hit, And Other Tales Of The Neurology Of Sports*. Henry Holt And Company, 2013.

Kolk, Bessel van der. *The Body Keeps The Score*. Penguin, 2015.

Kotler, Steven. *The Rise Of Superman*. New Harvest, 2014.

Lahey, Jessica. *The Gift Of Failure*. Harpercollins, 2015.

Lawrence-Lightfoot, Sara. *Respect*. Perseus Books, 2000.

Lewis, Michael. *The Undoing Project*. W.W. Norton & Company, 2016.

Lieberman, Daniel Z. Long. *Molecule Of More*. Benbella Books, 2019.

Lockhart, Paul. *A Mathematician's Lament*. Bellevue Literary Press, 2009.

Mauboussin, Michael J. *The Success Equation*. Harvard Business Review Press, 2012.

McGilchrist, Iain. *The Master And His Emissary*. Yale University Press, 2019.

Mischel, Walter. *Marshmallow Test*. Little, Brown And Company, 2014.

Mlodinow, Leonard. *The Drunkard's Walk*. Pantheon Books, 2009.

Mullainathan, Sendhil, and Eldar Shafir. *Scarcity*. Picador, 2013.

Muller, Jerry Z. *Tyranny Of Metrics*. Princeton University Press, 2019.

Newport, Cal. *How To Become A Straight-A Student*. Broadway Books, 2007.

Newport, Cal. *Be So Good They Can't Ignore You*. Business Plus, 2012.

Nichols, Tom. *Death Of Expertise*. Oxford University Press, 2019.

Olson, Jeff, and John David Mann. *The Slight Edge*. Greenleaf Book Group Press, 2013.

O'Reilly, Tim. *What's The Future And Why It's Up To Us*. Harper, 2017.

Owens, David-. *Creative People Must Be Stopped*. Jossey-Bass, 2012.

Pink, Daniel H. *Drive*. Canongate Books, 2018.

Pink, Daniel H. *When*. Random House, 2018.

Pollard, Matthew, and Derek Brandon Lewis. *The Introvert's Edge*. AMACOM, 2018,

Robinson, Ken, and Lou Aronica. *Creative Schools*. Penguin Books, 2016.

Rose, Todd. *The End Of Average*. Allen Lane, 2016.

Saltz, Gail. *The Power Of Different*. Flatiron Books, 2017.

Sandel, Michael J. *Justice*. Farrar, Straus And Giroux, 2009.

Sapolsky, Robert M. *The Trouble With Testosterone*. Scribner, 2014.

Schulz, Kathryn. *Being Wrong*. Harper Collins, 2010.

Seife, Charles. *Proofiness*. Penguin Books, 2014.

Silver, Nate. *The Signal And The Noise*. Penguin Books, 2015.

Sinek, Simon. *Start With Why*. Joosr Ltd, 2016.

Smith, Rupert. *The Utility Of Force*. Knopf, 2007.

Stanford, Michele. *Informed Consent*. Author Academy Elite, 2017.

Stone, D, and Sheila Heen. *Thanks For The Feedback*. Viking, 2015.

Sunstein, Cass R. *Going To Extremes*. Oxford University Press, 2011.

Taleb, Nassim. *Fooled By Randomness*. Random House, 2005.

Taleb, Nassim. *The Black Swan*. Allen Lane, 2011.

Tetlock, Philip, and Dan Gardner. *Superforecasting*. Random House Books, 2016.

Thaler, Richard H, and Cass R Sunstein. *Nudge*. Yale University Press, 2008.

The Holy Bible. American Bible Society, 1986.

Tough, Paul. *How Children Succeed*. Mariner, 2012.

Tracy, Jessica L. *Take Pride*. Houghton Mifflin Harcourt, 2016.

Voss, Christopher, and Tahl Raz. *Never Split The Difference*. Harper, 2016.

Wheelan, Charles J. *Naked Statistics*. Norton, 2013.

Willink, Jocko. *Discipline Equals Freedom*. St. Martin's Press, 2017.

Wiseman, Liz. *Rookie Smarts*. Harper Collins, 2014.

45720284R00163

Made in the USA
Middletown, DE
19 May 2019